IMAGES
of America

REEDLEY

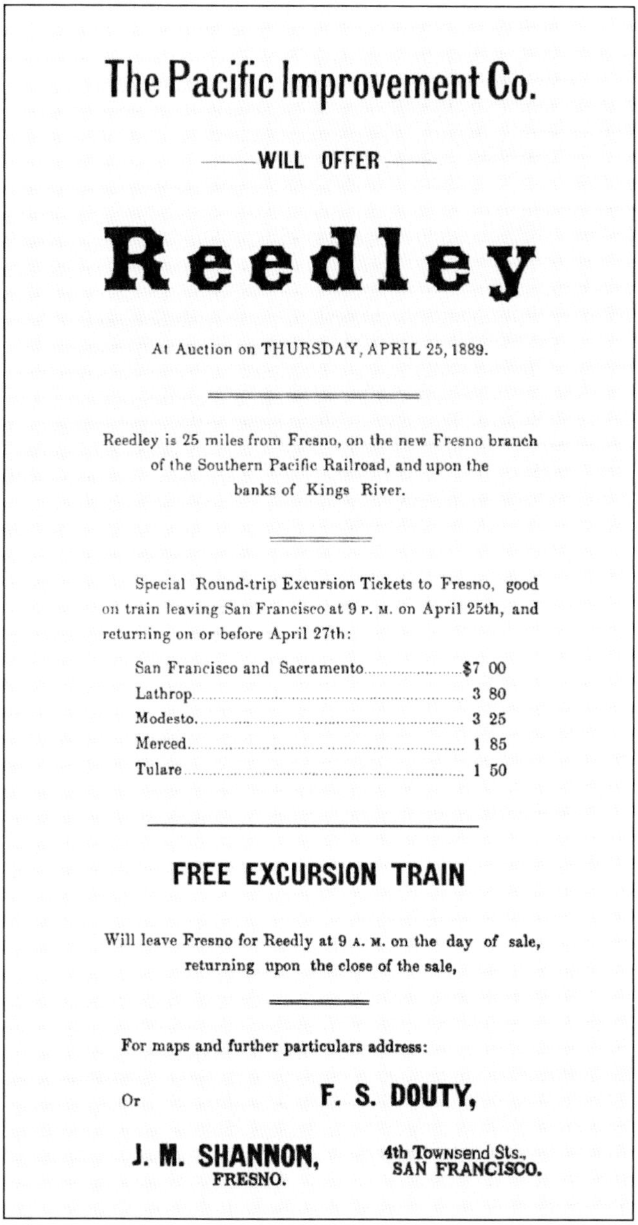

The Pacific Improvement Co.

—WILL OFFER—

Reedley

At Auction on THURSDAY, APRIL 25, 1889.

Reedley is 25 miles from Fresno, on the new Fresno branch of the Southern Pacific Railroad, and upon the banks of Kings River.

Special Round-trip Excursion Tickets to Fresno, good on train leaving San Francisco at 9 P. M. on April 25th, and returning on or before April 27th:

San Francisco and Sacramento	$7 00
Lathrop	3 80
Modesto	3 25
Merced	1 85
Tulare	1 50

FREE EXCURSION TRAIN

Will leave Fresno for Reedly at 9 A. M. on the day of sale, returning upon the close of the sale,

For maps and further particulars address:

F. S. DOUTY,
4th Townsend Sts., SAN FRANCISCO.

Or

J. M. SHANNON,
FRESNO.

The first auction sale of town lots in Reedley occurred on April 25, 1889. The *Traver Advocate* published this advertisement in its April 13 and 20 issues. It was later reported that an excursion train from Fresno, with six coaches "packed to the doors," arrived for the sale. (Author's collection.)

ON THE COVER: One of many entries in the Fourth of July parade of 1911 was Allen E. and Sarah McClanahan's elaborately decorated E-M-F automobile (founded by Everitt, Metzger, and Flanders). Allen McClanahan came to California in 1898 as a nine-year-old and was one of Reedley's earliest citizens. He was a partner of T.L. Reed in the development of the town. An active community volunteer, he received recognition for his work with the Red Cross during World War I. (Courtesy of the Reedley Historical Society.)

IMAGES
of America

REEDLEY

Kenneth Zech

ARCADIA
PUBLISHING

ISBN 978-1-4671-3267-1

Published by Arcadia Publishing
Charleston, South Carolina

Printed in the United States of America

Library of Congress Control Number: 2014942963

For all general information, please contact Arcadia Publishing:
Telephone 843-853-2070
Fax 843-853-0044
E-mail sales@arcadiapublishing.com
For customer service and orders:
Toll-Free 1-888-313-2665

Visit us on the Internet at www.arcadiapublishing.com

Contents

ACKNOWLEDGMENTS

This book would not have been possible without the work of dedicated individuals who, through the years, have recorded and preserved the history of Reedley. Deserving special mention are three persons: John C. McCubbin, a Traver and Reedley pioneer, was the earliest chronicler of Reedley area history. Many years later, Katharine Nickel, an elementary school teacher, undertook the task of compiling and publishing the first book on Reedley's history. In more recent years, Budd Brockett, longtime editor of the *Reedley Exponent*, pored over decades of newspaper reportage so as to acquaint modern readers with the countless details of Reedley's origins and development.

And then there were the photographers. We do not know all their names, but we know some of the most important. Charles C. Curtis probably made more photographs of Reedley in its first few years than anyone else. He was based in Traver and was a onetime member of the utopian socialist Kaweah Colony. George Besaw, who specialized in postcards, had his studio in Reedley. His postcards of Reedley and other California towns are now highly sought collectors' items. August Nelson opened his studio in Reedley in 1919. His son Arthur joined the business in 1920. For decades, they were on the scene to record Reedley events and development.

Thank you to Pamela Melville and Michael J. Semas, who graciously lent photographs from their collections for use in this book. Unless otherwise noted, all photographs in this book are from the collections of the Reedley Historical Society Museum.

Thank you to Diana Bulls, who kindly agreed to review the manuscript before it was sent to the publisher.

Finally, thanks must go to the Reedley Historical Society volunteers. Since 1976, dozens of enthusiastic and hardworking members have labored to preserve and record the history of the Reedley area. All share in the authorship of this book.

All the author's royalties earned from the sale of this book will go to support the Reedley Historical Society.

Introduction

Thomas Law Reed was just 10 days short of his 37th birthday when he arrived in Fresno County with 11 horses and mules and some borrowed money. The date was March 3, 1884.

Several shareholders of the 76 Land and Water Company persuaded Reed to try his hand at farming here. The 76 Company was founded in 1882 with the idea of building an irrigation project that would bring Kings River water to 130,000 acres of southern Fresno County and northern Tulare County. They would make money by selling the land and the water. By their calculation, T.L. Reed was just the sort of man who could prove, by example, the land's value.

Reed took up temporary residence in the abandoned Smith's Ferry Hotel. For the better part of that first month, Reed labored, turning furrows on land that had never known a plow. When he was done, he had planted a modest 200 acres in wheat. He returned to his home in Yolo County later in the year to harvest his last crop. In November, he came back to "76 Country," this time with his wife, Amantha, and their four children. They were here to stay.

The Reeds were not the first white settlers in what would become Reedley. That distinction goes to the family of James and Martha Smith, who arrived in 1855. In fact, the Smiths had built the abandoned hotel that the Reed family later occupied. The Smiths came to the area to conduct a ferry service on the Kings River and to operate a way station for weary travelers, both of which were located on the east bank of the river, near the present-day Olson Avenue bridge. By all accounts, it was a successful business, until the encroachment of civilization rendered the ferry obsolete. The railroad had advanced down the valley, and wagon bridges were being built. The ferry and hotel were abandoned in 1874.

Just as the Reeds were not the first white settlers, the Smiths were not the first people to live here. The Reedley area's earliest residents were, of course, Native Americans. The Yokuts people, comprised of close to 50 distinct tribes, had once occupied the entirety of the San Joaquin Valley. The late Oscar Noren identified 20 of their habitation sites within a five-mile radius of Reedley. By the time the Reed family arrived to farm along the Kings River, dispossession, disease, and worse had already taken a severe toll on the Yokuts.

In 1885, T.L. Reed increased his wheat acreage and planted Egyptian corn. The next year, he purchased two sections of land along today's Reed Avenue. Ultimately, he would have thousands of acres under cultivation.

Getting his wheat to the railroad for shipment was not an easy task. The nearest rail stop was 12 miles away, in Traver. Reed's opportunity to solve this problem came when the Southern Pacific Railroad decided to build a branch line on the east side, from the city of Fresno to Kern County. Reed made a deal with Southern Pacific. In exchange for a half interest in 360 acres of Reed's farmland, the railroad would build a depot along its eastern branch and help develop a townsite. It was the sort of deal that landowners all along the right-of-way were eager to make.

So, in 1888, the Southern Pacific laid its rails and built its depot. The railroad's land development subsidiary, the Pacific Improvement Company, began "selling" the town. Reed did, too. Lots on the townsite were sold, as were colony lots adjoining the townsite. The name the railroad chose for this new town was Reedley.

It was mostly European Americans who arrived in Reedley in the very first years. Some were recent immigrants or the children of immigrants. Also among the arrivals were the Chinese, along with a number of German Jews. Many early settlers were descended from families who, over several generations, had continued to move west across the United States.

Reedley's ethnic mix greatly expanded after the turn of the century. A settler would arrive, then tout the region to his countrymen, and others would follow. The colony system of land development tended to encourage this, and the railroad promoted it. In the first two decades of the 20th century, Reedley saw the development of several distinct ethnic communities. These groups included Japanese, Mexicans, Armenians, Mennonites, Lebanese, Finns, Danes, Filipinos, and Koreans.

Mexicans had, of course, been regular visitors to the valley for many years. After all, they used to own the place. And when gold was discovered in 1848, Mexican gold rushers would pass through the valley just like everybody else. But it was the continuing violence of revolution in Mexico, starting in 1910 and lasting a miserable 10 years, that prompted so many families to head north to places like Reedley.

For all their differences, it is the similarities in each group's immigration story that are most striking. The common reasons for migration included religious, ethnic, or political persecution; war; an entrenched class system; and the lack of hope for economic advancement. Miss Liberty might as well have been standing in the Kings River instead of New York Harbor.

Did everybody get along? No, of course not. Each group has its oral histories that detail the challenges they faced. But persevere they did. Hard work and good character had a way of helping earn others' respect.

The squabbles that made the news were not ethnic. They were political and, sometimes, personal. A quarrel significant to Reedley history was incorporating the city. For many, the importance of Reedley's incorporation was indisputable. The apparatus of government was necessary for progress. A city government could secure a reliable water supply, build and maintain streets, provide law enforcement and fire protection, and beautify the town. The primary dispute, however, was about alcohol. The wets feared that teetotalers would take control of city government and pass an ordinance closing the town's saloons. So long as there was no city government, county law would prevail. Fresno County allowed saloons.

Incorporation was put to a vote in 1910. The proposition failed. The wets had won. On February 14, 1913, the people of Reedley were once again asked whether they wished to incorporate Reedley as a city. This time, it passed 310 to 88. A remarkable turnaround? Not exactly. The booze issue had been rendered moot by two events. First, Fresno County voters had outlawed the sale of alcohol in the unincorporated areas in August 1912. Reedley was already "dry." Second, California had given women the right to vote in 1911. And women were not going to elect anyone to the city council who would propose an ordinance permitting the sale of alcohol.

But this is just one of the anecdotes from Reedley's early history. The 228 photographs that follow will tell more stories. But this book is not comprehensive. It offers only a sampling. Presented here are images from the earliest days to 1940. Each caption is no more than 70 words, when 700 could have been written. And for each photograph selected, there were seven others in the vault that were just as good.

One

Beginnings

With the establishment of the railroad depot, the stage was set for the development of Reedley. Settlers were ready to come. New towns offered the potential of future prosperity. A would-be shopkeeper could buy a town lot for a relatively small price. And with another small investment, he could open a business. Those who came early would have an advantage. As more settlers arrived, the town would grow, and this would raise land prices and increase the shopkeeper's business.

T.L. Reed lost no time building some of the essentials. A grain warehouse was erected along the railroad tracks. Farmers' mule-pulled grain wagons would no longer have to make the 12-mile journey to Traver, which was then the nearest rail stop. Reed built a hotel and a livery stable. He provided land for a school and contributed to the establishment of two churches.

Reedley had a post office within months of its founding. And, in three years, it had a newspaper to report on the great developments in the town and surrounding area. The railroad offered reduced fares to those in San Francisco and parts north to come see Reedley and what it had to offer. The railroad built the New Reedley Hotel, a giant three-story brick structure just a block from the depot. A schoolhouse was constructed that was even more substantial. Would a prospective settler dare ignore such buildings? This was a town with a future!

Emil Hirschfeld opened Reedley's first general merchandise business in the year the town was founded. Telephone service came the following year, when Hirschfeld's store was connected to the 76 Company's private line, which ran from Traver to the Wahtoke headgate. A druggist came to town, as did a jeweler. In less than a decade, a second railroad arrived. Wheat farming gave way to orchards and vineyards. The economy was diversifying. Not long after the turn of the century, a chamber of commerce was formed, and local businessmen founded a bank.

Reedley was on its way.

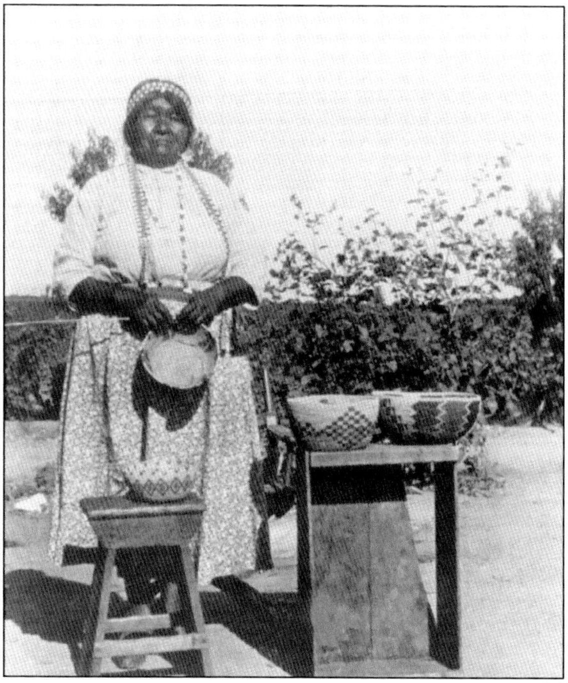

Julia Hughes Davis is pictured here in 1932. Her father was the last chief of the Choinumni Yokuts, who populated the area along the Kings River north of Reedley. Davis was a valuable source of information for anthropologists studying the life of the Native American people. Local historian Oscar Noren was one of those who, with Davis's help, gathered and recorded the history of local Native Americans.

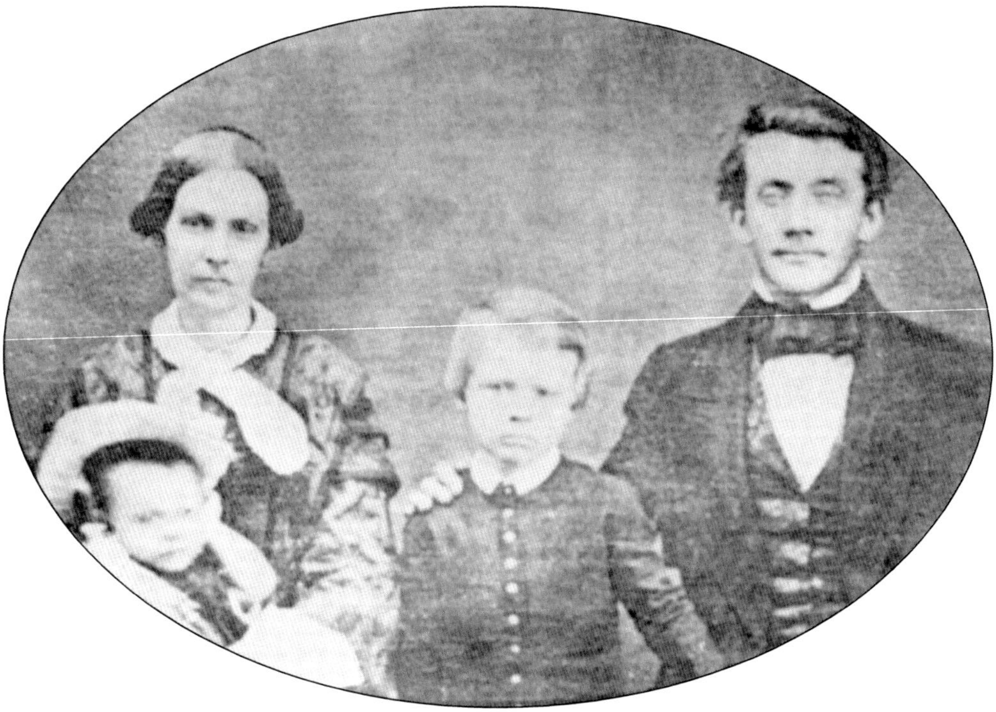

In 1855, James Smith established a ferry service and hotel on the east side of the Kings River in what would later become Reedley. This 1854 portrait shows James with his wife, Martha, and their children, John Parks Hamilton and Harriet Lucretia. Smith died in 1862, leaving Martha to run the business on her own. A new husband helped for a time, until he departed. Too little business resulted in the ferry and hotel closing in 1874.

The Thomas Law Reed family is shown here about 1892. They are, from left to right, (first row) Dollie, Amantha, Thomas, and Imogene; (second row) Jessie, Horace, Nina, and Edmond.

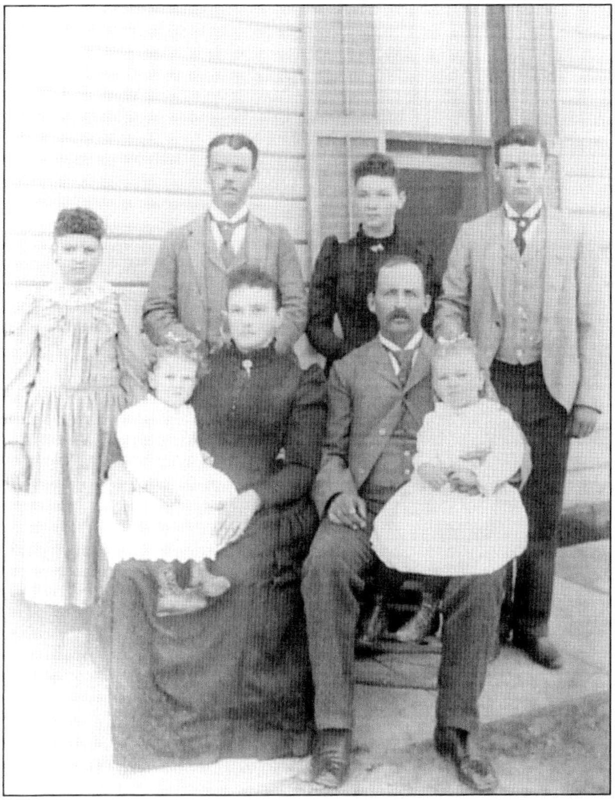

The construction of the Southern Pacific Railroad bridge across the Kings River in 1888, along with the establishment of the Reedley depot one mile to the east, marked the beginning of Reedley as a town. The old wagon bridge at what is now Manning Avenue is visible in the background.

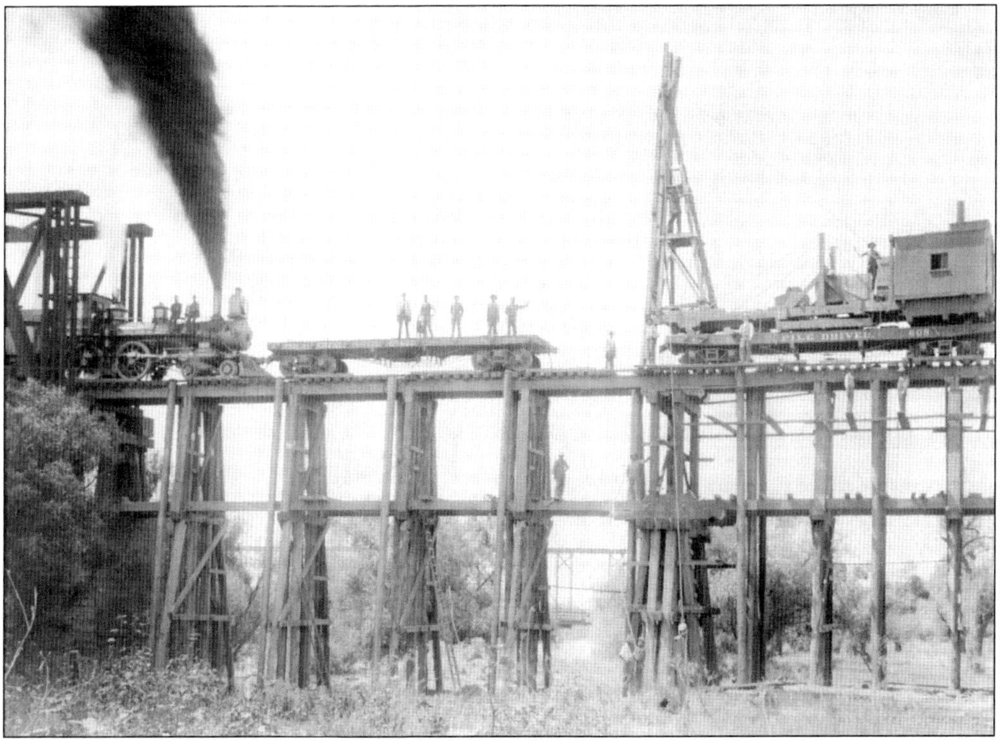

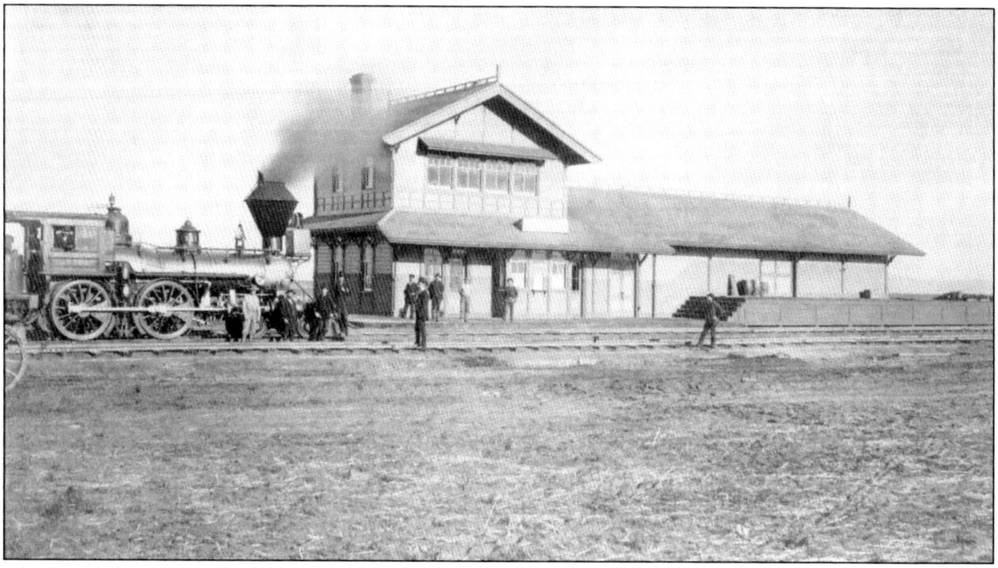

This well-known 1888 photograph documents the first train arriving at Reedley's new Southern Pacific Railroad depot, located on the south side of Eleventh Street. No other structures are visible in the background. The building of a town could now begin. The depot was demolished in 1972.

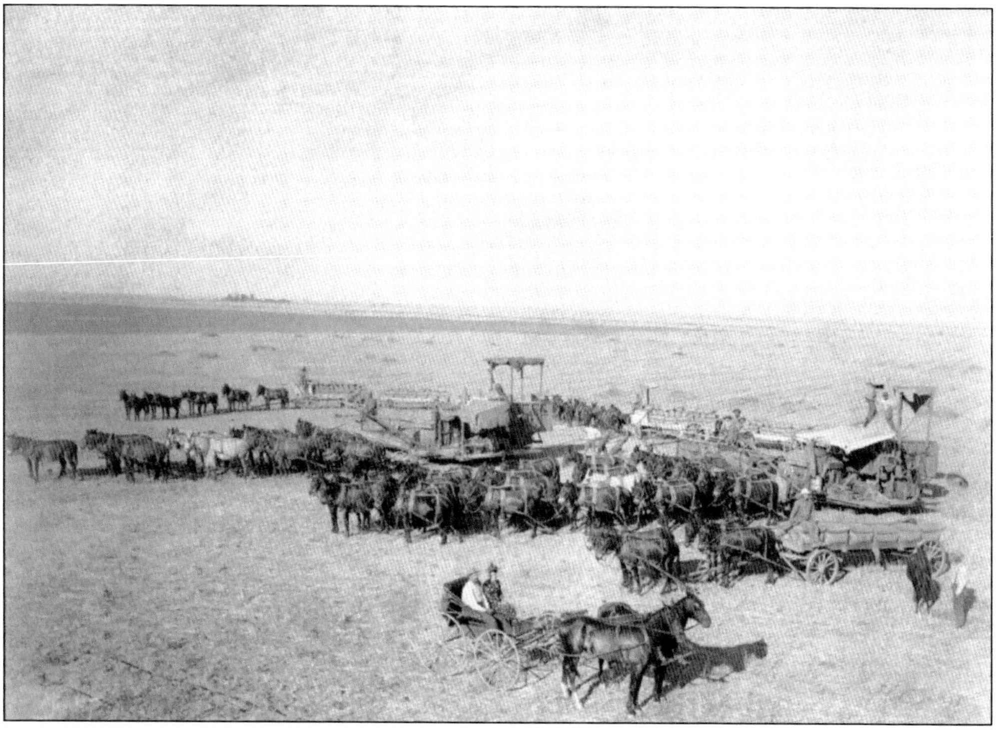

T.L. and Amantha Reed are pictured in their buggy on harvest morning, August 15, 1892. (Photograph by J.S. Wintemute.)

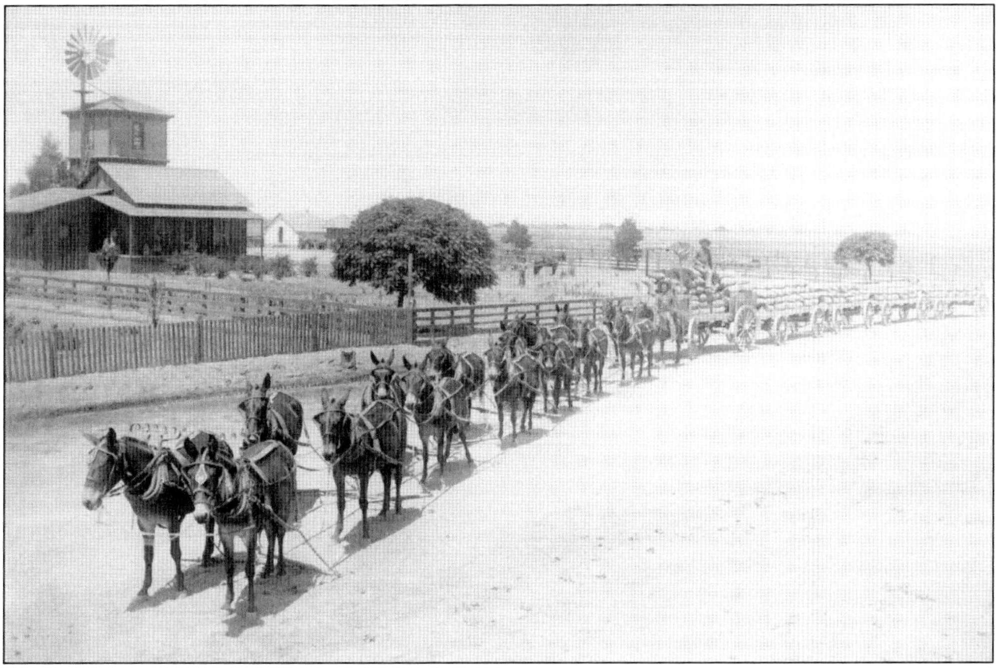

Around 1891, a mule team hauls five wagons of harvested wheat grain at the T.L. Reed "home ranch," as identified in the image's handwritten caption. The ranch property is now the campus of Reedley College. (Photograph by C.C. Curtis.)

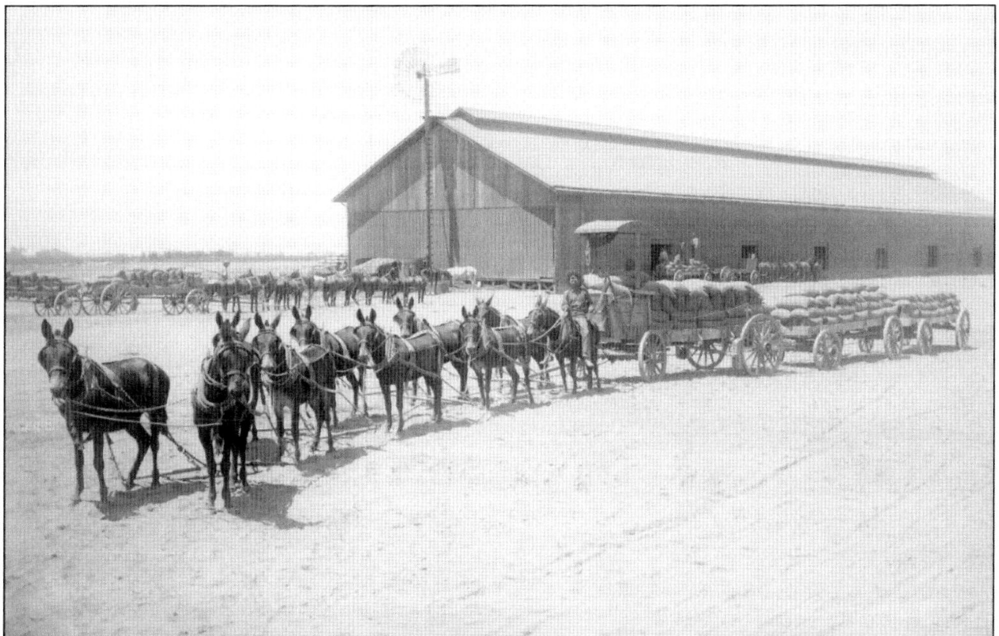

In 1888, T.L. Reed purchased 250 feet of the 500-foot-long Traver warehouse, owned by the 76 Land and Water Company. Reed's half of the structure was hauled to Reedley and was ready in time for his 1889 grain crop. The warehouse, the first in Reedley, was located along the Southern Pacific Railroad tracks on the north side of Eighth Street. (Photograph by C.C. Curtis.)

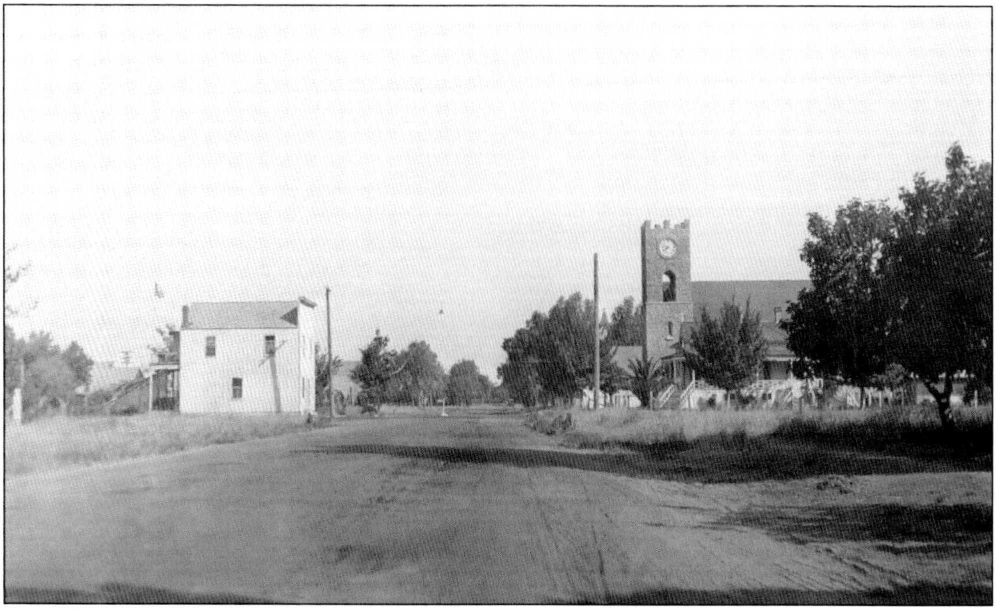

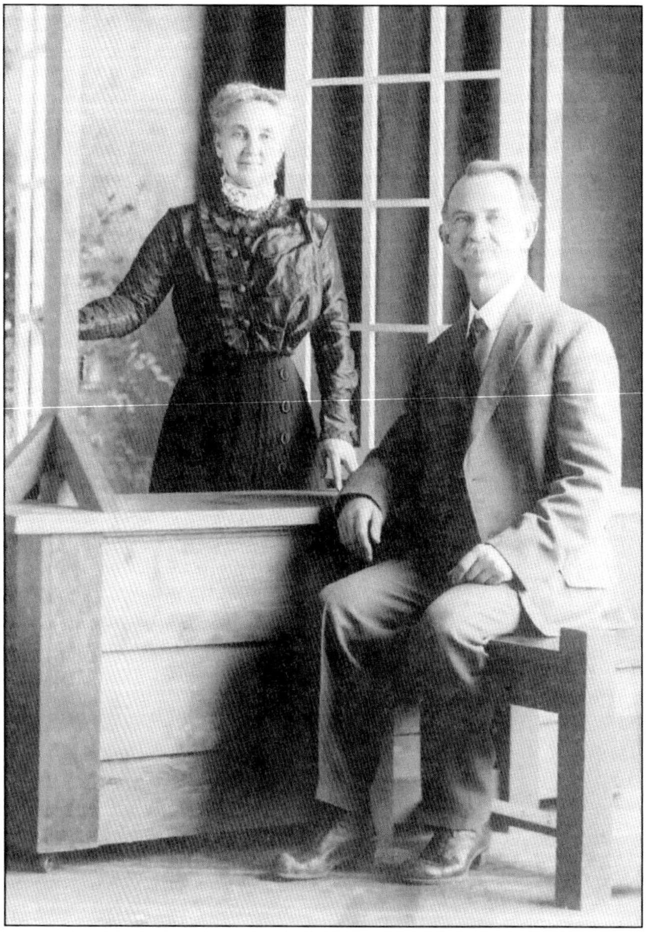

Frank and Flora Knauer's home (left) was the first residential building erected on Reedley's townsite. It was built at the corner of F and Eleventh Streets in 1888. In that same year, their home became Reedley's first post office, with Flora as the first postmaster. Reedley's Catholics began construction of their first church, across the street, 19 years later.

Flora and Frank Knauer played significant roles in Reedley's early years. Flora was Reedley's first postmaster, a position she held for 32 years. Frank was an early teacher at the old Smith's Ferry School. He also served as a bookkeeper for the 76 Land and Water Company, Reedley's first city clerk, and an organizer of Reedley's first city band.

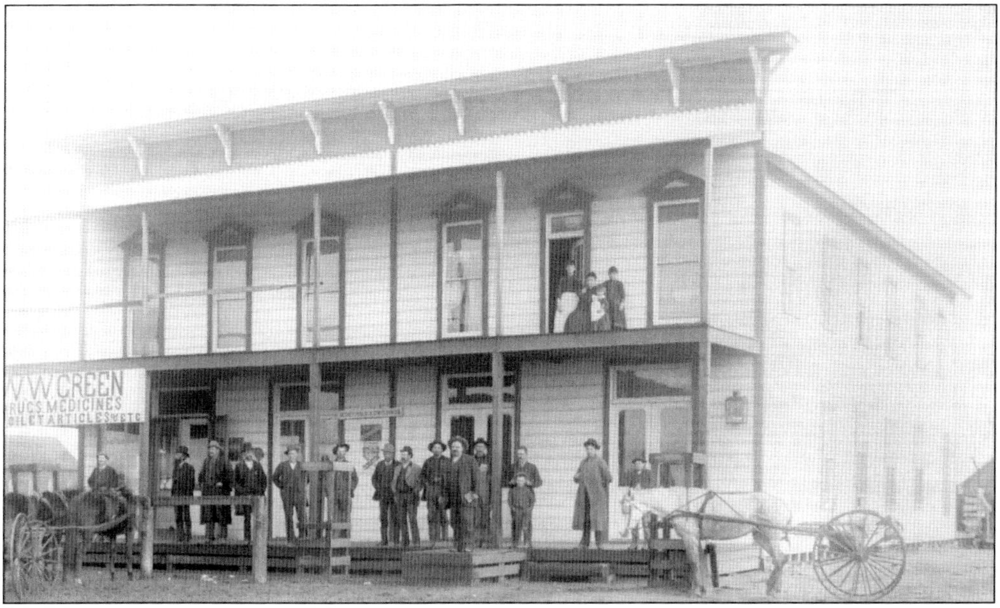

The first hotel in town was the Reedley Hotel, built at G and Eleventh Streets in 1889. T.L. Reed owned the hotel, and H.E. Barnum operated the business. The Simpson family purchased the hotel in 1892 and served as its proprietors for many years. Around town, it became known as the Simpson Hotel. This is the earliest-known photograph of the hotel, dating from about 1891. (Photograph by C.C. Curtis.)

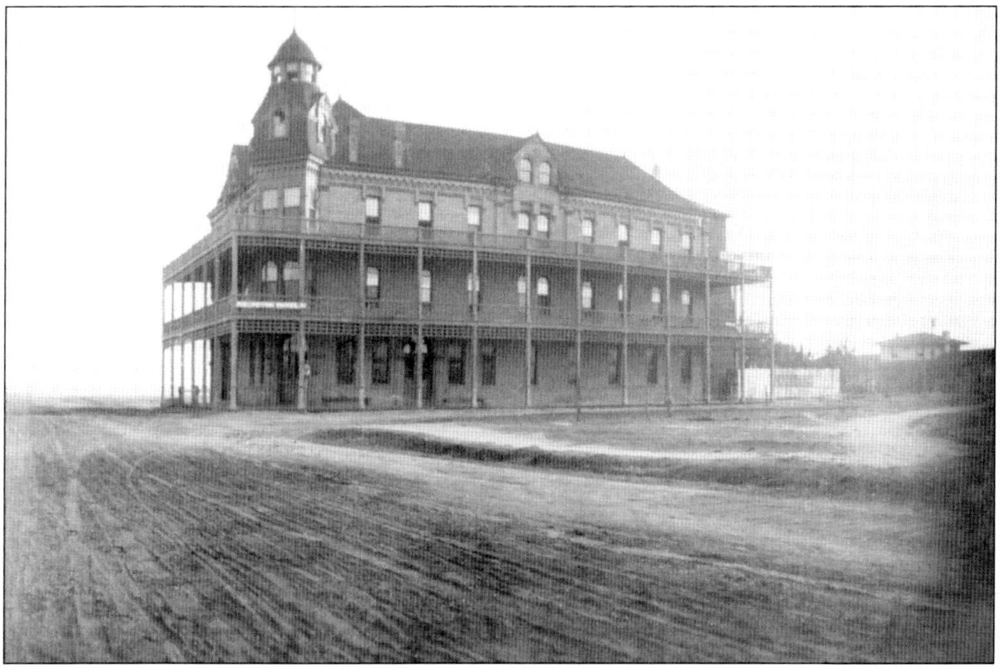

The Pacific Improvement Company, a subsidiary of the Southern Pacific Railroad, built Reedley's second hotel in 1891–1892. The massive three-story New Reedley Hotel was located at G and Twelfth Streets. This photograph dates from the period of 1899–1904, when it was known as the Arlington Hotel. The Santa Fe Railway depot is on the far right.

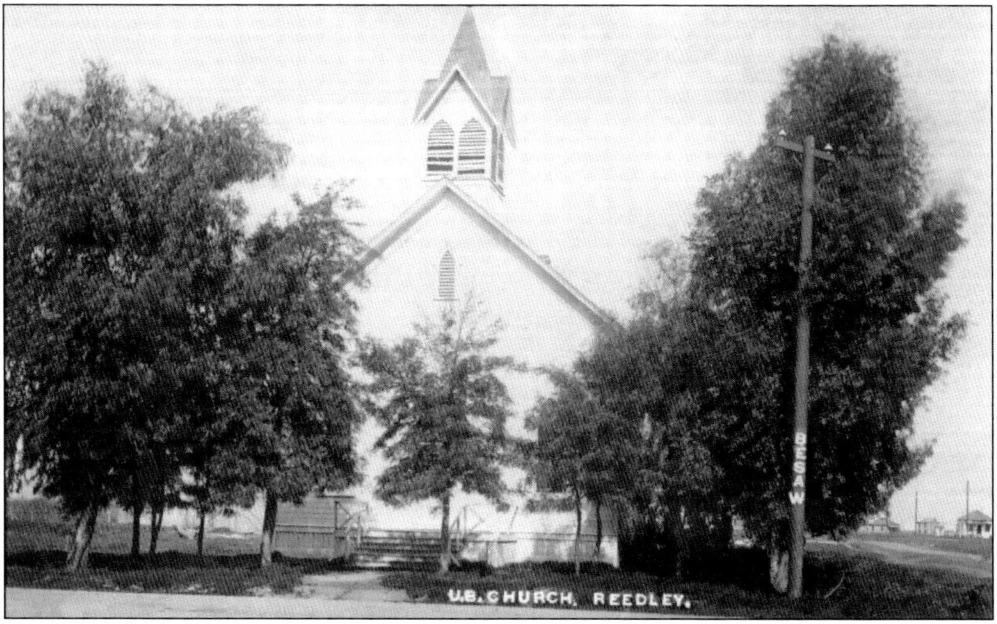

Reedley's first church was the United Brethren Church, at the corner of F and Tenth Streets. It was built in the fall of 1889, but finishing touches had to await the collection of funds to complete the project. It was officially dedicated in January 1892. The congregation disbanded in 1917 and sold the building to the Finnish Evangelical Lutherans. (Photograph by George Besaw.)

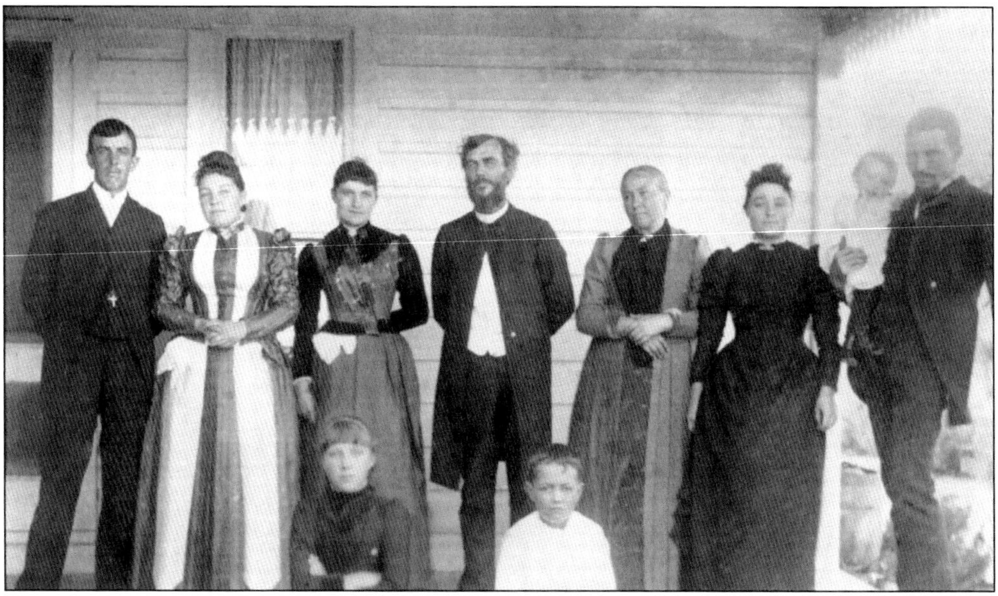

The 1890 marriage of Lyle Reed and Lelah Bauder was the first to occur in Reedley. Those gathered for the wedding are, from left to right, (seated) Laura and Talmage Bauder; (standing) Lyle Reed, Lelah Bauder, Myrtle Bauder, Rev. T.J. Bauder (the bride's father), Electa Bauder, Minnie Bauder Winter, and Lewis Winter (holding baby Ethel). Reverend Bauder, founder of the United Brethren Church, officiated the ceremony. The wedding took place at the Bauder home, which still stands, at 109 South Reed Avenue.

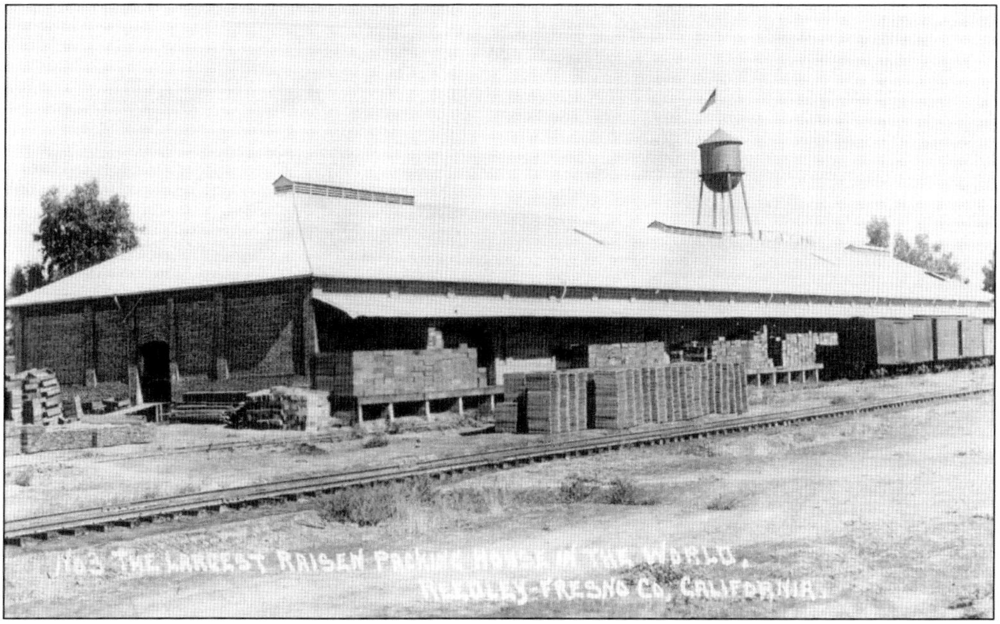

The Grangers' Bank of California built this huge grain warehouse on the north side of Tenth Street in 1892. In 1914, the California Associated Raisin Company, predecessor to Sun-Maid Raisin Growers, purchased the 62-foot-by-351-foot building. Many believe that no building still standing is more important to the story of Reedley's origins than the Grangers' warehouse. This photograph was taken sometime between 1915 and 1922.

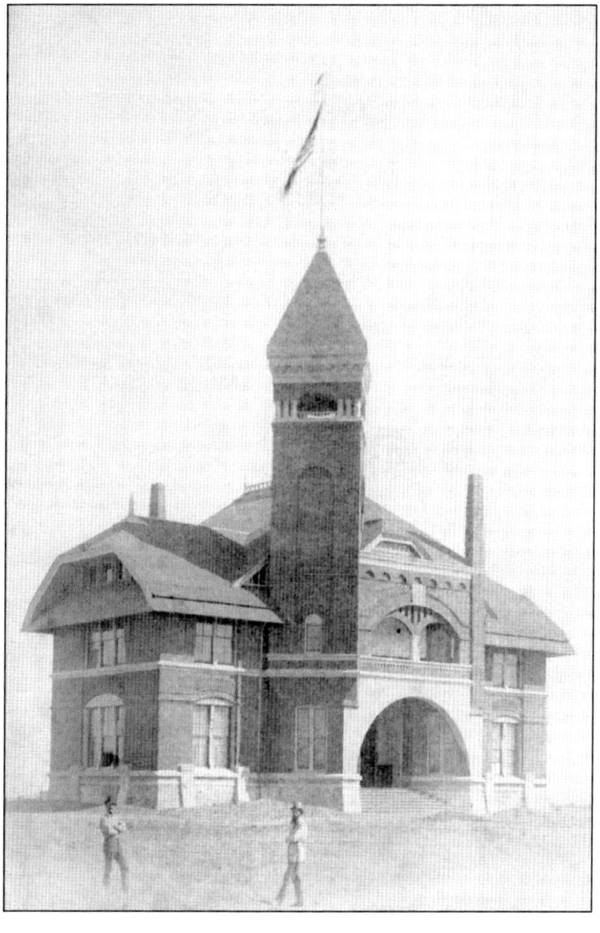

The new Reedley Grammar School opened in September 1891. This photograph probably dates from that same year. The construction of this towering structure was a measure of the community's commitment to education. The school was renamed West Side School in 1912, and it became Washington School in 1918. The building was demolished and replaced by the present-day Washington School in 1950. (Photograph by C.C. Curtis.)

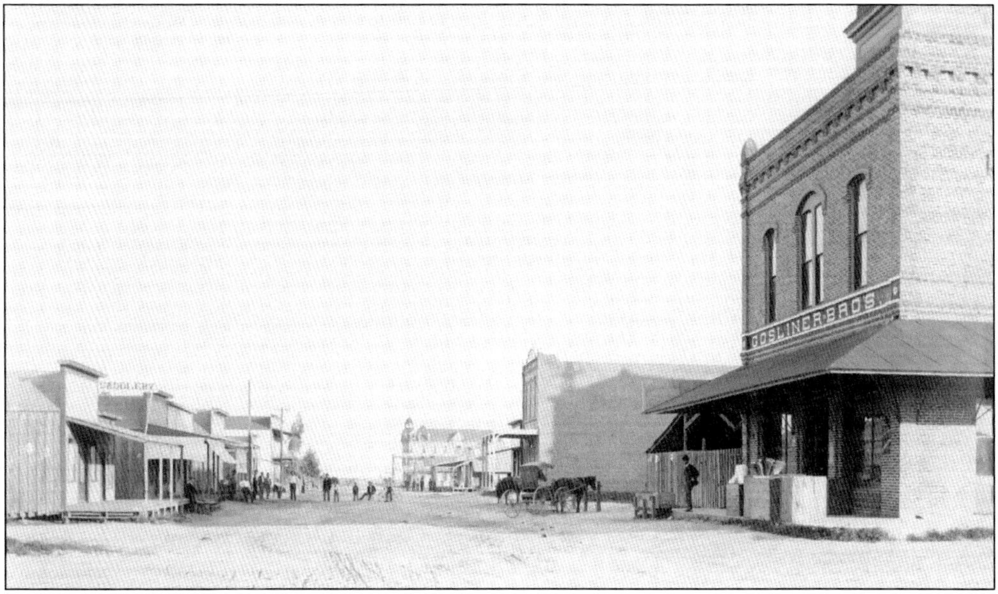

Looking from Tenth Street, this 1895 photograph shows G Street, the main street through town. The two-story brick building on the right is the Gosliner Brothers general merchandise store. At center, in the distance, is the New Reedley Hotel.

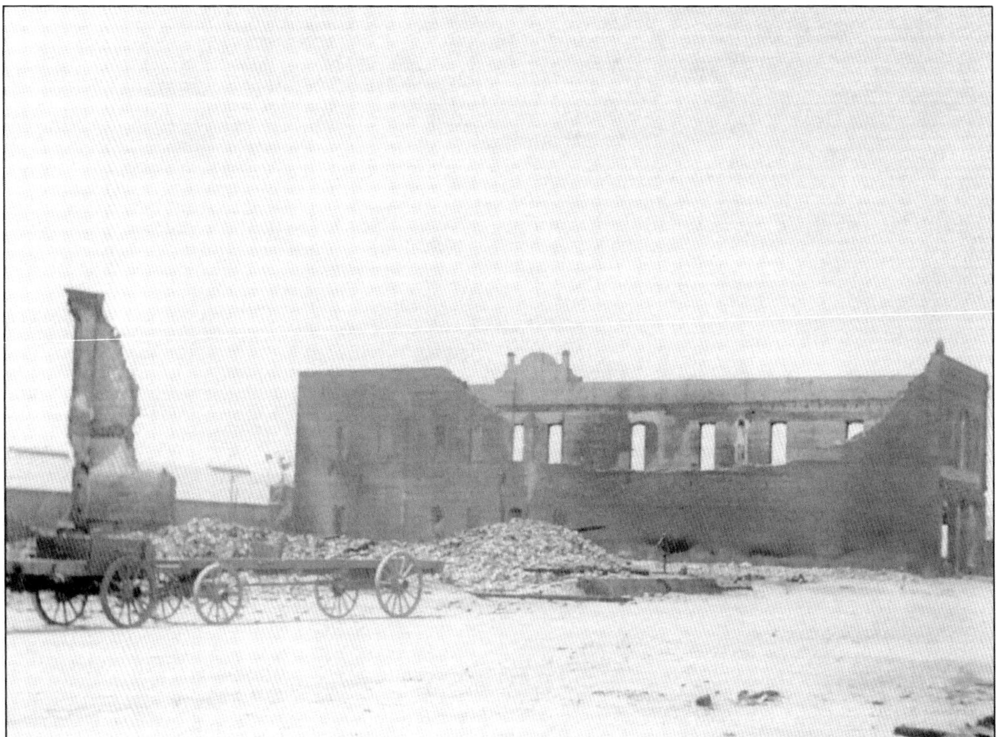

The remains of the Gosliner building are pictured here after an early-morning fire on August 11, 1902. This was the worst of the three downtown fires that plagued Reedley in its first 22 years of existence. On this day, 15 businesses were lost.

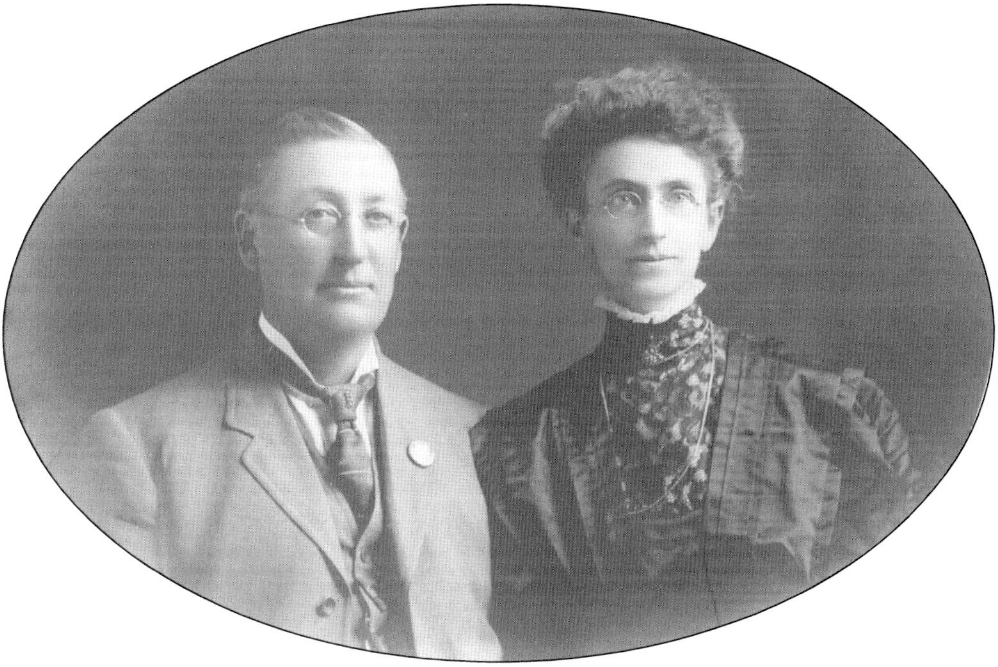

Jesse Jansen, a Danish immigrant, pictured here with his wife, Helen Miller Jansen, came to Reedley in 1890 to work as a buying agent for the McNear wheat grain company. In 1902, he organized the Reedley Store and Hall Company, which built the Jansen Block and Opera House. The building complex is now listed in the National Register of Historic Places. He was a founder of Reedley's first bank, the Reedley State Bank.

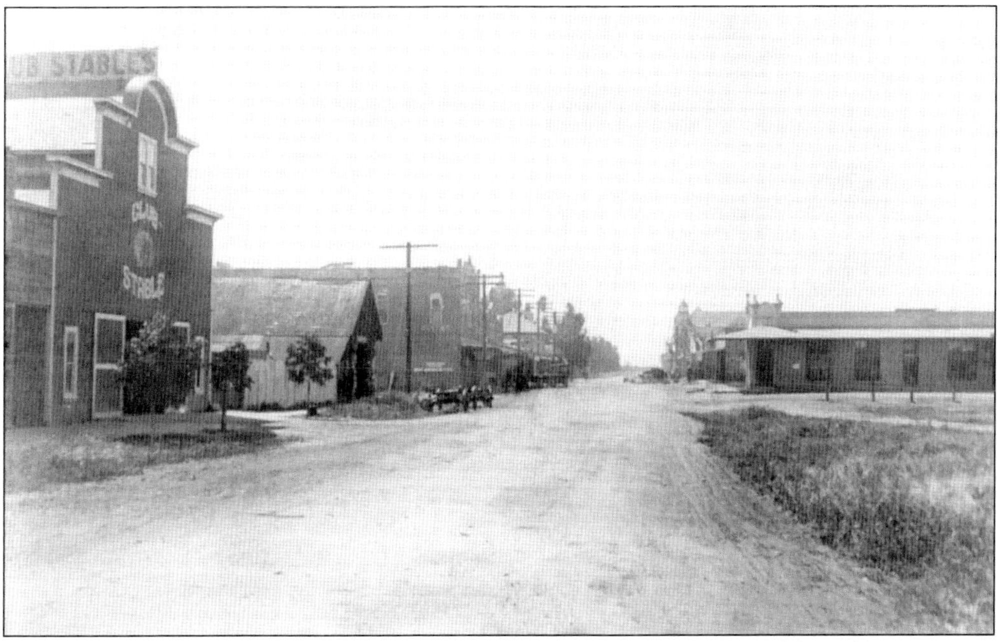

Downtown Reedley is seen here about 1905. On the left is John Marlar's Club Stable. Next to it is Manuel Enos's blacksmith shop. On the right is the Jansen Block building, at the corner of G and Tenth Streets.

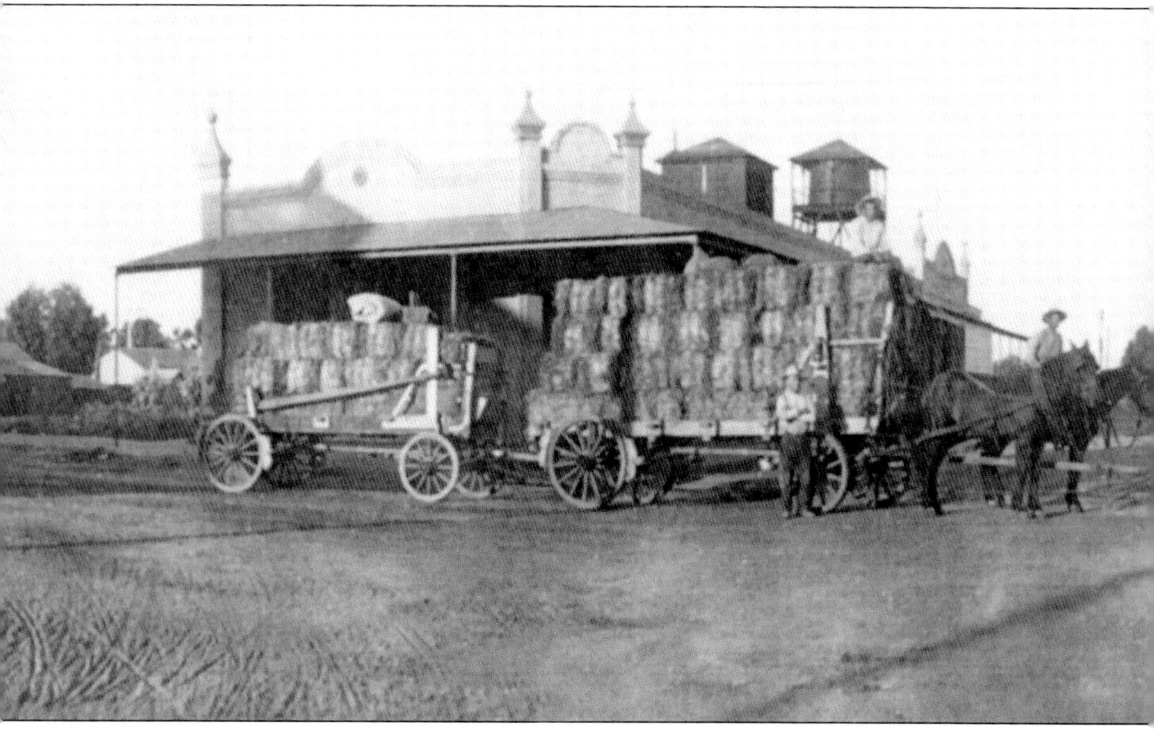

In July 1906, hay wagons could still be seen coming down main street. The crew has stopped at the Tenth Street intersection in front of the Jansen building. In the distance, just right of center,

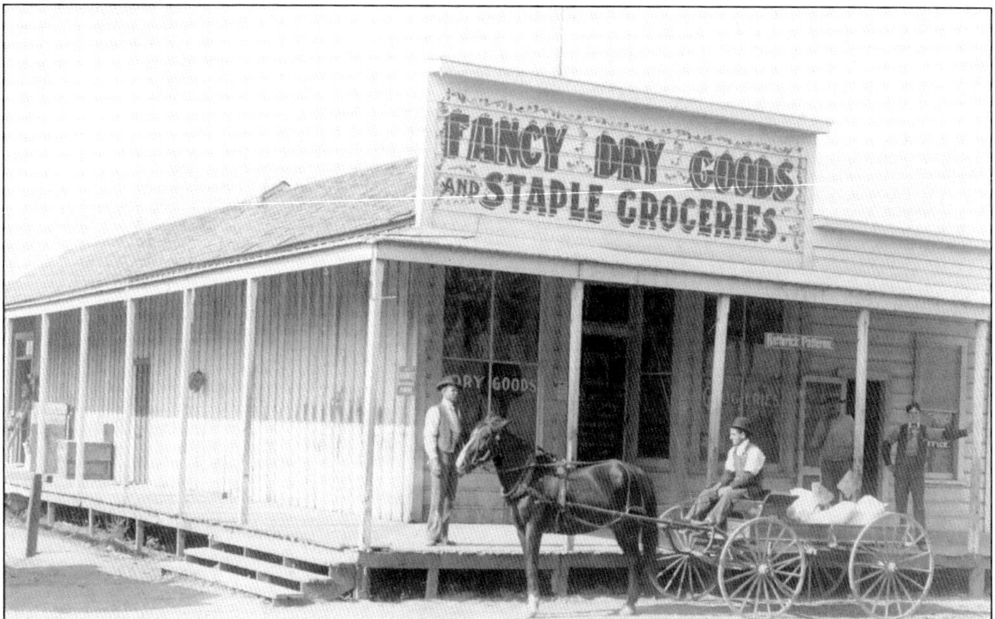

The H.D. Bollin family arrived in Reedley in early 1899. Within a few months, Bollin was in business as the proprietor of a dry goods and grocery store. This photograph, likely from 1899 or 1900, shows his first store.

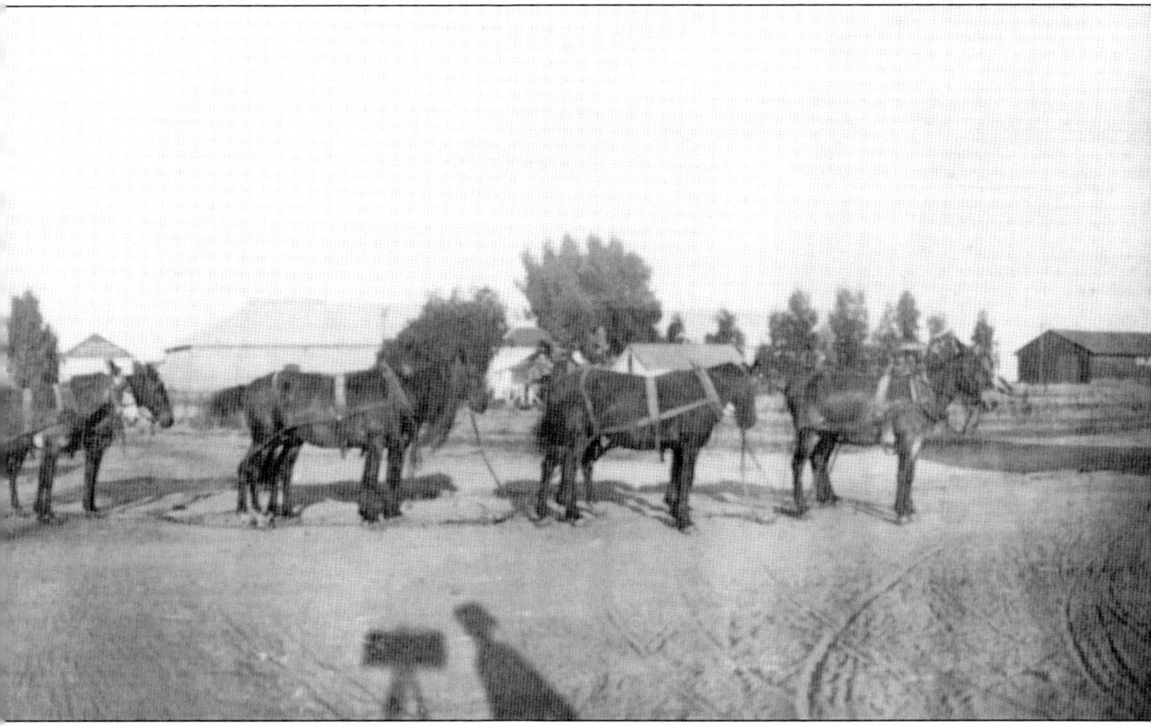

is the Grangers' warehouse. On the far right is the old 76 warehouse that was hauled in from Traver. The photographer (or at least his shadow) even managed to get into the picture.

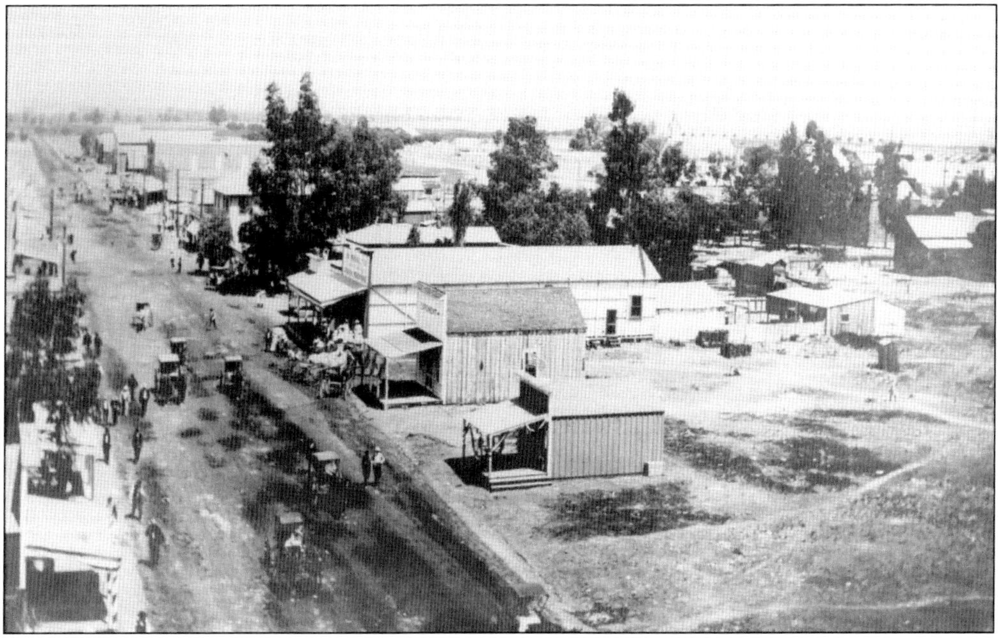

This c. 1906 photograph was taken from an upper floor of the Hotel Grand, at G and Twelfth Streets. This is what downtown looked like after 18 years of existence. The building at the very center, second from the bottom, is the office of the *Exponent*.

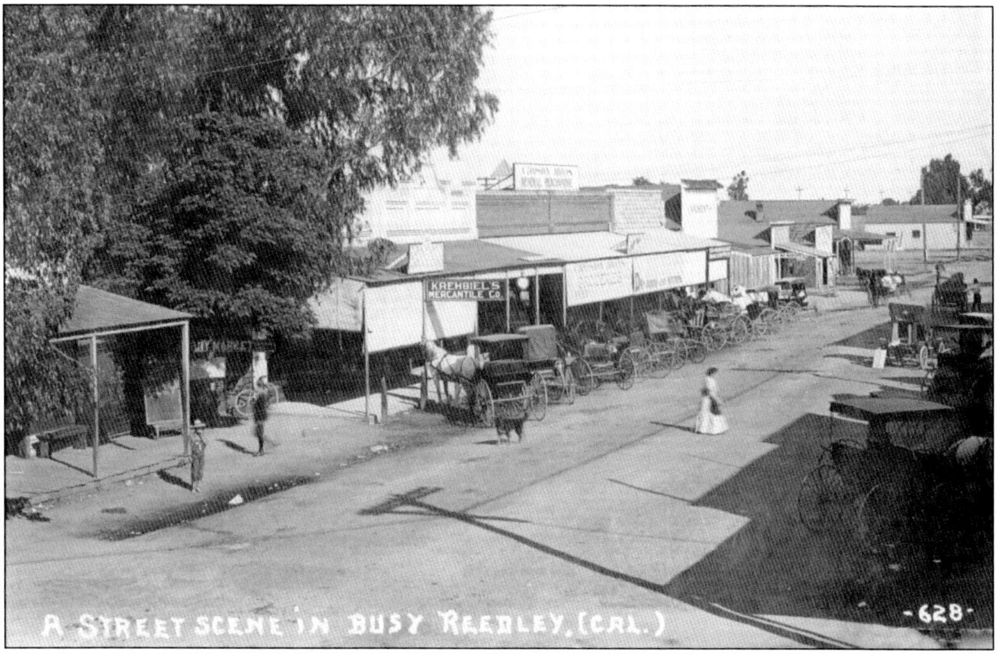

The east side of the 1100 block of G Street is seen here about 1908. Businesses in this scene are, from left to right, S.D. England's market, Krehbiel's Mercantile, Crosby Brothers Groceries and Dry Goods, Mueller Real Estate, the *Exponent*, and the Home Bakery. (Photograph by George Besaw.)

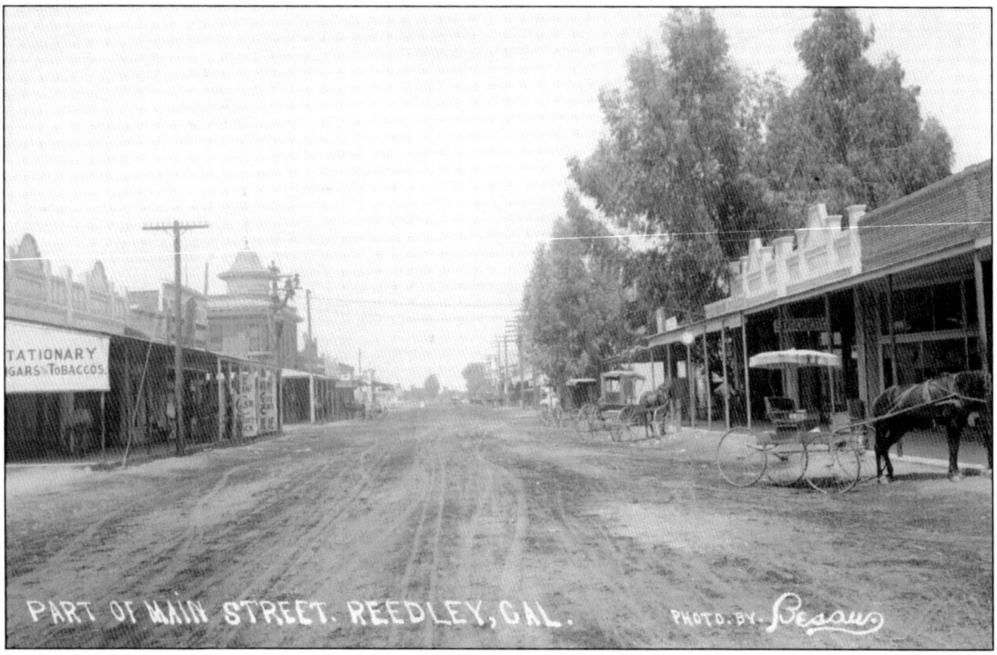

The 1100 block G Street is photographed on a quiet day about 1908. The First National Bank is seen on the corner of G and Eleventh Streets. Eymann Hardware is next door. On the left, closer to the photographer, are a druggist and a store offering cigars, tobacco, and "stationary." A competitor across the street offers "stationery." (Photograph by George Besaw.)

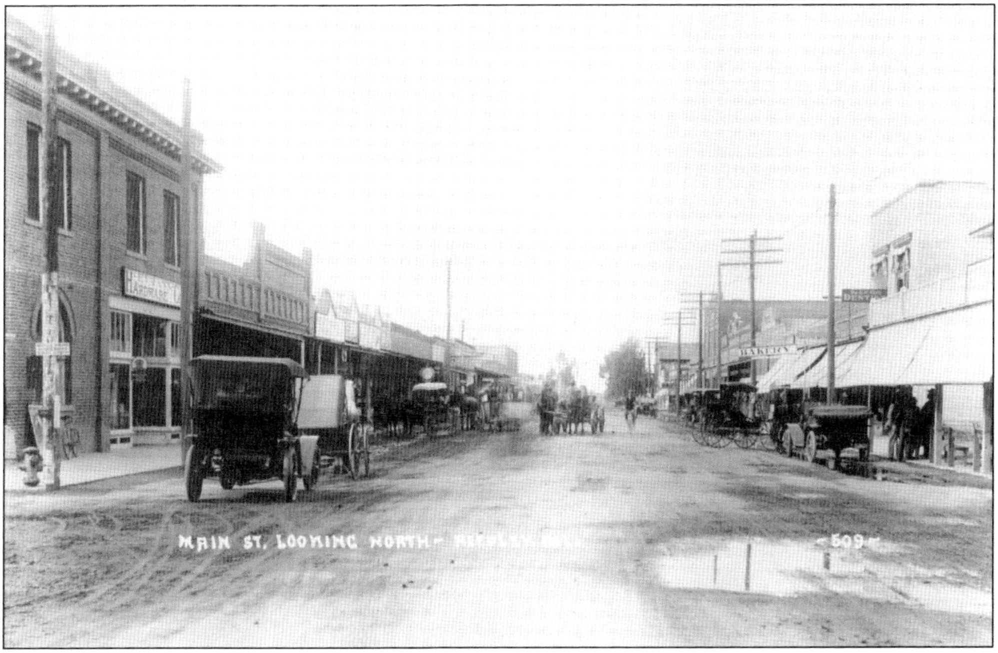

This c. 1912 photograph of G Street, taken from Eleventh Street, shows that the transition from horses and buggies to automobiles is under way. At left, in the distance, the post office now occupies the corner spot in the Jansen building. It would remain there until 1917. (Photograph by George Besaw.)

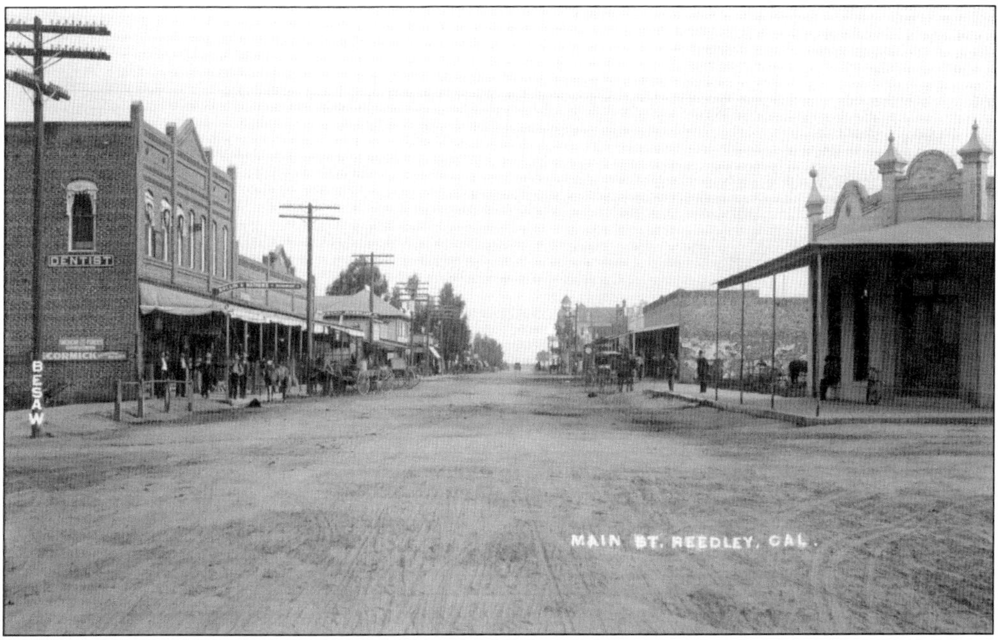

The 1902 fire convinced many business owners to use brick in their reconstruction, as evidenced by this c. 1905 photograph of G Street. Prominent on the left is the Bollin & Matthews building. On the right is the Jansen building. (Photograph by George Besaw.)

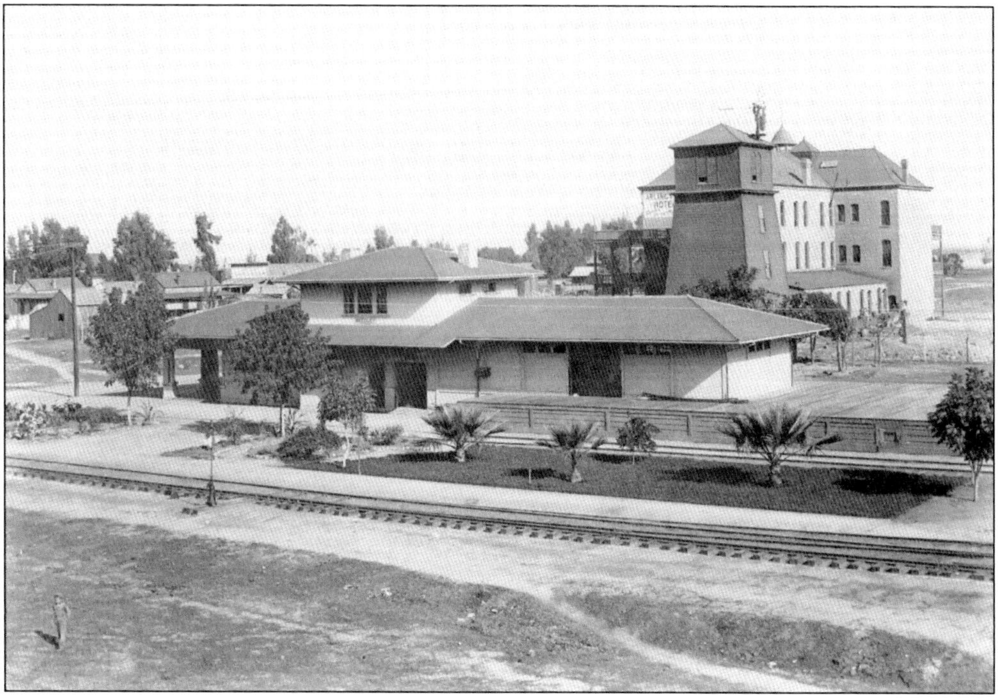

In 1897, the San Francisco & San Joaquin Valley Railroad built a line through Reedley and established a depot. The "Valley Road" was viewed as a welcome competitor to the despised Southern Pacific. The Santa Fe Railway purchased the Valley Road in 1898. The depot was located on the south side of Twelfth Street. The Arlington Hotel stands in the background.

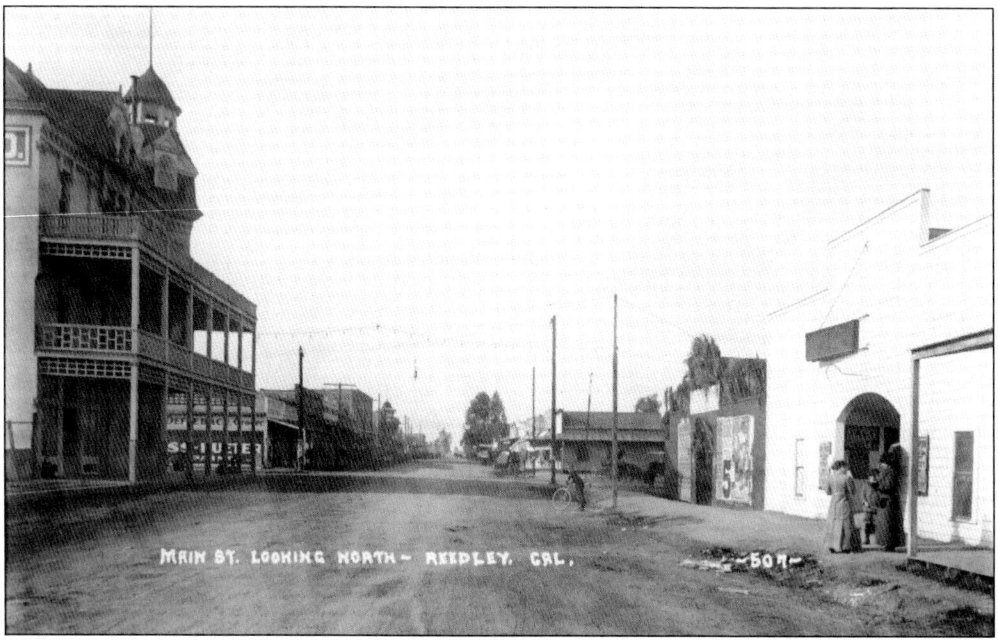

G Street is seen in this c. 1908 photograph, taken from just south of Twelfth Street. On the left is the Hotel Grand (the former Arlington Hotel). Reedley's open-air theater—known as the "Airdome" for a time—is on the right. (Photograph by George Besaw.)

Harry F. Winnes came to Reedley in 1889 as a carpenter, but he quickly became one of the town's most successful entrepreneurs. At one time, he owned and operated a furniture store, a general merchandise and grocery store, and a funeral parlor. Among his other pursuits were developing real estate, building the Winnes Hotel, and serving as one of the founders of Reedley's first bank. He is pictured here in 1887 at age 27.

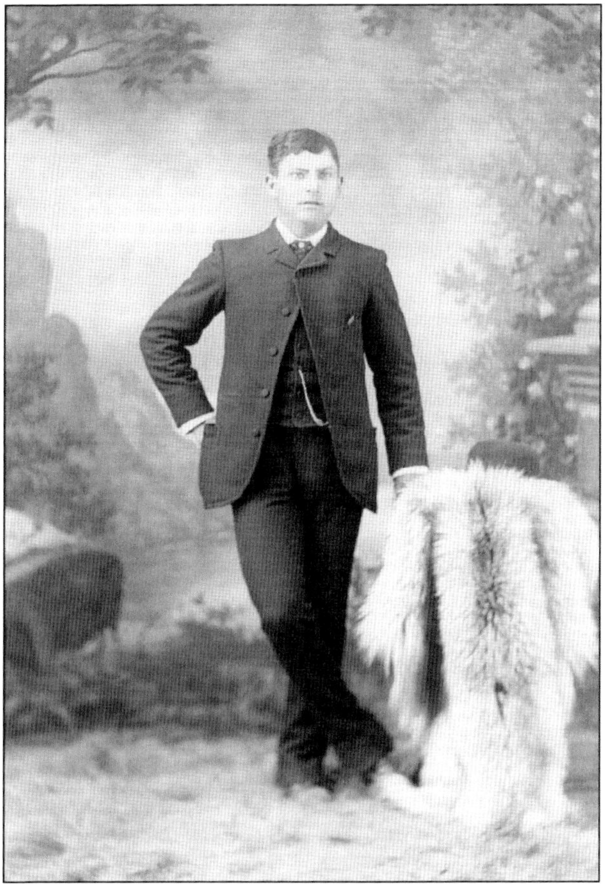

This rare photograph, taken in 1912 or 1913, shows the Winnes Hotel under construction at G and Eleventh Streets. The hotel was on the second floor, and stores occupied the ground floor. Reedley's post office was located in the corner space for a few years, starting in 1917. Later, C.H. Howell's stationery store was there before moving across the street.

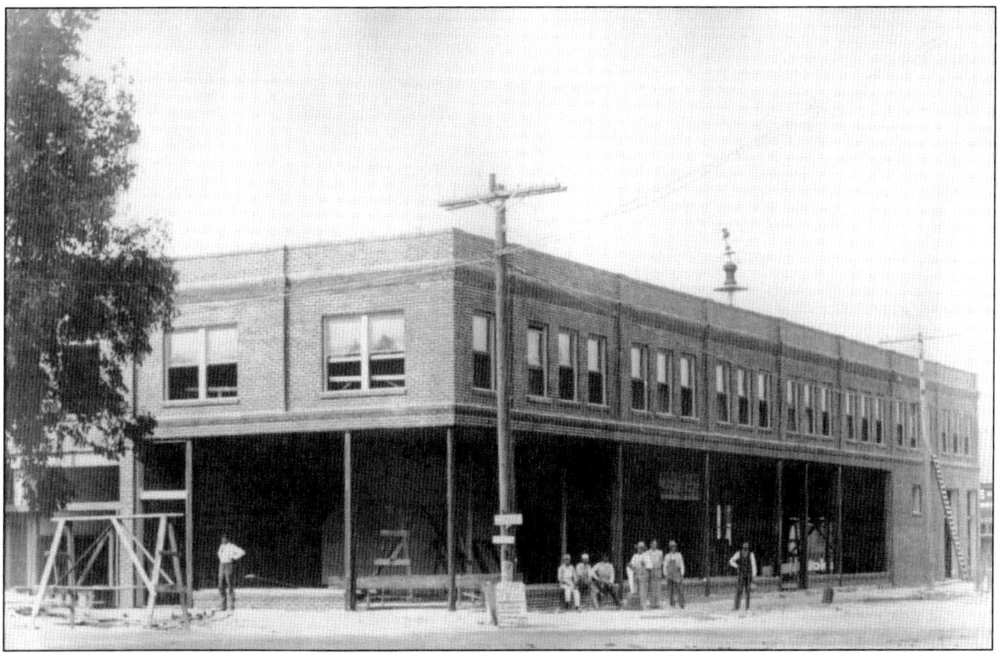

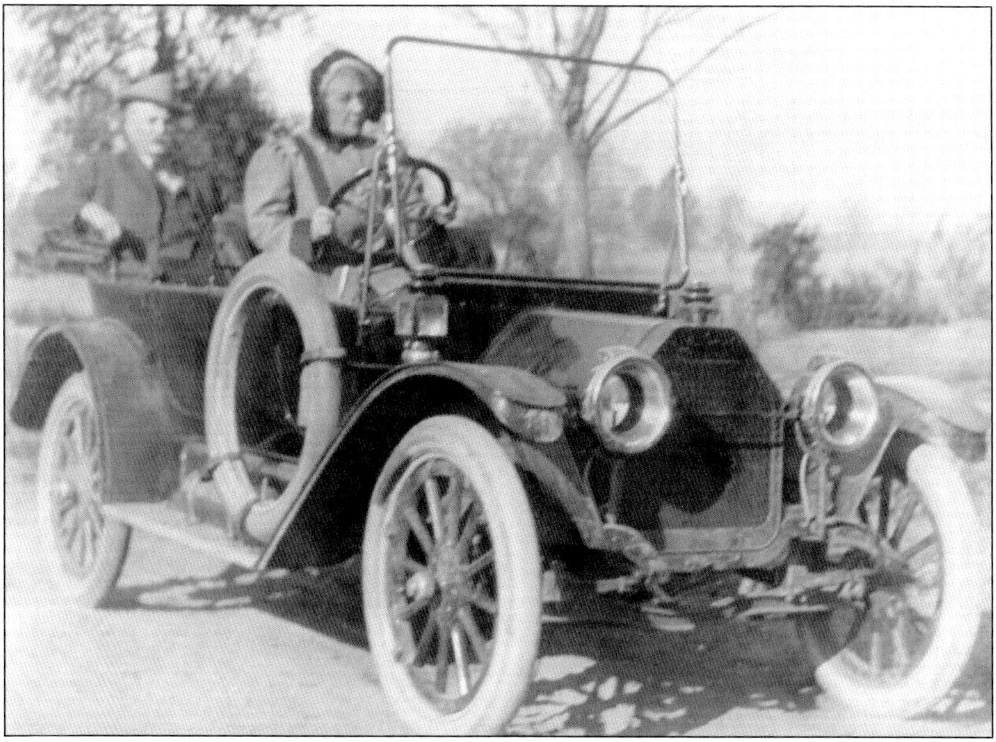

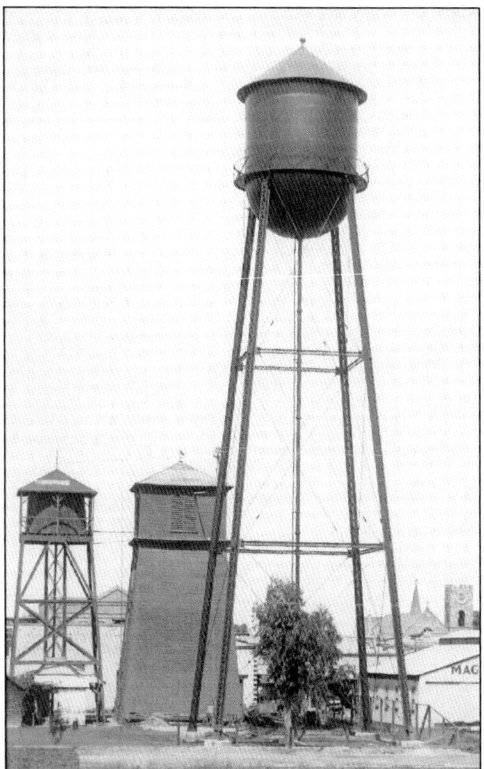

Dr. George Hawkins is seen in his 1912 Buick, being chauffeured by Cammie Simpson. Hawkins was one of Reedley's first physicians and one of the first persons in Reedley to own an automobile. He lived in the Reedley Hotel, where he also had his office. Simpson's parents owned and operated the hotel. The automobile was kept in a nearby livery stable.

The town's waterworks was privately owned in the early years. The City bought the facility in March 1914 and immediately contracted for the installation of a steel tower and a 60,000-gallon tank. The old wooden towers were demolished. A second steel tower was added in 1923. The distinctive twin water towers became, and remain, an iconic feature of Reedley's downtown skyline.

John C. McCubbin first came to Traver in 1886. He moved to a small ranch just south of Reedley in 1895. His writings, which chronicled early happenings in both Traver and Reedley, are an invaluable resource for present-day historians. This 1908 photograph shows McCubbin with what he called his Wild West moustache.

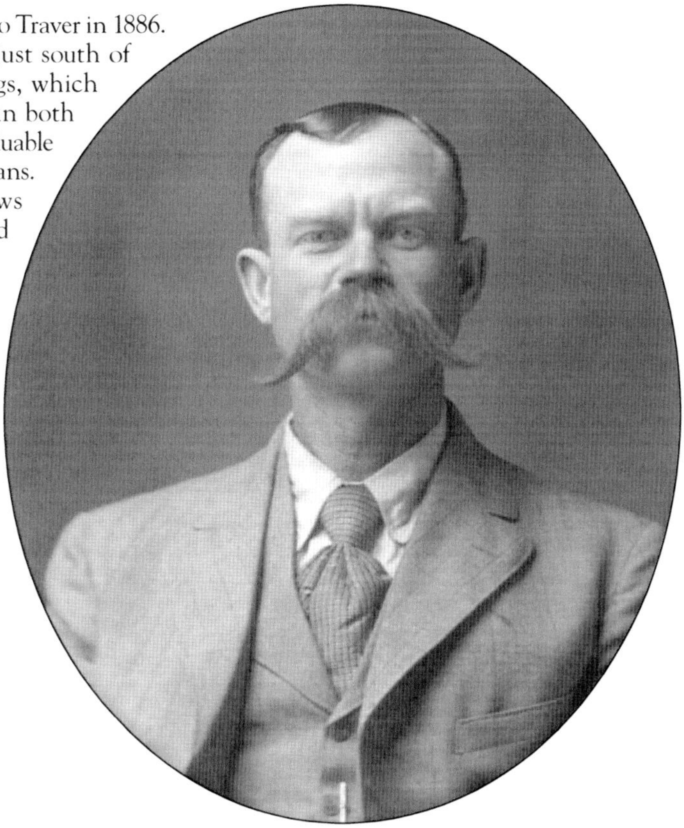

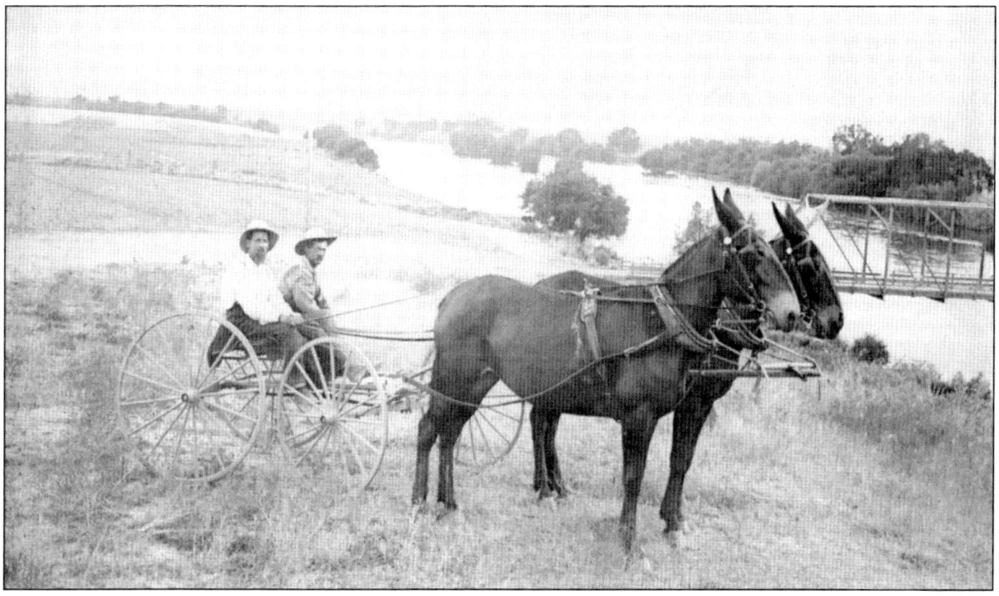

T.L. Reed (left) and J.H. Harris, along with their mules Madam and Matt, pose for a photograph on Reed's ranch property on the east side of the Kings River in 1887. Reedley would have its birth the following year. At right is the old wagon bridge, built in 1885 at what is now Manning Avenue. (Photograph by C.C. Curtis.)

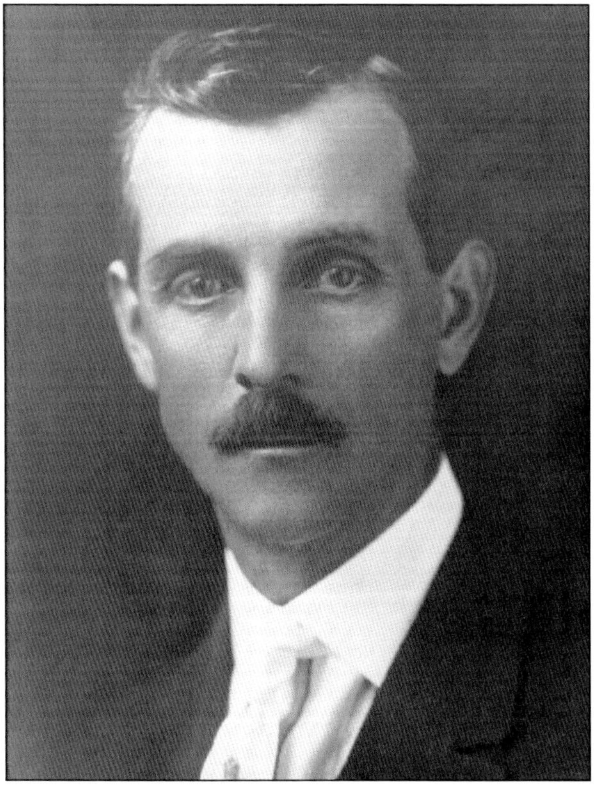

Jacob John Eymann became Reedley's first mayor when the town incorporated in 1913. After arriving in Reedley in 1904, Eymann went into the lumber business and, later, real estate, insurance, and banking. Eymann's father, Daniel T. Eymann, promoted settlement in Reedley by those Mennonites who would found Reedley's First Mennonite Church.

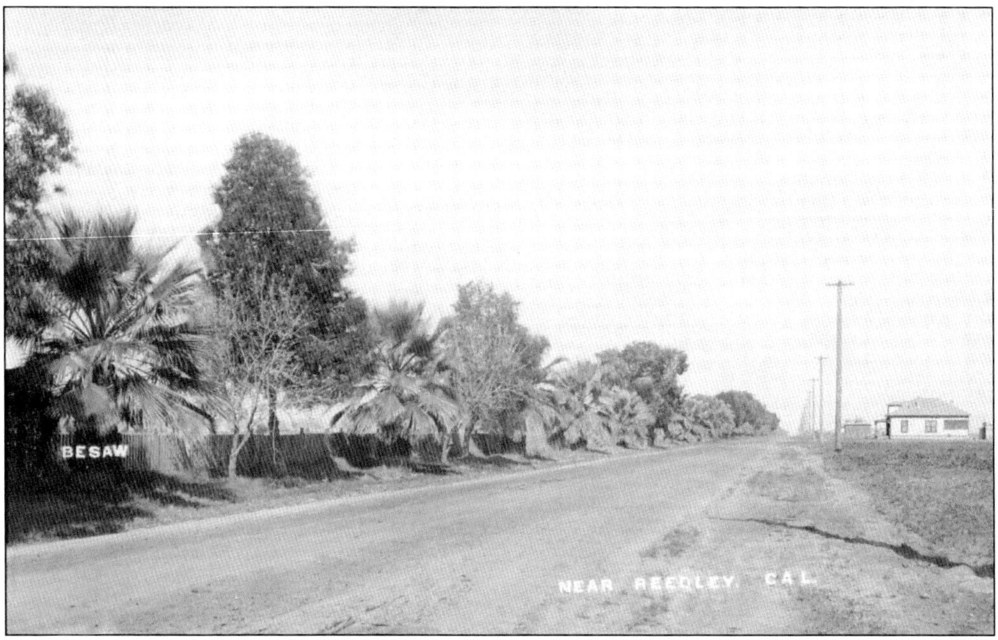

The border trees and palms along Reed Avenue mark the south and east boundaries of the T.L. Reed ranch, as seen in this c. 1904 photograph. These historic California fan palms, still standing along Reed Avenue, are a magnificent reminder of Reedley's beginnings as a community. (Photograph by George Besaw.)

Two

Agriculture

The white settlers who arrived in the Central Valley in the 1850s found an arid plain. But this was not a source of disappointment for these hardy pioneers. Livestock could be raised here, and the rapidly growing population of coastal California would provide a nearby market for their production. By the 1860s, newer settlers were venturing into wheat farming. Rainfall was minimal, but wheat could be dry-farmed.

Wheat production grew tremendously in the last quarter of the 19th century. This was attributable, in good part, to two factors. The railroad had arrived in Fresno and Tulare Counties in 1872. Shipping wheat to distant markets was now easy. And with the passage of the No Fence Law of 1874, farmers now had recourse when their neighbors' cattle damaged their crops. The era of the free range was effectively at its end.

T.L. Reed was among the beneficiaries of these developments. His arrival in Fresno County in 1884 marked the beginning of large-scale wheat production in the Reedley area. Within a few years, California's San Joaquin Valley became the leading producer of wheat in the world.

Just as wheat production was accelerating, steps were being taken for the next phase in agricultural development. The big player in what would become the Reedley area was the 76 Land and Water Company. Its plan was to sell land with access to water from an irrigation system the company would build. The pitch was simple. Irrigation would allow farmers to produce crops far more profitable than wheat. Fewer acres would be needed to support a family. The pace of settlement quickened, as did the transition from growing wheat to growing grapes and tree fruit.

Agriculture would experience another transition at the turn of the century when the modern age reached the farm. The steam-powered tractor had a brief life, but it foreshadowed things to come. Gasoline-powered tractors and trucks, rural electrification, advanced irrigation systems, and so many other improvements changed the farming game. It was an age of increased efficiency and productivity.

Reedley was ready to feed the world.

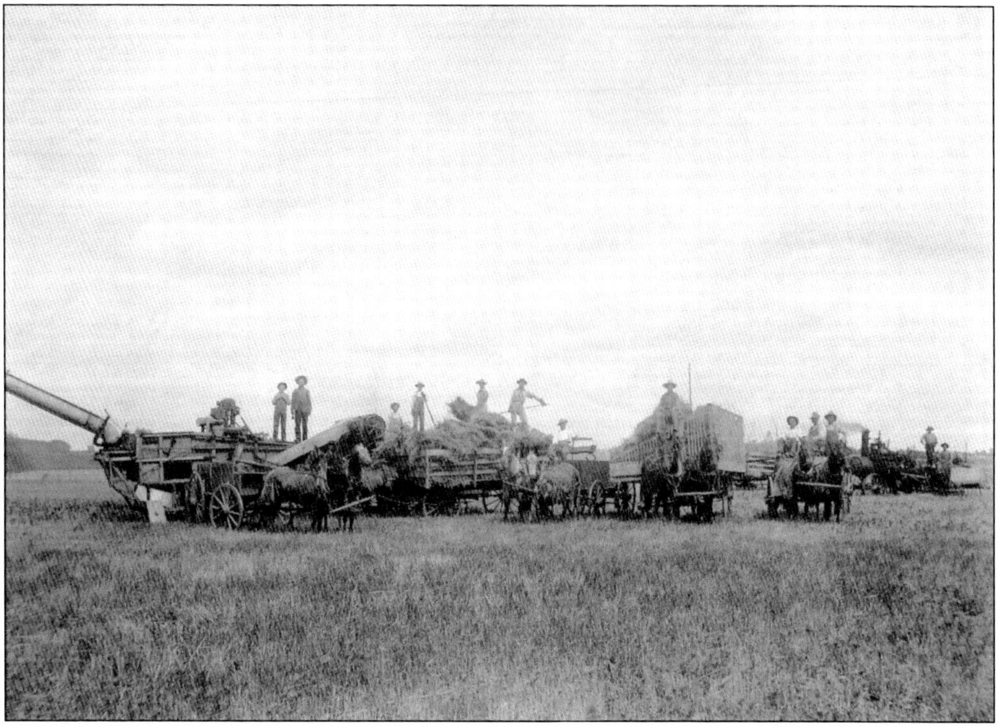

Wheat threshing is depicted on a Reedley-area ranch around the turn of the century. While mules provide most of the motive power in this operation, a transition is under way. A steam tractor is at work in the background on the right.

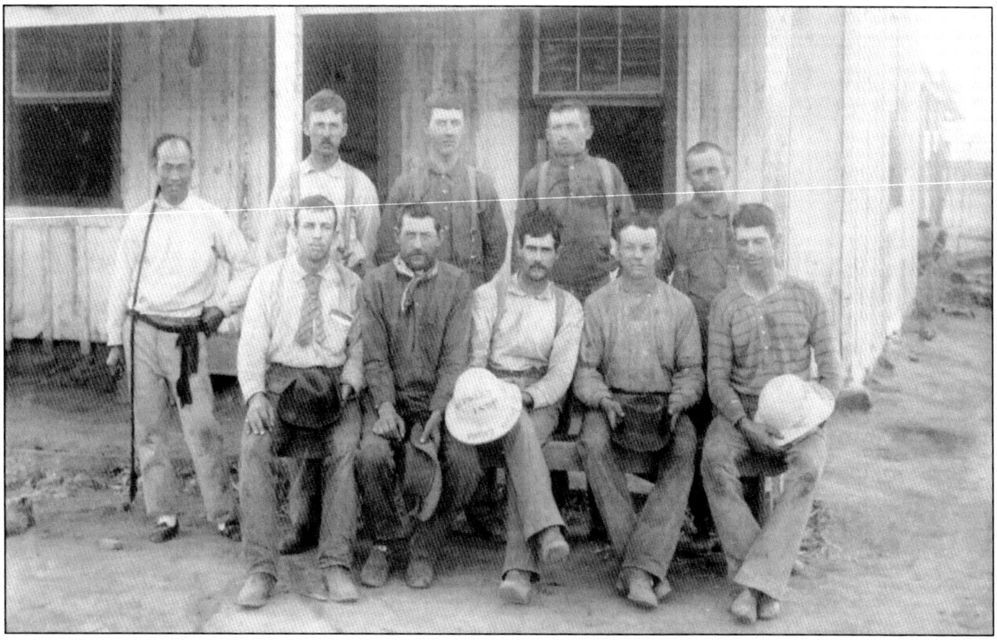

The wheat-threshing crew from the John R. Reed ranch poses for a photograph in 1890. Louie Lee (or Li), on the far left, was the cook. John Reed was T.L. Reed's brother. (Photograph by C.C. Curtis.)

Wheat grain is stacked to the rafters in this Reedley warehouse prior to shipment. Gene Jones, shown leading the horse, was paid $1 per day for his work.

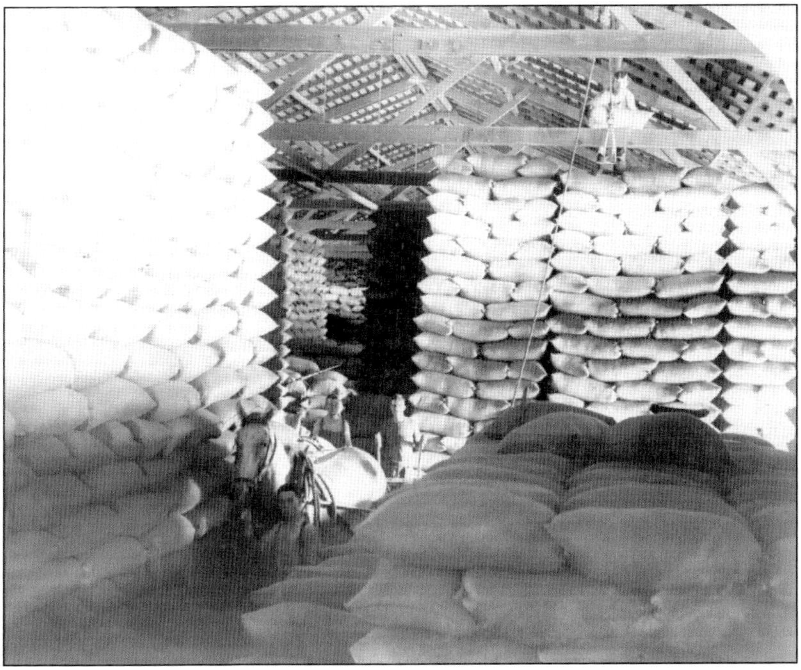

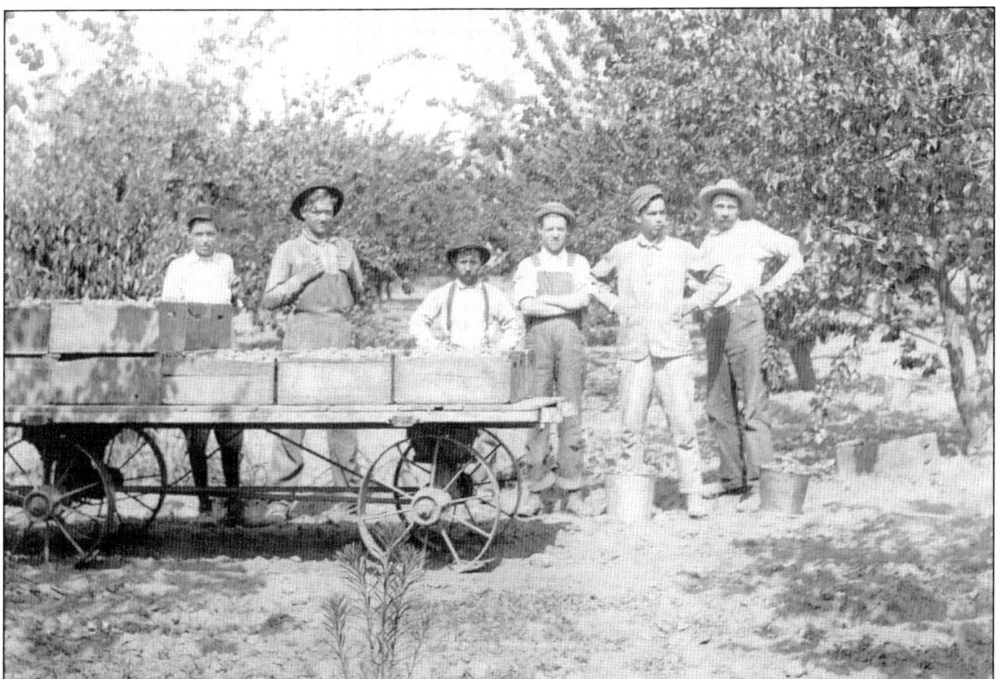

These men strike a pose for the photographer in a Reedley-area orchard. A century later, farms are still very much dependent on the manual labor and hard work of farmhands.

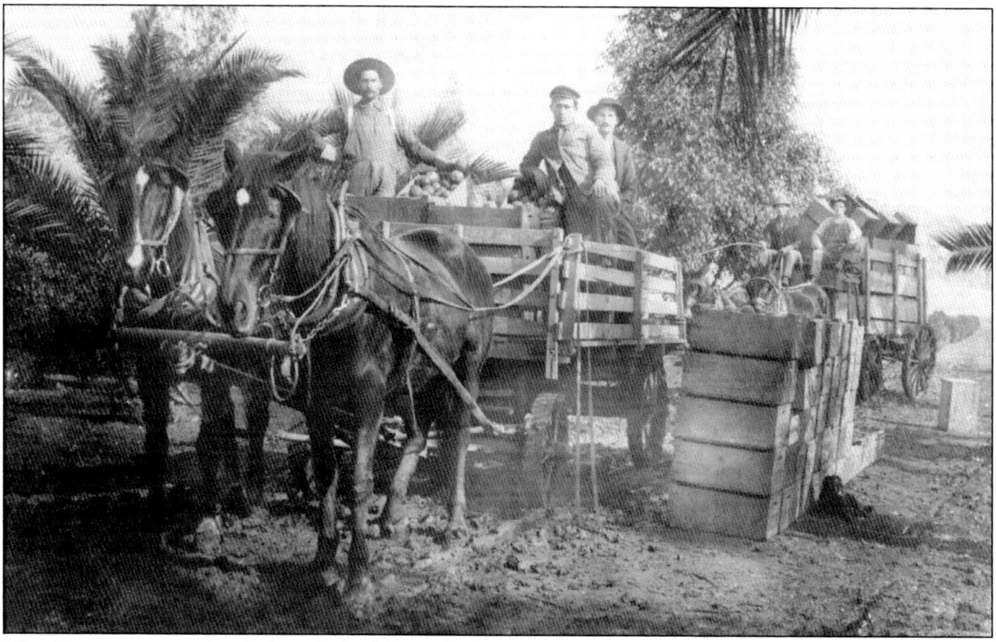

The front wagon is loaded with freshly picked fruit ready to be taken to the packing shed. The rear wagon carries empty boxes that the pickers would fill next.

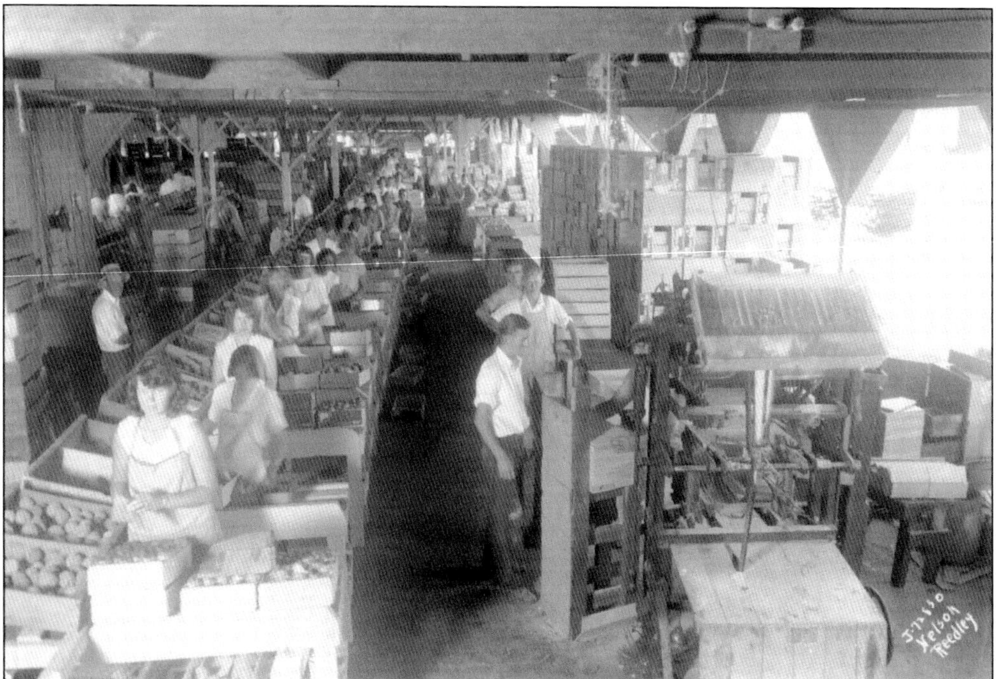

Workers pack tree fruit at the Reedley Grape Growers packinghouse in 1930. The local packinghouses provided seasonal and some year-round employment for many area residents. An early box-making machine is seen on the right. (Photograph by Nelson Studio.)

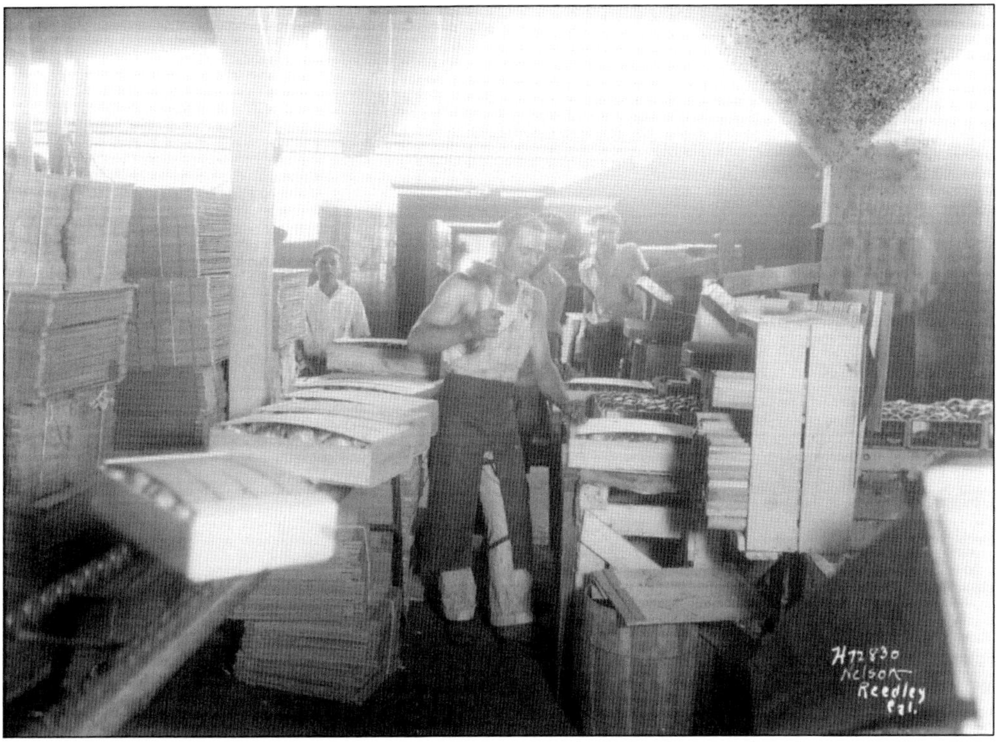

The electrically operated nailing press had not yet reached this fruit packinghouse in the 1930s. Here, a worker is attaching the lid to a lug box in the original way it was done—by hand. (Photograph by Nelson Studio.)

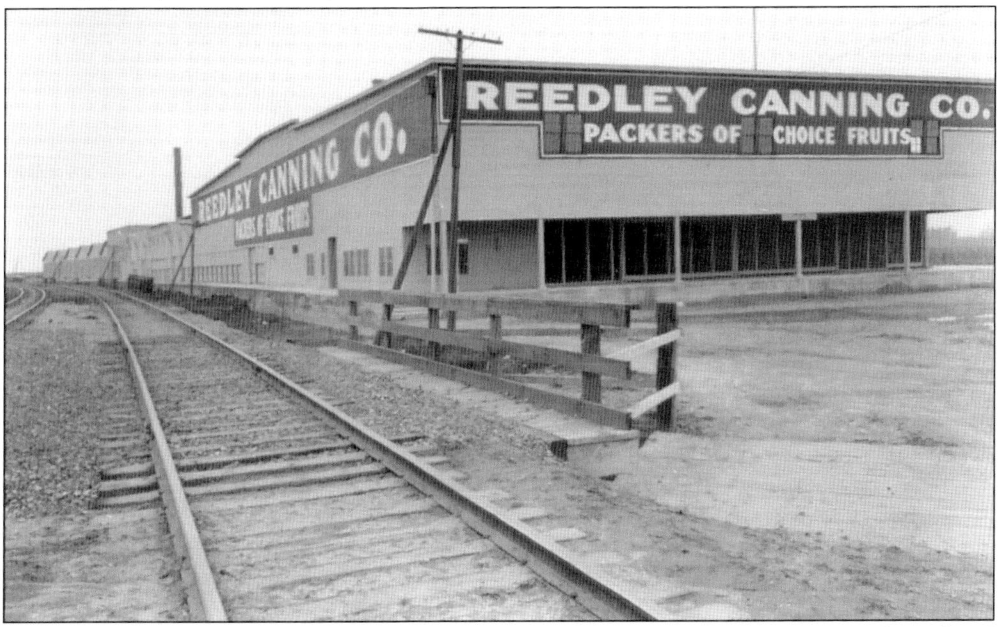

The Reedley Canning Company opened in 1919. The large facility was located along the railroad tracks, just south of Dinuba Avenue. The plant was sold two years later to the San Jose–based Herbert Packing Company, which continued to use the facility as a fruit cannery.

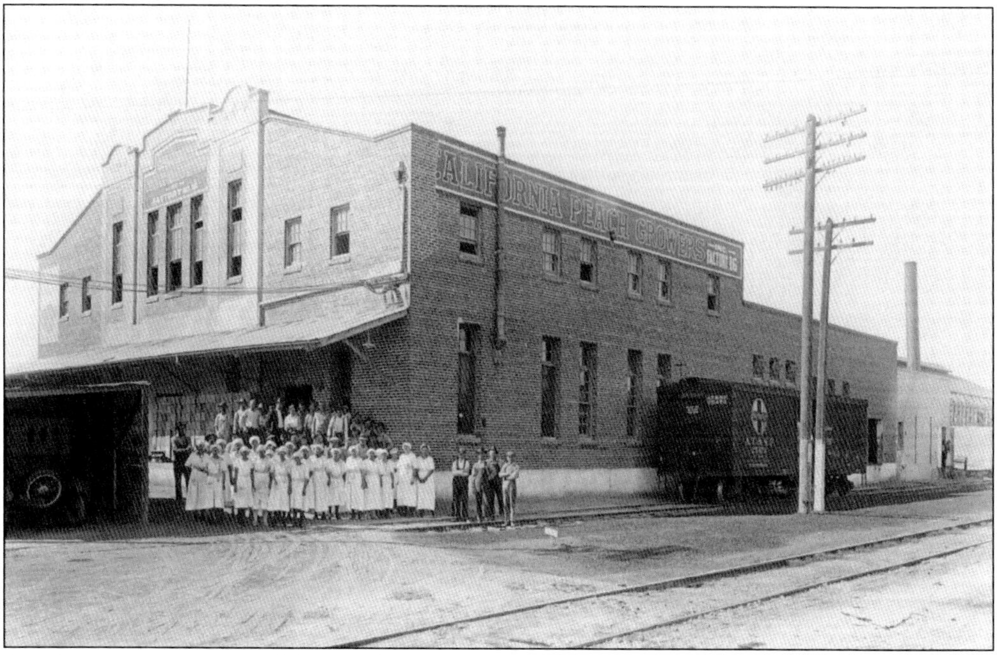

The brick packinghouse of the California Peach Growers was built in 1917, directly in front of the old 76 warehouse on the north side of Eighth Street. Employees of what was known locally as the "peach house" pose for a photograph in the 1920s.

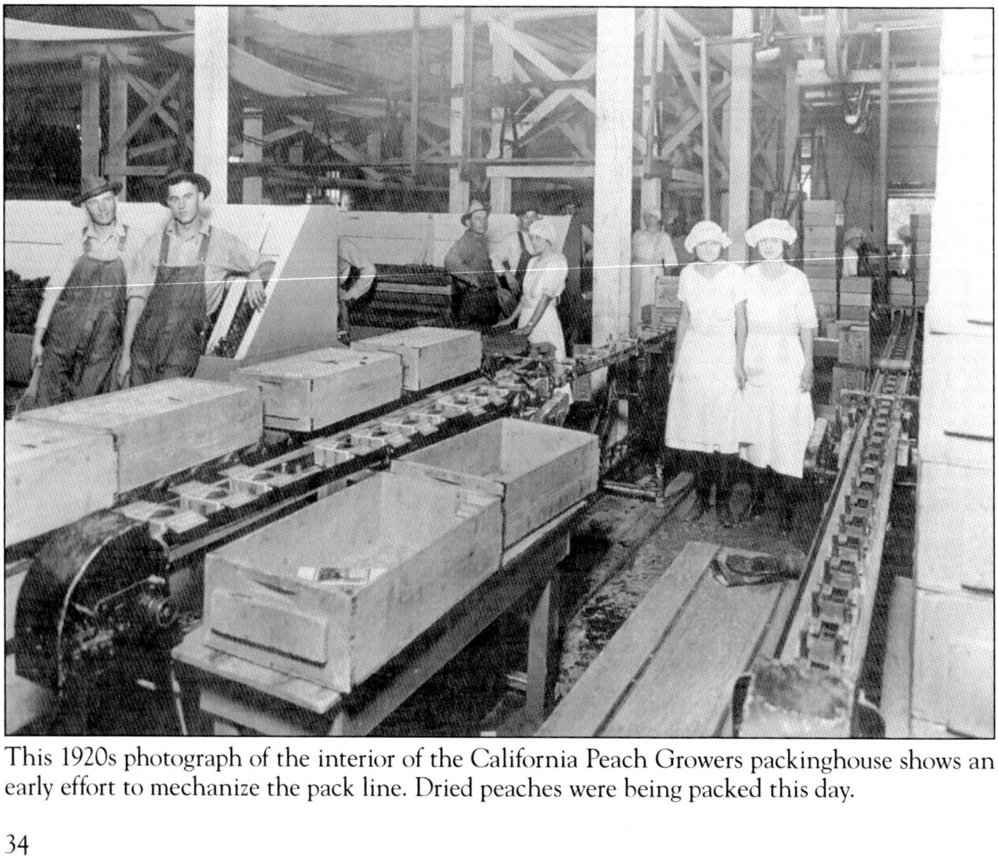

This 1920s photograph of the interior of the California Peach Growers packinghouse shows an early effort to mechanize the pack line. Dried peaches were being packed this day.

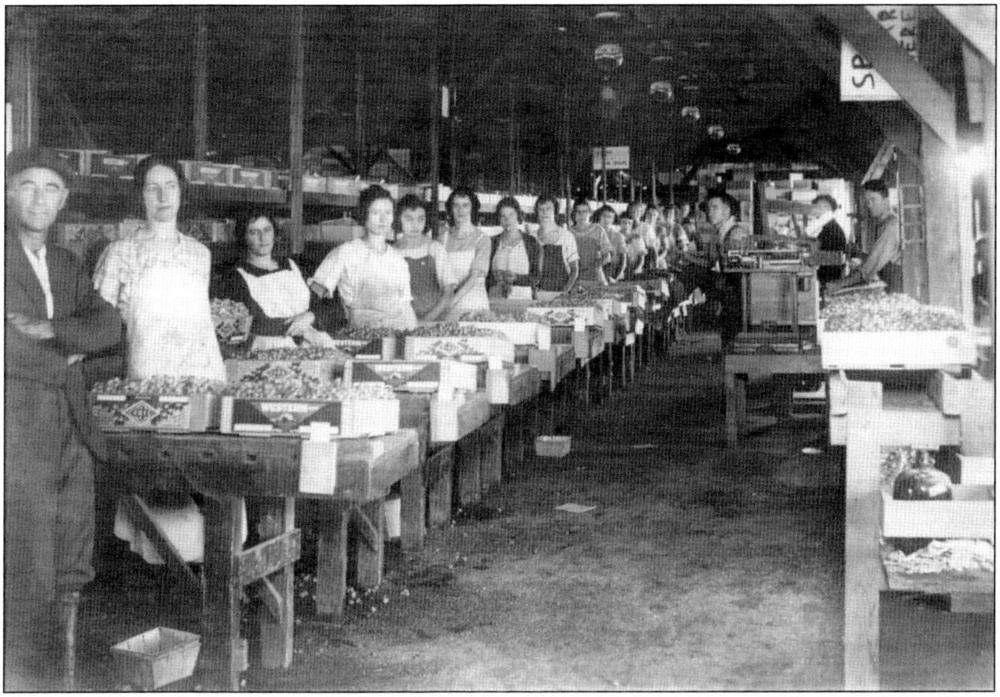

Grapes are being packed in this photograph, taken between 1920 and 1925. Sometimes packers would use two different labels, as seen here, for marketing varying grades of fruit—a practice still in use today.

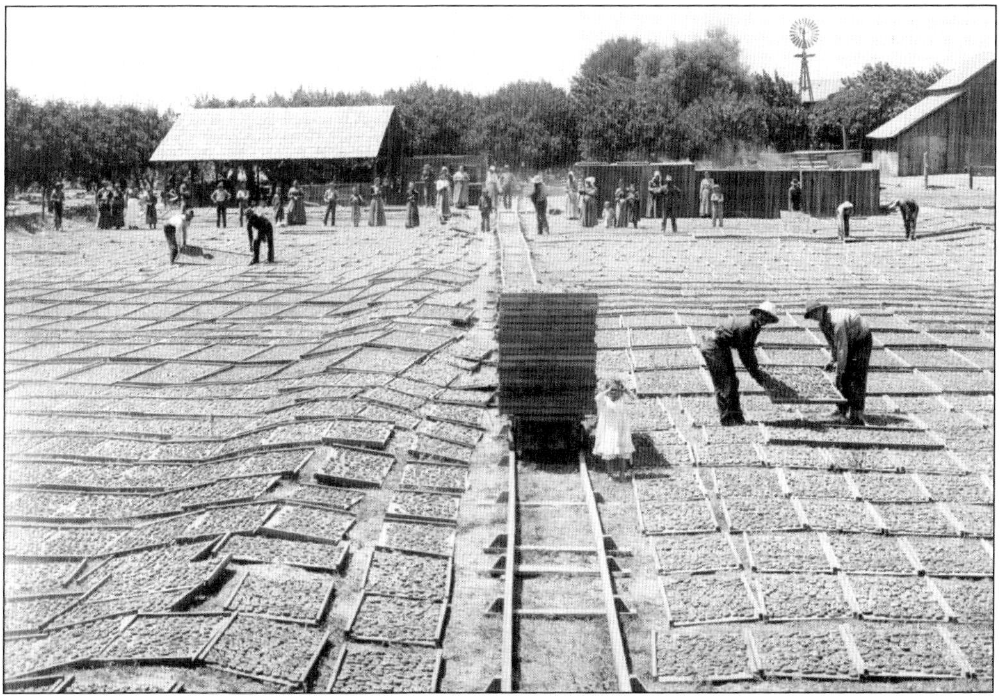

Cut peaches are laid out for drying at the Bollinger ranch. This photograph probably dates from the first decade of the 20th century. (Photograph by H.H. Alexander.)

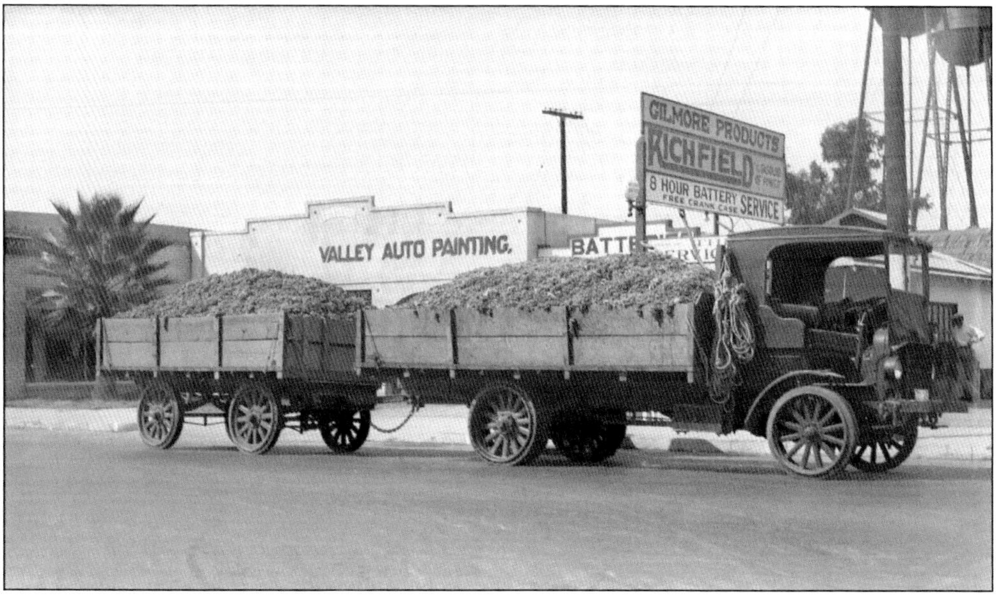

These grapes are likely headed to a local winery. The driver has parked his truck on Eleventh Street and is seen at right chatting with someone at the gas station. His dog watches from the cab of the truck. The photographer, whose studio was directly across the street, seized the opportunity to capture this image around 1926. (Photograph by Nelson Studio.)

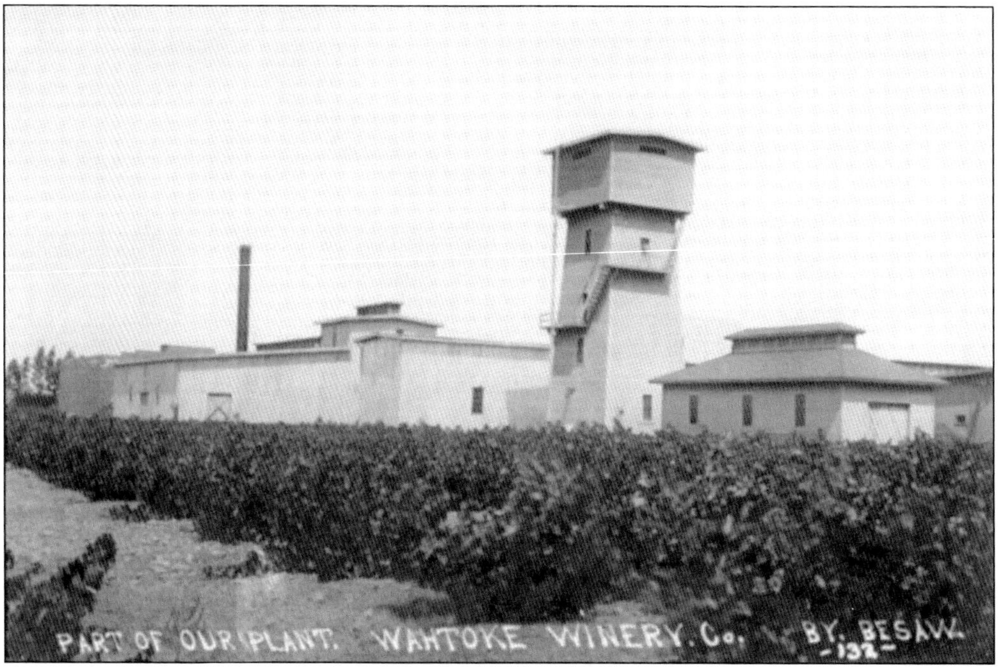

In 1905, the California Wine Association built the Wahtoke Winery amid 2,500 acres of vineyards north of town. Additional buildings were added to the facility in 1907. This photograph was taken about 1908. Some of the original structures are still in use today by the Franzia company. The winery is located at 2916 South Reed Avenue. (Photograph by George Besaw.)

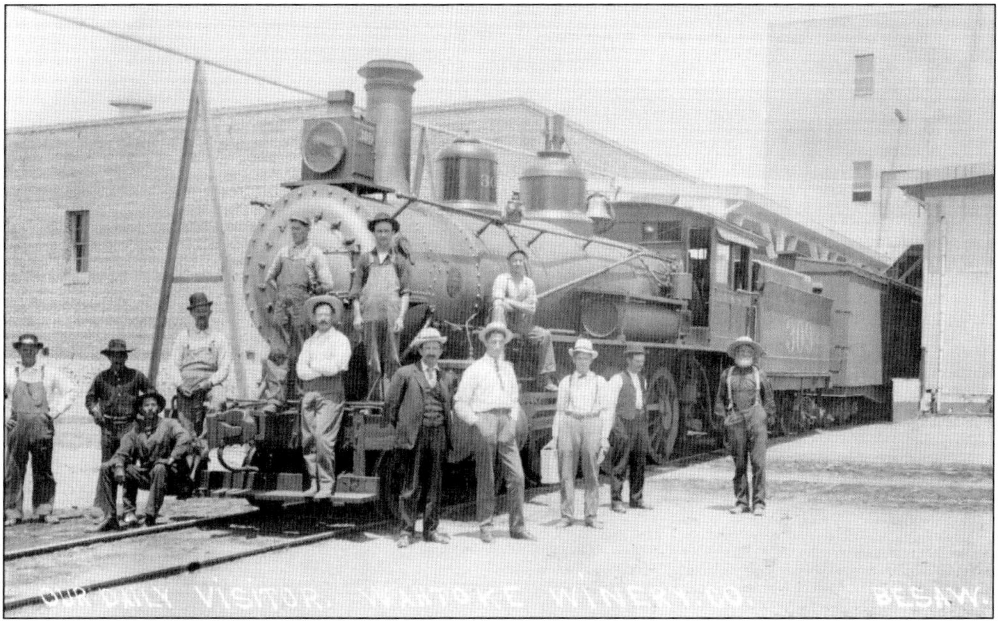

The Santa Fe Railway branch line from Reedley to the Wahtoke Winery was completed in 1906. Five years later, the line was extended from the winery to Piedra. Passenger service was also offered along this line. (Photograph by George Besaw.)

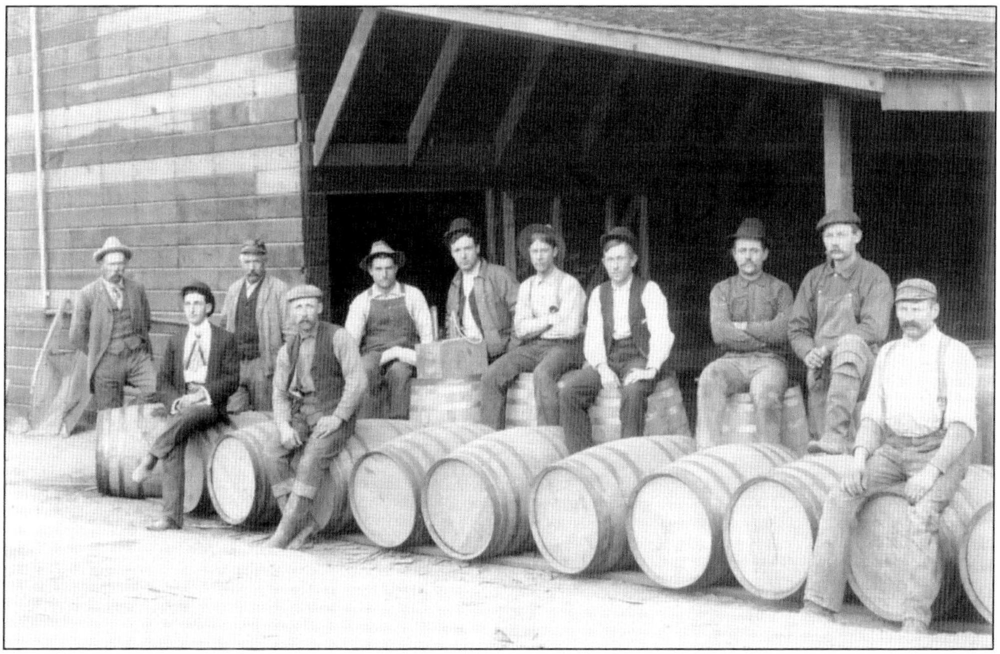

Workers at a local winery pose with some of their recent product. The photograph likely dates from between 1905 and 1910.

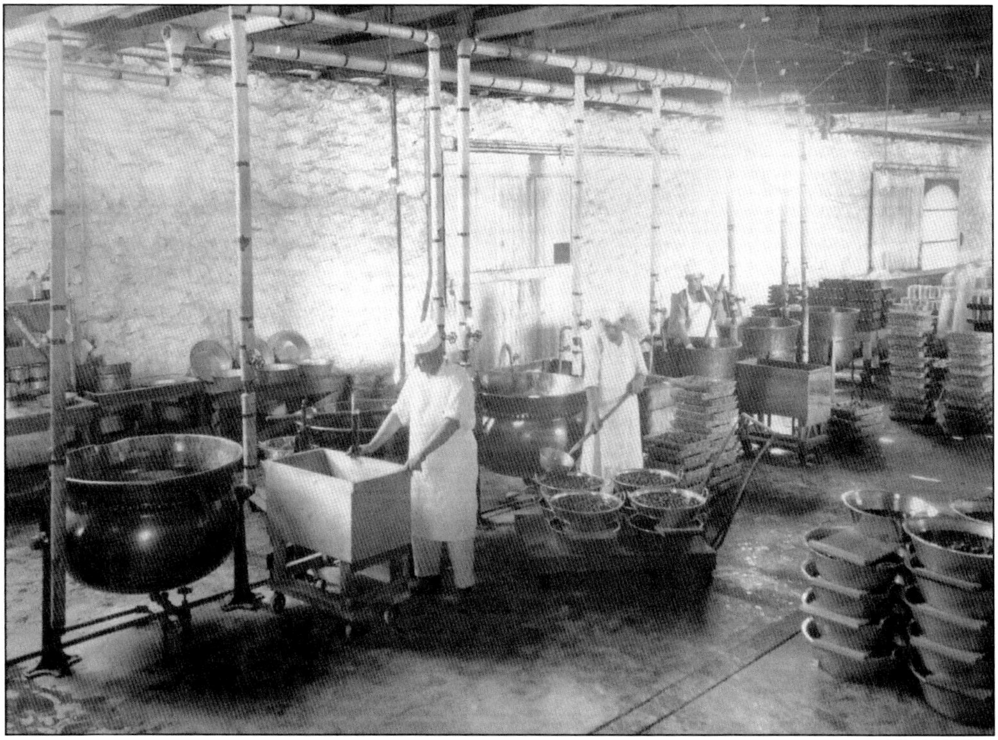

The interior of the Beckwith fig plant shows the steam kettles that were used to cook the figs. Beckwith's operation was located at 1760 Thirteenth Street in the old stone warehouse that still stands along the old Santa Fe Railway right-of-way.

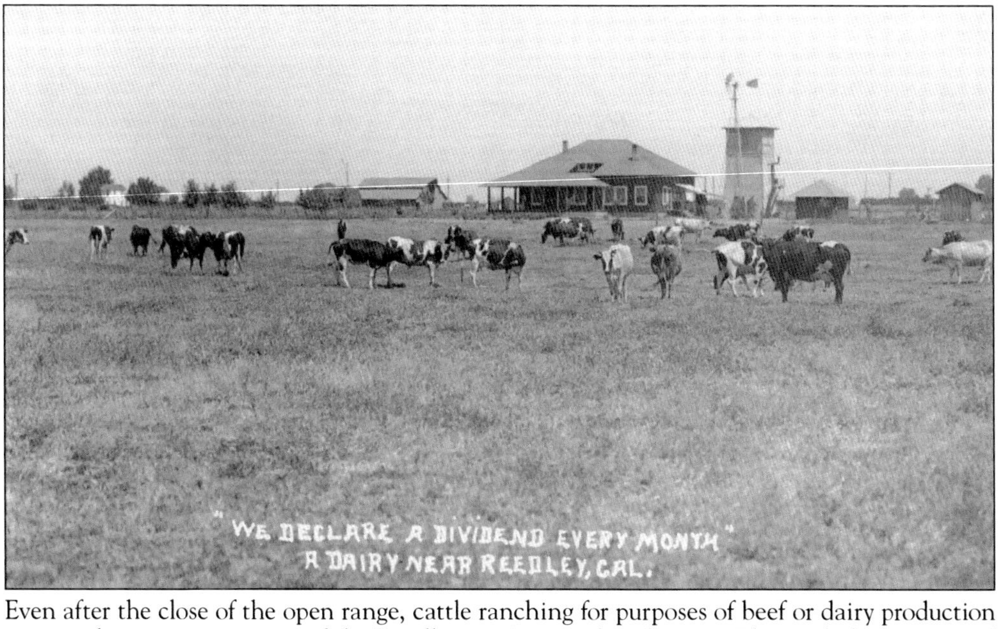

Even after the close of the open range, cattle ranching for purposes of beef or dairy production remained an important part of the Reedley area's agricultural scene. This real-photo postcard from about 1908 was an effort to promote this aspect of the local economy. (Photograph by George Besaw.)

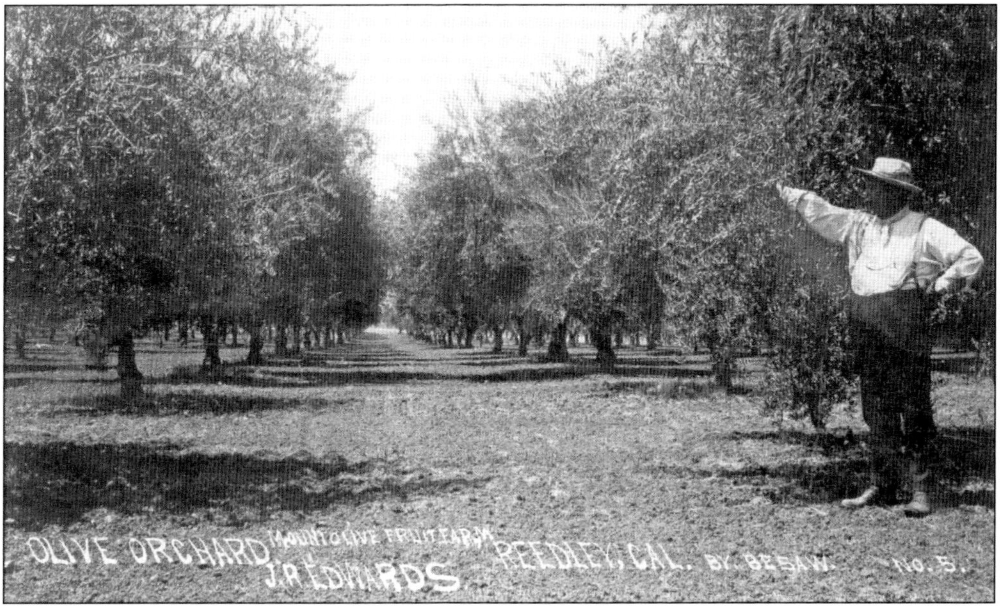

The Mount Olive Ranch, located several miles east of Reedley, was first developed in 1887 by the California Fruit and Wine Land Association of San Francisco. The ranch acquired its name from the fact that a mound at the center of the property was planted with olive trees. By the time this photograph was taken, J.R. Edwards had acquired some of the original ranch property. The man at right is unidentified.

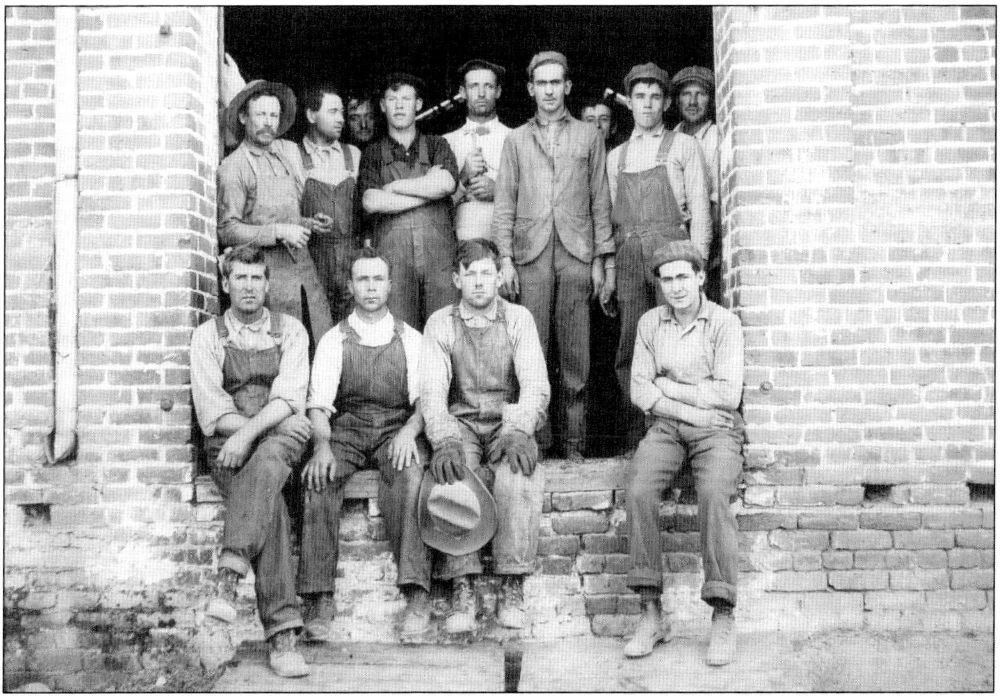

The north loading dock of the historic Grangers' warehouse served to frame this portrait of its workers at the turn of the century. The bricks used to build the Grangers' warehouse came from the kilns of Reedley's own brickyard.

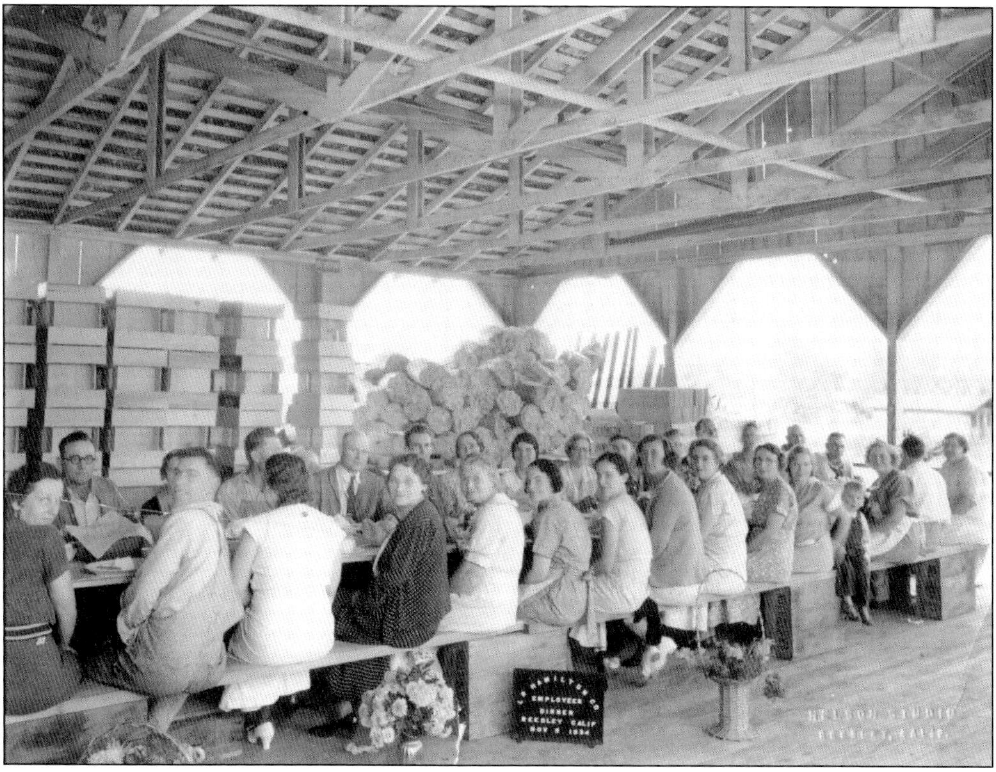

A custom that continues to this day is the packinghouse employee luncheon or dinner held to conclude the harvest season. The hard work and long hours of the L.R. Hamilton company workers are being acknowledged at this dinner in November 1934. (Photograph by Nelson Studio.)

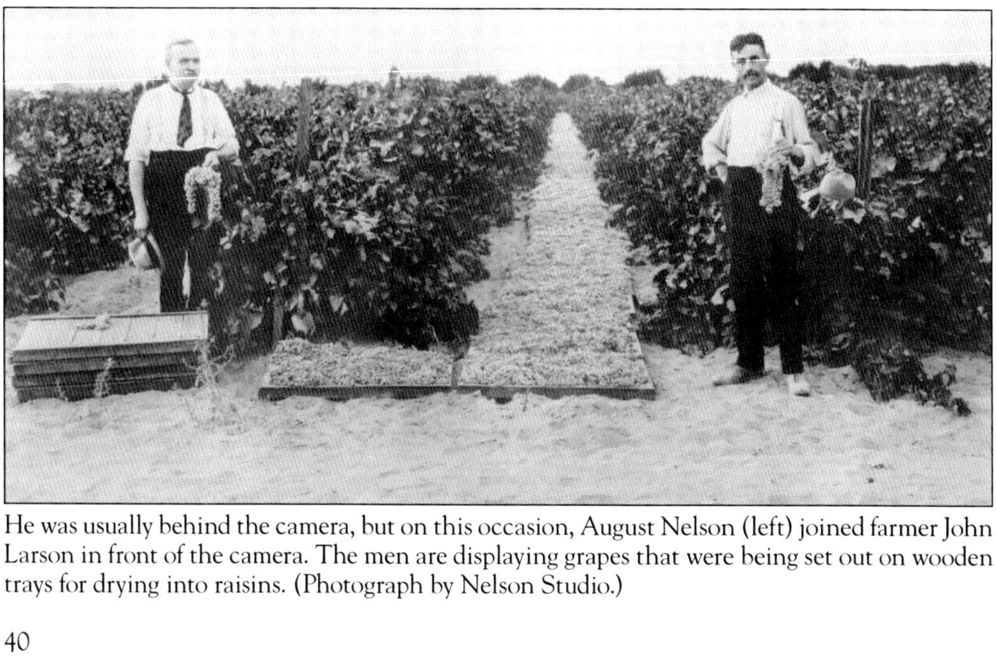

He was usually behind the camera, but on this occasion, August Nelson (left) joined farmer John Larson in front of the camera. The men are displaying grapes that were being set out on wooden trays for drying into raisins. (Photograph by Nelson Studio.)

Three

Business

The first business in Reedley was the railroad; the second was probably Emil Hirschfeld's general merchandise store. The post office opened, and so did the Reedley Hotel. Grocers and butchers went into business. There were blacksmiths and hardware stores. A livery stable opened, and then another. A newspaper was established. Bricks were made in town. A lumberyard experienced brisk demand.

Early Reedley had restaurants and saloons. Candy stores and ice cream shops were there, too. The iceman took orders and made deliveries. Doctors and dentists opened practices. A veterinarian attended to animals. Druggists came to dispense medications. An opera house was built to host traveling entertainers.

Warehouses and fruit packinghouses lined the railroad tracks from one end of town to the other. Sellers of farm implements promoted the latest tool or machine that would make farming easier or increase production. Clothing stores, shoe stores, and hat shops found customers. There was a jeweler and a photographer. There were two bicycle shops and a harness maker. Barbers cut hair, and a steam laundry cleaned clothes. And when death came, an undertaker was available.

Real estate was big business. Settlers continued to arrive, looking for farm property or a business they could start. A chamber of commerce was formed. Local businessmen founded two banks. New homes were built, completely furnished by what was found at a local furniture store.

The automobile age arrived. Machinists and liverymen became automobile dealers for Maxwells, Buicks, Overlands, and Fords. Service stations opened to sell gas, repair punctured tires, and fix troublesome engines. Then moving pictures came to town. An open-air theater opened on G Street in 1909, and within two years, another downtown theater was competing for customers.

Reedley was open for business.

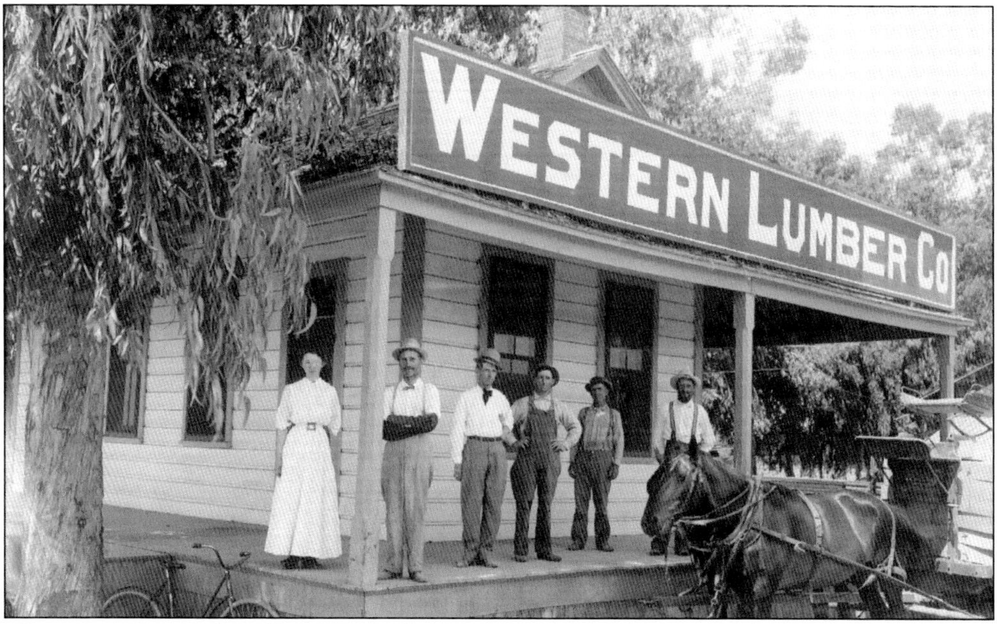

The growing town of Reedley supported at least two lumberyards. Western Lumber Company was one of the earliest and one of the longest lasting. The business, located at the corner of Eleventh and I Streets, was known as Citizens Lumber in later years.

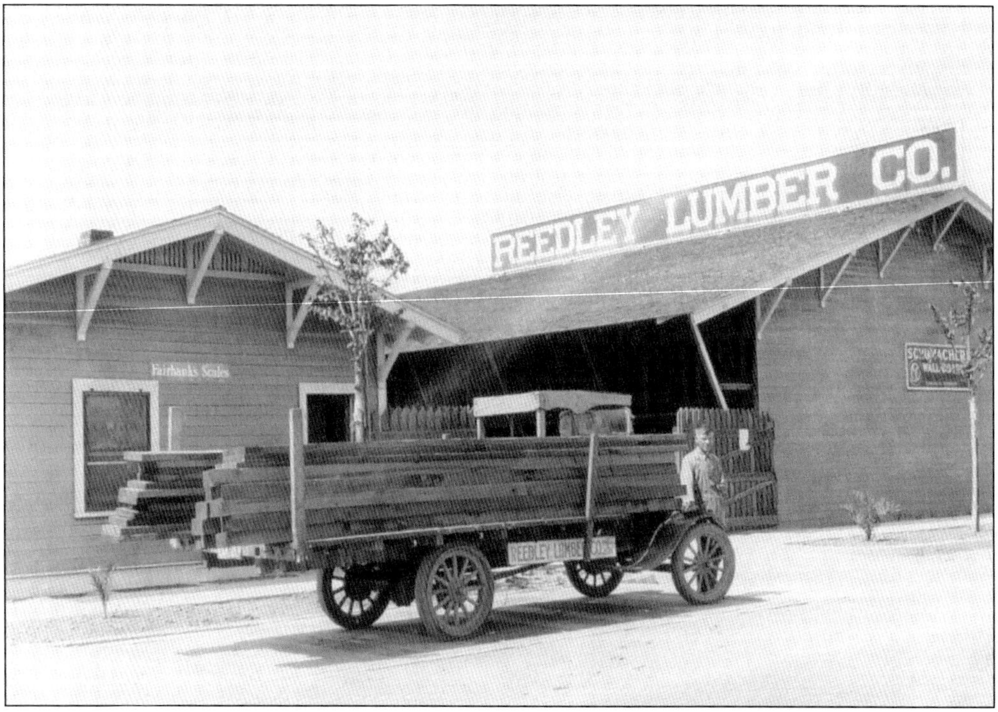

Reedley Lumber Company was founded in 1921 at 1547 G Street. The founding stockholders were Ernest P. Ruth, Rudolph Bergthold, C.F. Mueller, Bush Bondurant, Art Ruth, Rudy Ruth, and Ed Dettweiler. Despite two ruinous fires that took place 15 years apart, the family-owned business remains open today at the very same location.

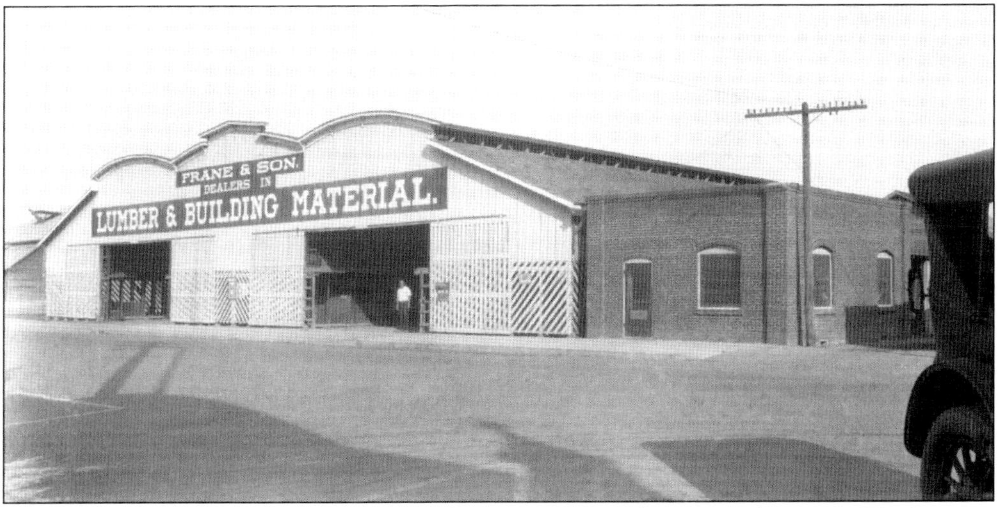

Frank Frane's lumber and building material company opened in September 1909. The business was located on Tenth Street, directly across the street from what is now the Reedley Museum. In later years, the building was used for the tractor department of Growers Supply Company. This photograph dates from the 1920s. (Photograph by Nelson Studio.)

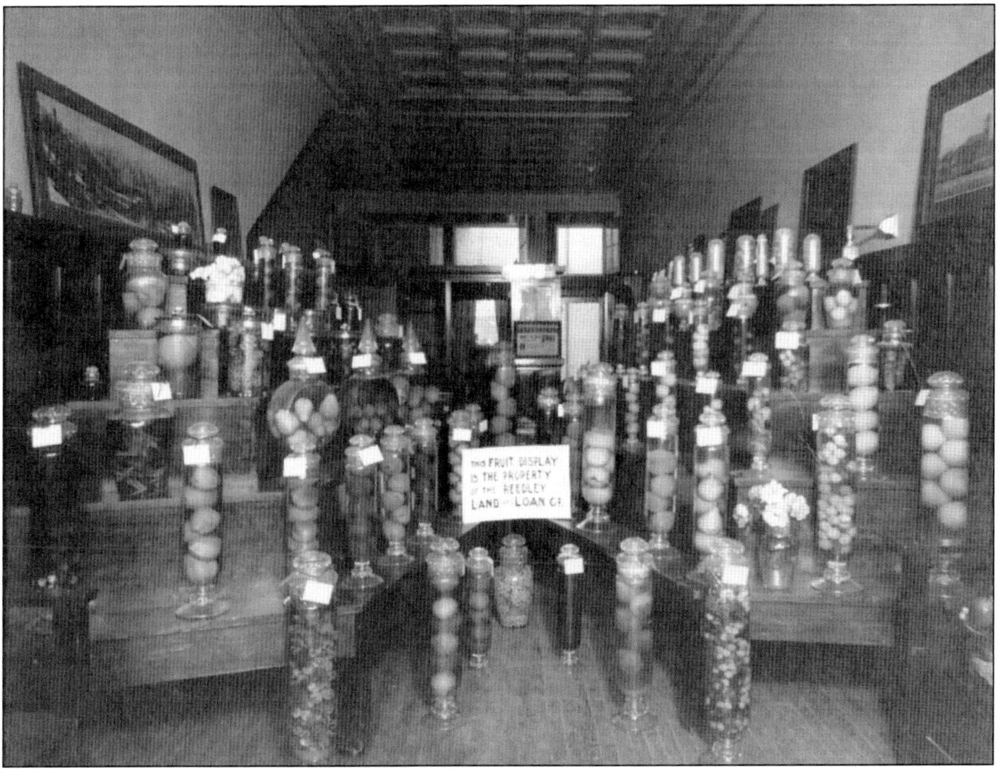

The Reedley Land and Loan Company created this display for its G Street office to demonstrate to prospective settlers the vast assortment of fruit that could be grown in the area. The framed photographs aided the marketing effort as well. On the left is an image of the Sierra Nevada mountain range, the source of the water that would irrigate their crops, and pictured on the right is the stately Washington School, where their children would get a good education.

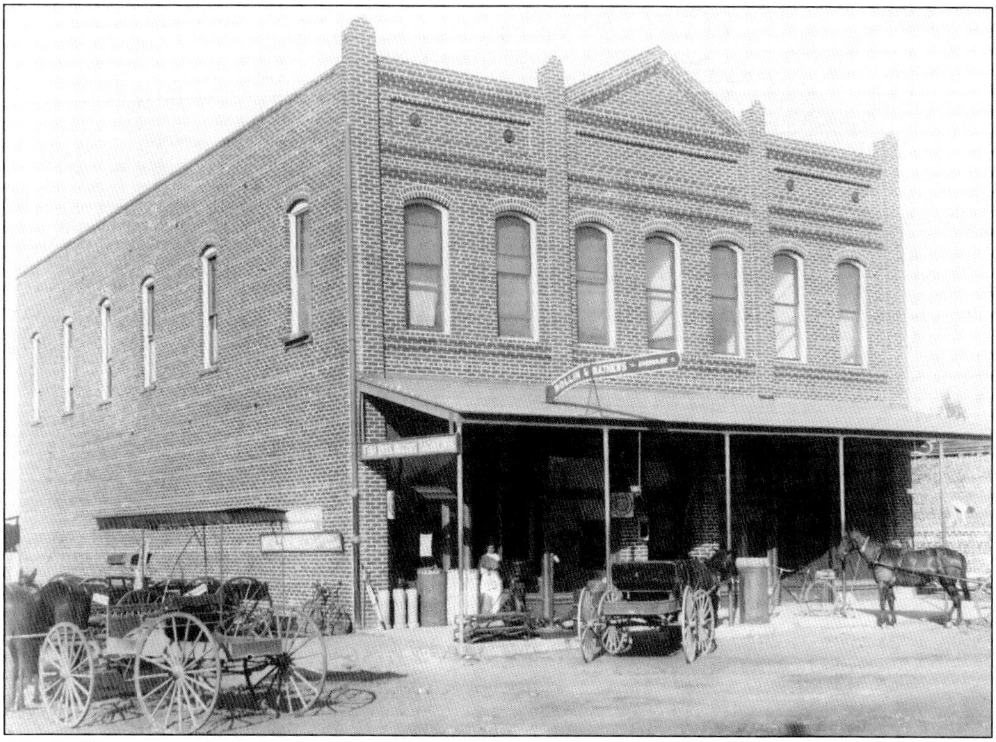

The Bollin & Matthews building at 1010 and 1012 G Street was built in 1903. It was one of the many brick buildings constructed in downtown Reedley during the aftermath of the 1902 fire. The ground floor housed the Bollin & Matthews Hardware Store and H.D. Bollin's General Merchandise Store. Today, the building houses the quilt store and offices of the West Coast Mennonite Central Committee.

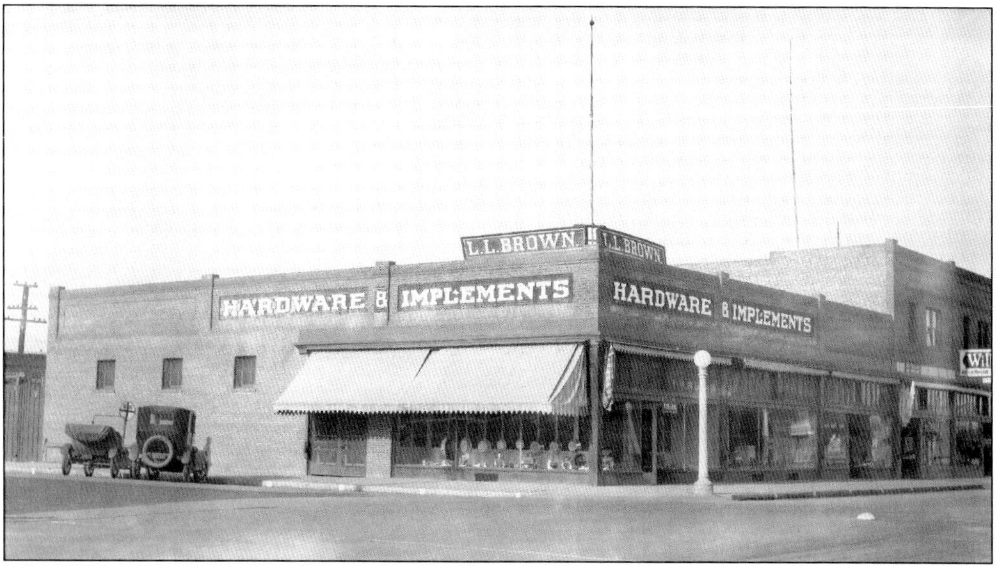

L.L. Brown's Hardware & Implements was a longtime business located at the corner of G and Tenth Streets. The current occupant of the building is Pioneer Equipment. Just like L.L. Brown's in its time, Pioneer meets the equipment and supply needs of local farmers.

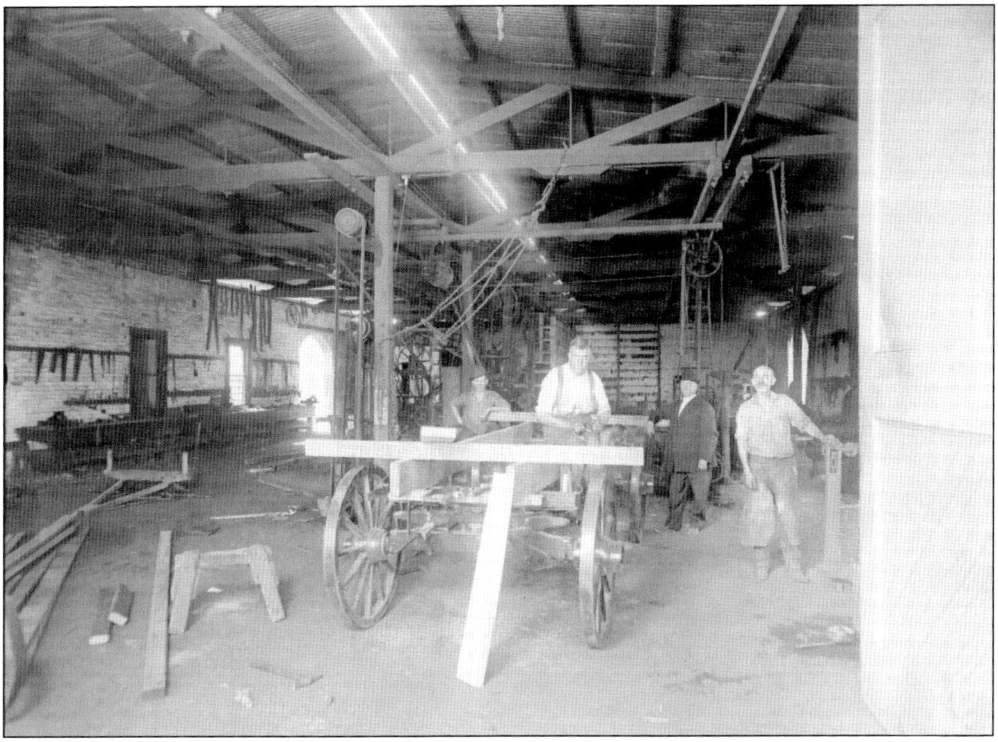

Workers at the blacksmith shop of Manuel Enos are building a bed for a Studebaker wagon around 1910. This was his new shop on the north side of Tenth Street, between G and F Streets.

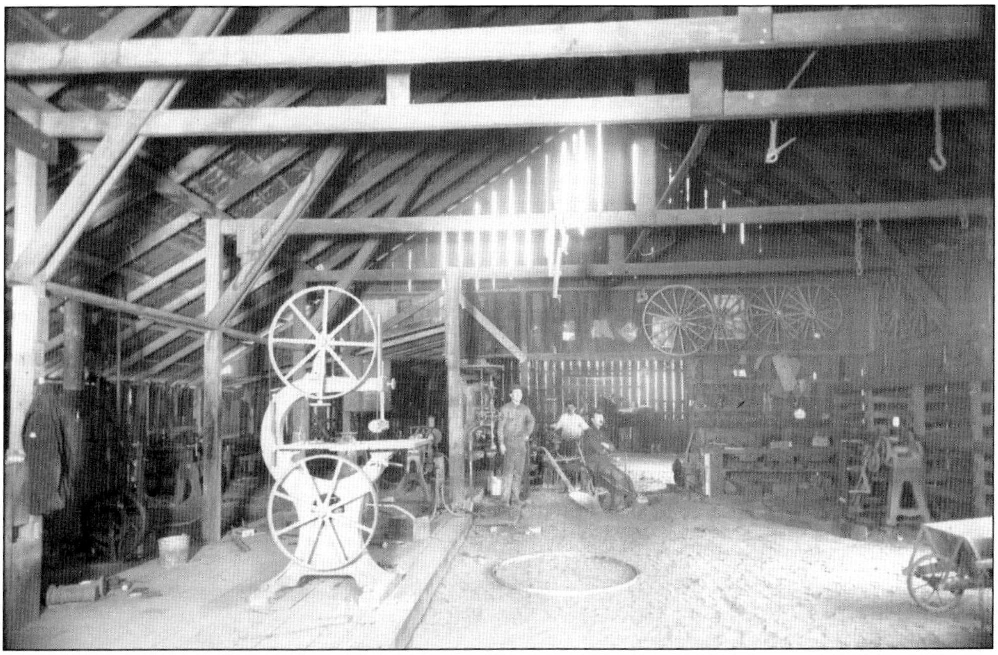

A growing agricultural community like Reedley was able to support several blacksmith and machine shops in its early years. This is an interior view of a shop that built and repaired all necessary equipment.

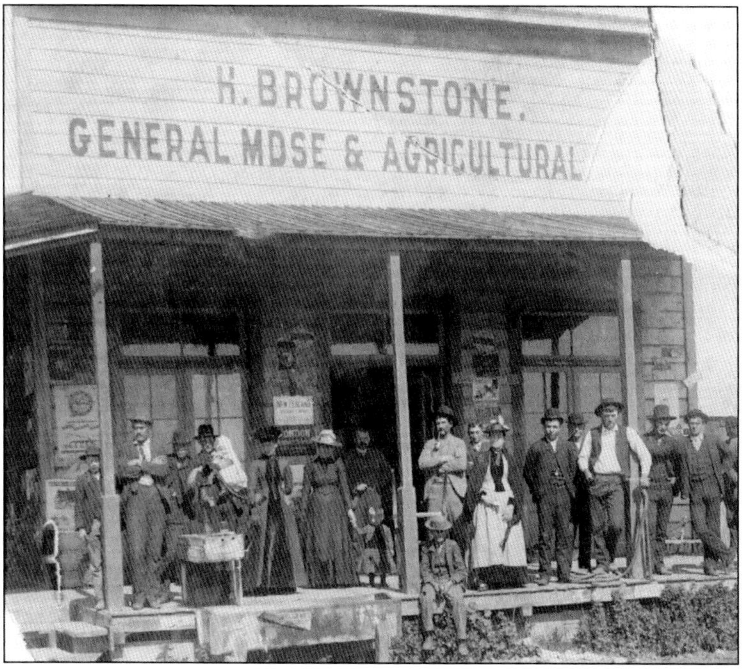

Henry Brownstone opened his general merchandise store in Reedley in August 1897. He had previously been in business in Traver, but left there when the town went into decline. Brownstone's building migrated, too. This former Traver building was hauled to Reedley and placed on the east side of the 1100 block of G Street, near the *Exponent* office. This damaged photograph is the only known close-up view of the store.

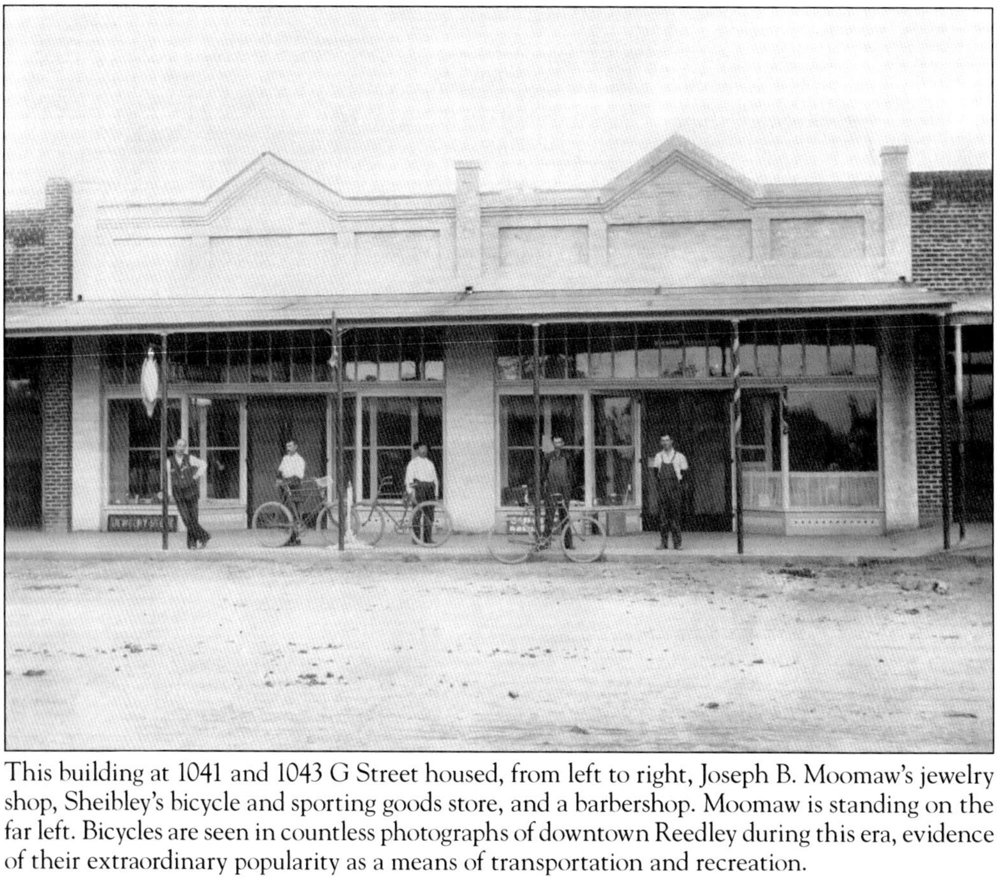

This building at 1041 and 1043 G Street housed, from left to right, Joseph B. Moomaw's jewelry shop, Sheibley's bicycle and sporting goods store, and a barbershop. Moomaw is standing on the far left. Bicycles are seen in countless photographs of downtown Reedley during this era, evidence of their extraordinary popularity as a means of transportation and recreation.

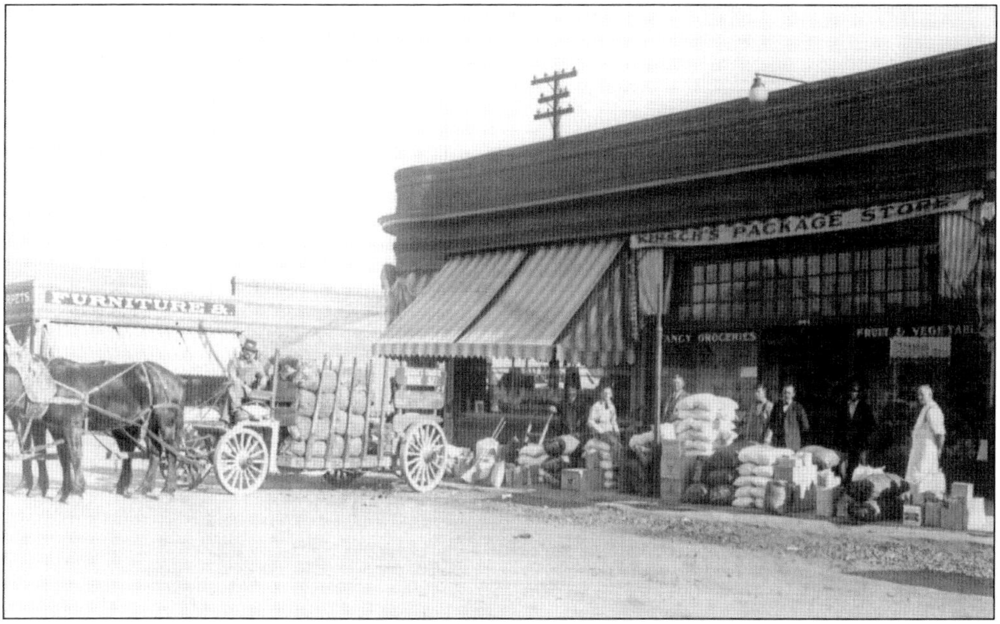

Segrue's Transfer freight wagon is making a delivery at Kirsch's Package Store in the 1910s. Next door, on the corner of G and Tenth Streets, is the Reedley National Bank. Across the street is Drath's Furniture Store.

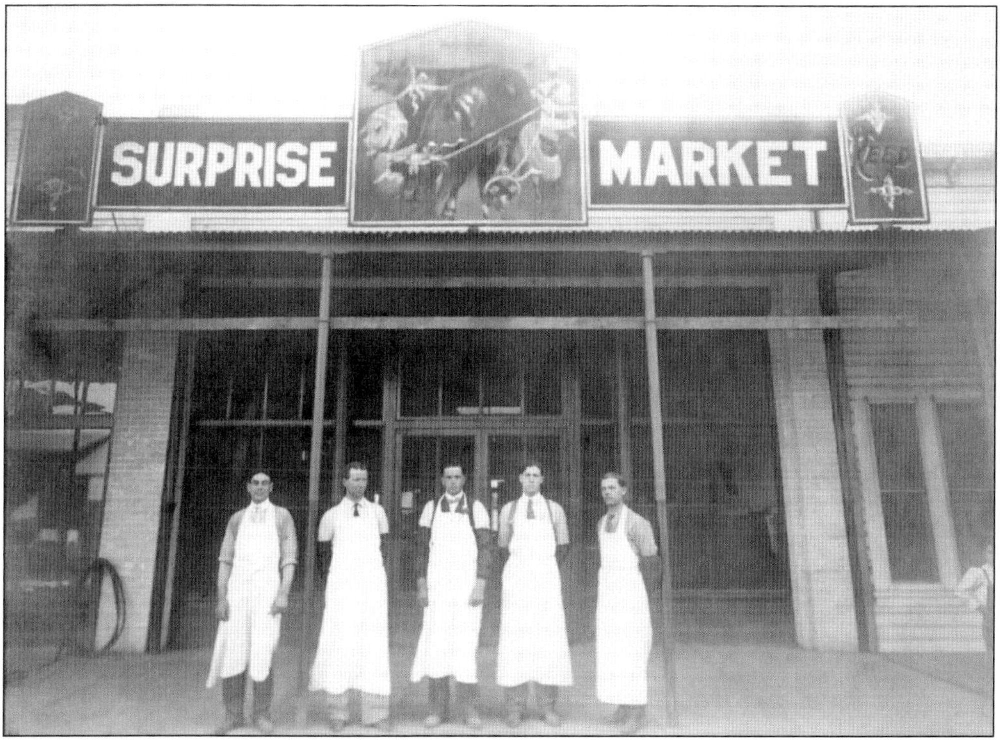

Edmond Reed and W.W. Parlier opened the Surprise Meat Market in early 1905. The butchers pose for a photograph in front of the store, which was located on the west side of the 1100 block of G Street.

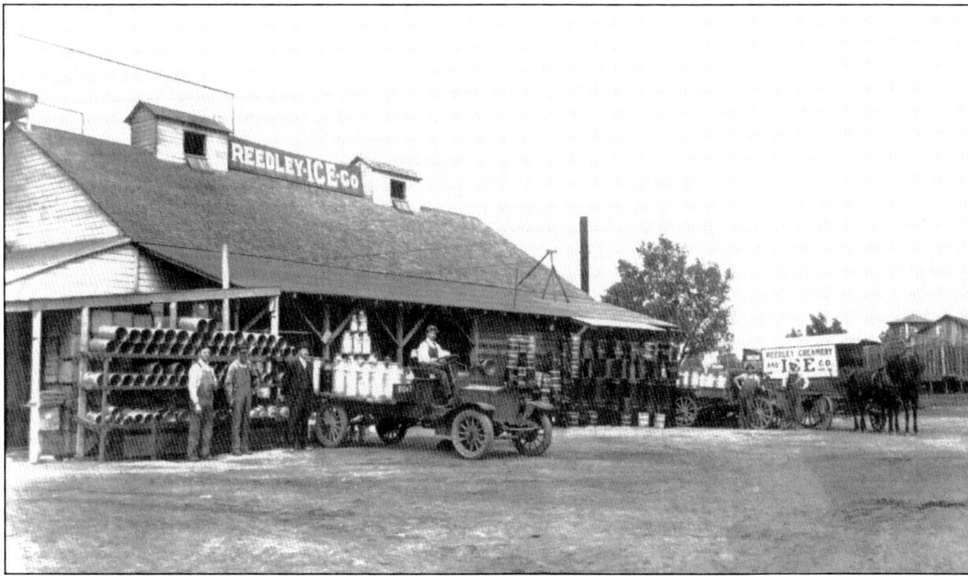

The Reedley Creamery & Ice Company was located at Fourteenth and H Streets. Standing in front of the empty milk containers are, from left to right, Floyd Caskey, Phil Schaffer, and Dick England. Butch Saile is on the far right, standing in front of the ice wagon. The other two men seen in this image are unidentified.

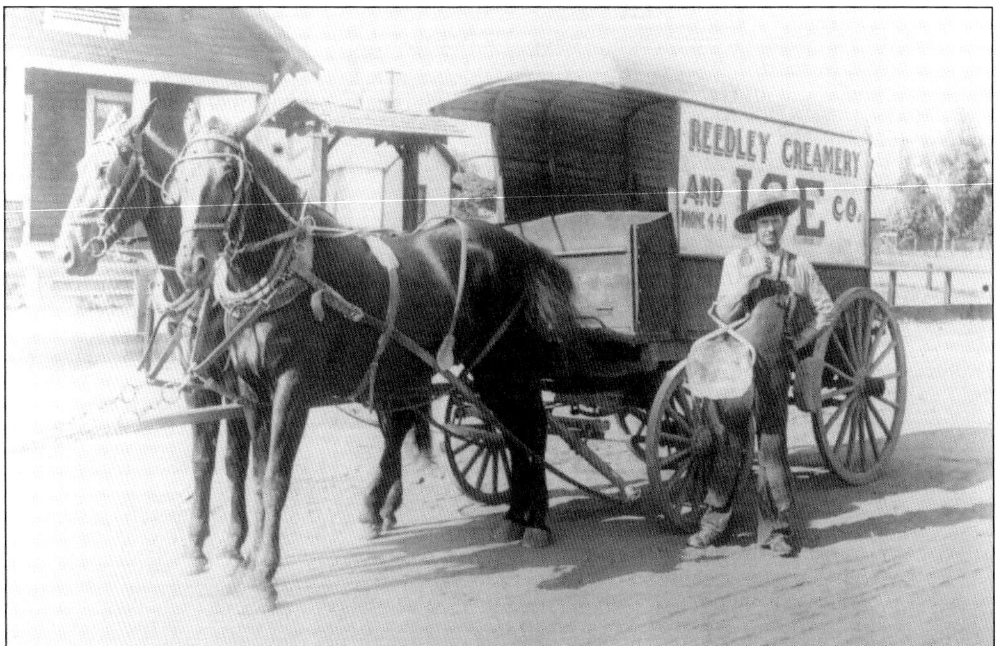

Isaac Koop, the iceman, is ready to make a delivery. The Reedley Creamery & Ice Company sold dairy products and delivered ice for household use.

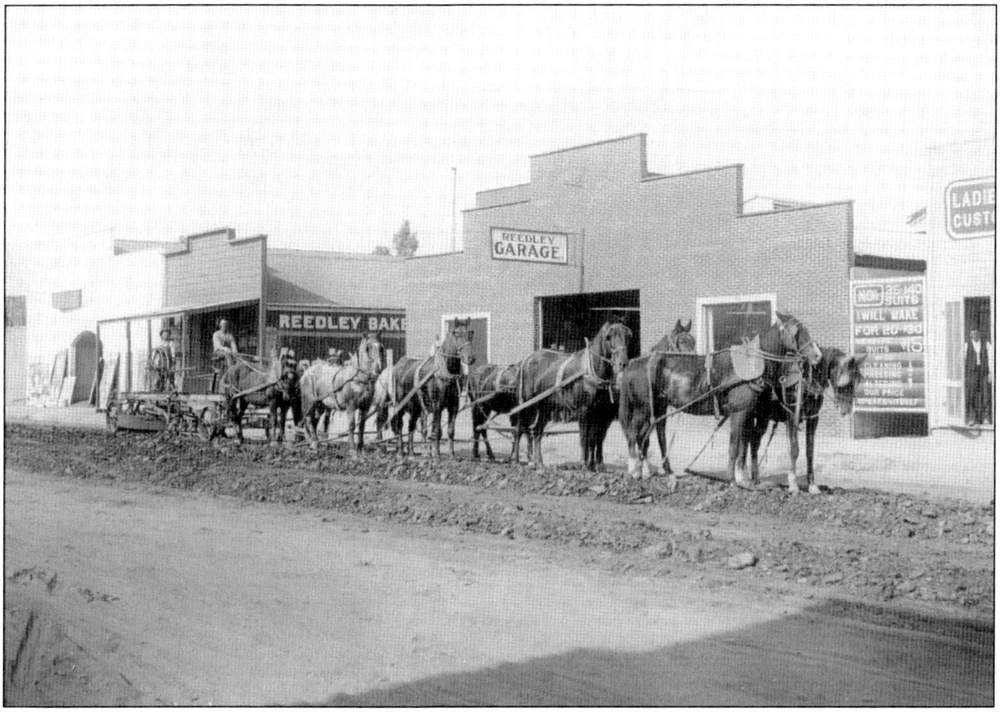

Street repair in Reedley around 1912 involved a Haynes Universal Road Machine, eight horses, and a skilled teamster. Joe Miller is at the reins. The businesses located in this section of the 1200 block of G Street are, from left to right, Reedley's open-air theater, a "noodle shop," a bakery, Reedley Garage, and a tailor and cleaning shop. Ben Rustigan was the tailor.

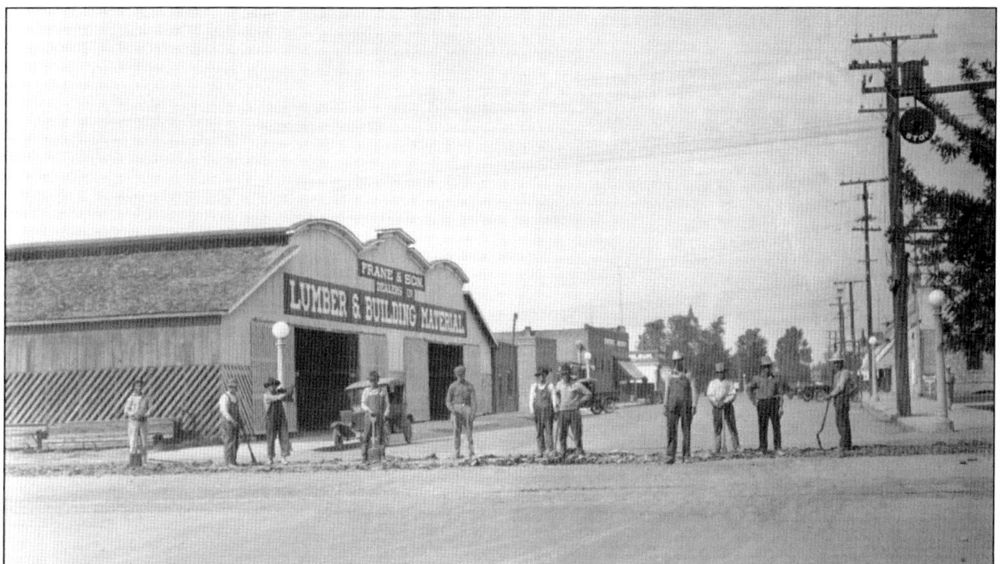

One can only imagine that crossing railroad tracks in an automobile was a pretty jarring experience in the old days. Here, a crew repairs the Santa Fe rail crossing at Tenth Street. (Photograph by Nelson Studio.)

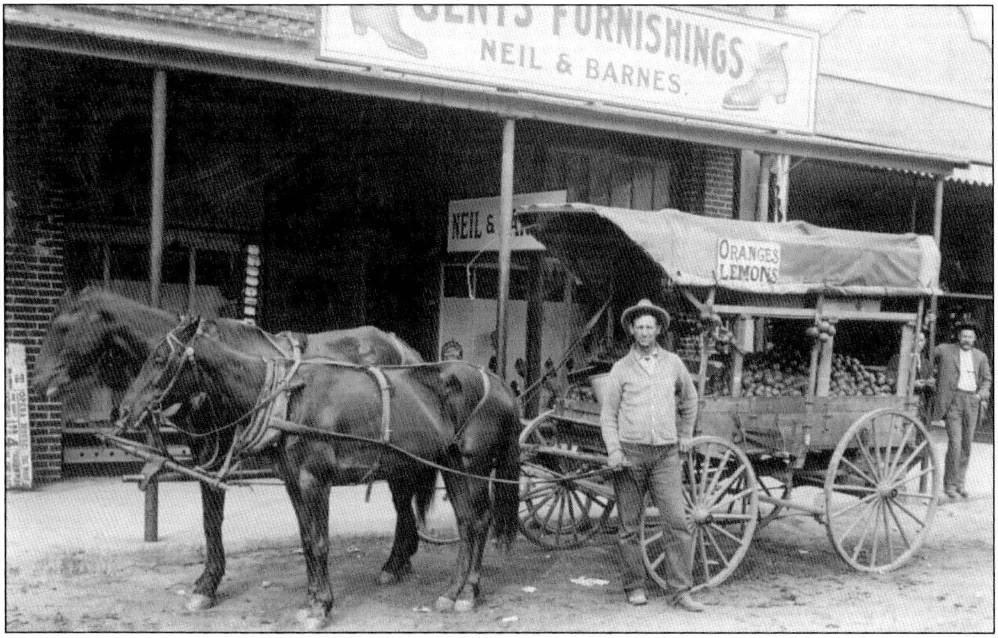

"Smith the Orange Man," as identified on this real-photo postcard, makes a stop on G Street with a wagonload of oranges and lemons that he is peddling.

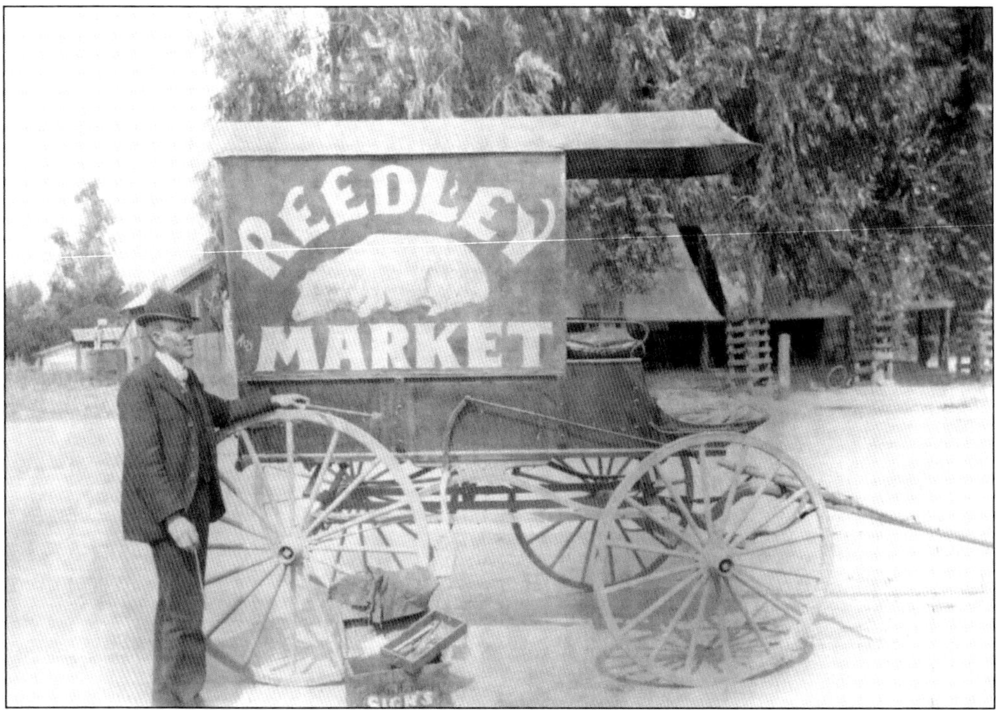

Charlie Ross, the sign painter, is seen here showing off his latest work—the signage and decoration of the Reedley Market delivery wagon.

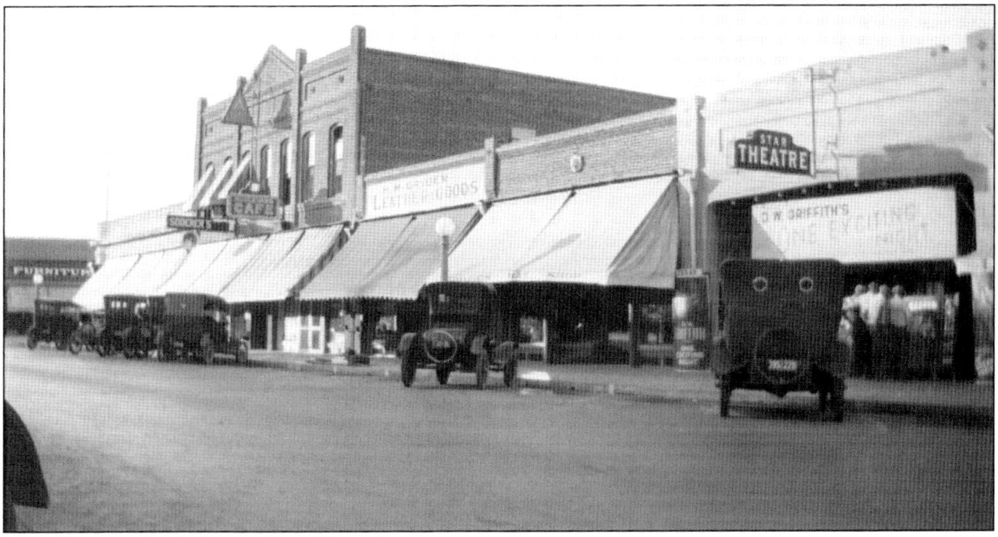

The east side of the 1000 block of G Street is seen here around 1926. Soderer's store and the Boulevard Café occupy the old Bollin & Matthews building, along with Reedley's Masonic Lodge upstairs. Next door is Grider's Leather Goods and Hodge's Hat Shop. The Star Theatre is showing D.W. Griffith's murder mystery *One Exciting Night*. The movie involved bootleggers and an orphan girl—the makings of a hit!

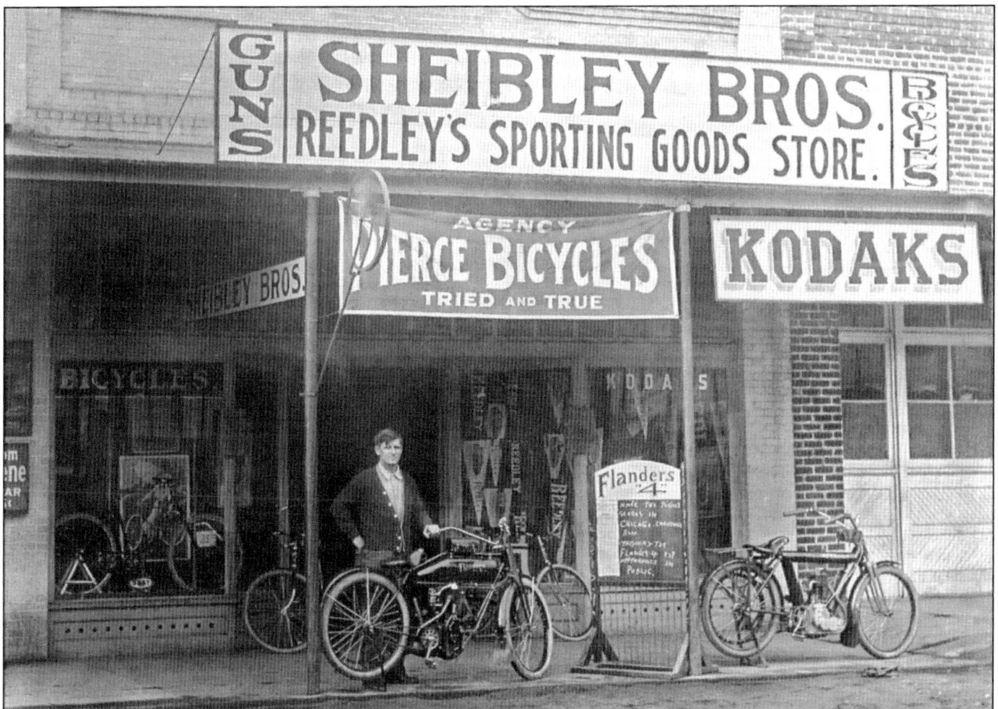

Sheibley's Elite Cyclery opened in 1901. In later years, the business took the name Sheibley Brothers and expanded its merchandise to include a variety of sporting goods, Kodak cameras, and Edison phonographs. This c. 1912 photograph of the shop shows that it also sold the Flanders 4 motorcycle.

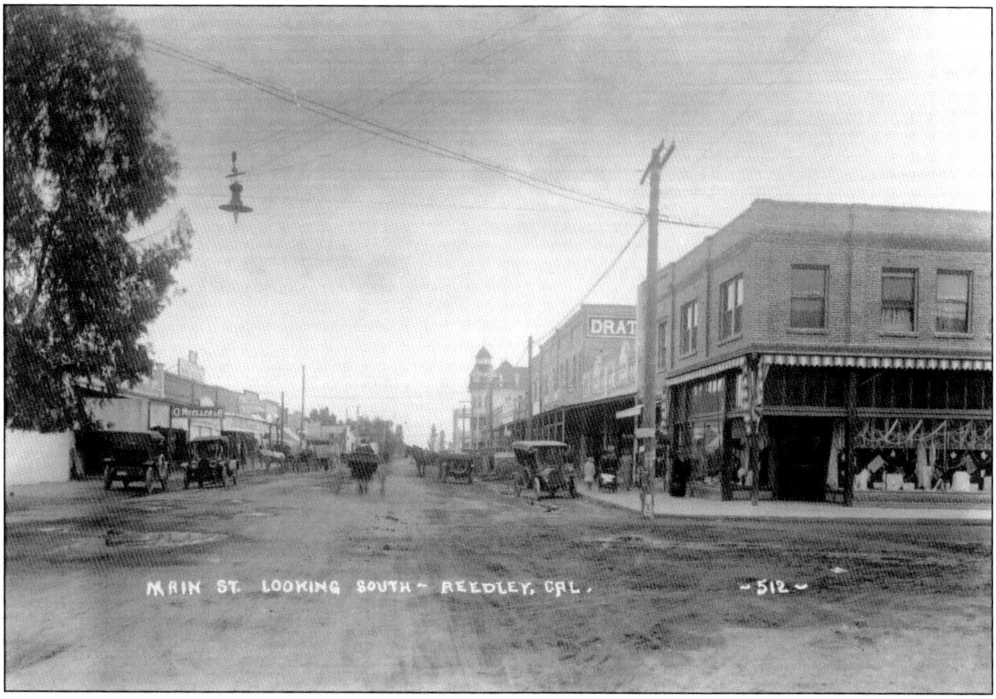

A buggy heads south on G Street in this c. 1913 photograph. The Winnes Hotel is on the corner at right. The dentist Dr. Acker had his offices upstairs, as did osteopath Dr. Glasgow. The two-story building a few doors down from the hotel is the Model Rooming House. The large block letters painted on the side of the building is a partial view of a sign advertising the photographic studio of Frank Drath. (Photograph by George Besaw.)

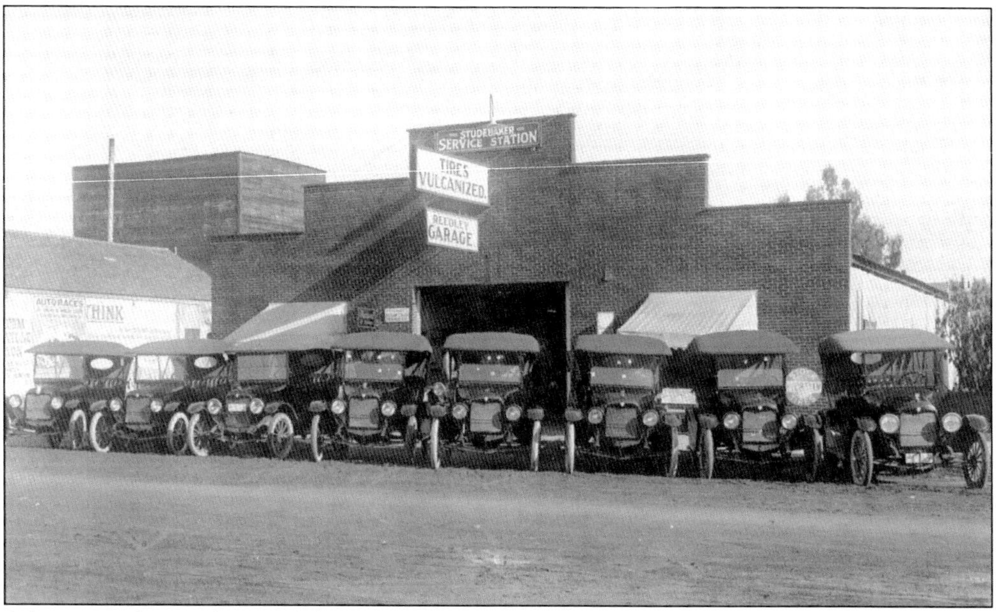

Sylvester "Tib" Smith owned the Reedley Garage, located on the east side of the 1200 block of G Street. Smith was also a dealer in Maxwell automobiles, as this c. 1916 photograph illustrates. Smith lost his garage to a fire in 1917.

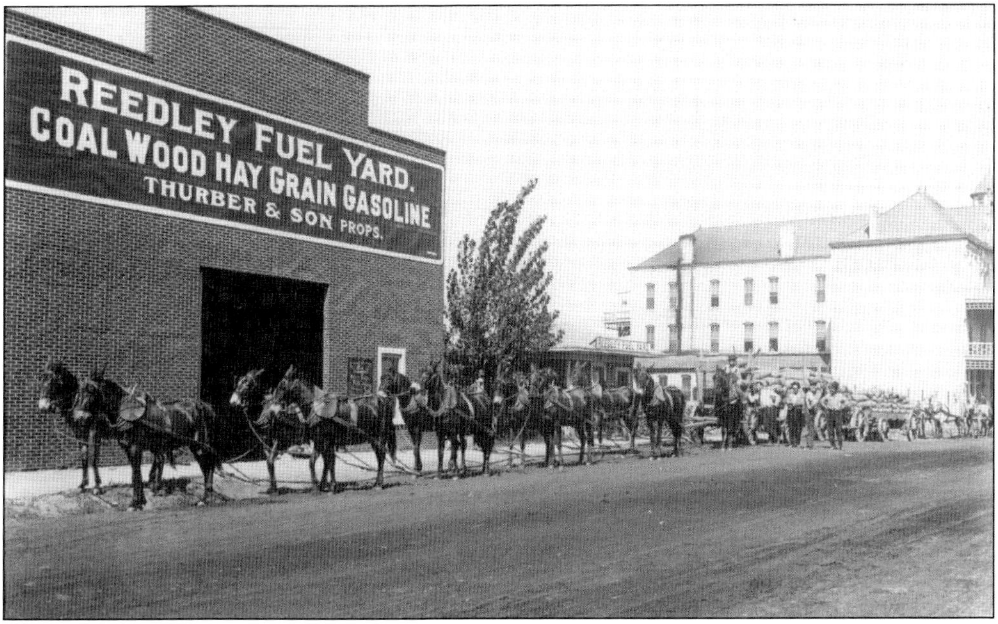

The Reedley Fuel Yard was directly across the street from Smith's garage. As the sign indicates, all kinds of fuel were available for sale. The yard also operated a platform scale, which drew a parade of grain wagons. According to his recollection published in *Beginnings in the Reedley Area* (1961), Smith recalls seeing master teamster Bert Belknap weigh his load, make a U-turn on G Street, and head back down the street to the old Grangers' warehouse. (Photograph by J.A. Baller.)

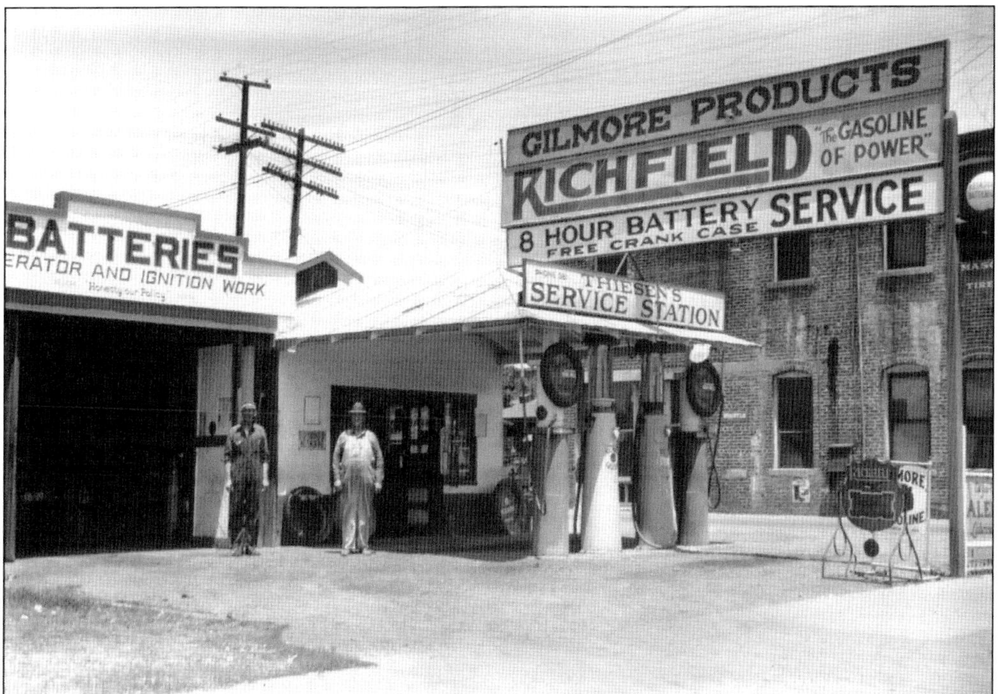

Thiesen's Service Station was located on the north side of Eleventh Street, adjacent to the alley between G and H Streets. (Photograph by Nelson Studio.)

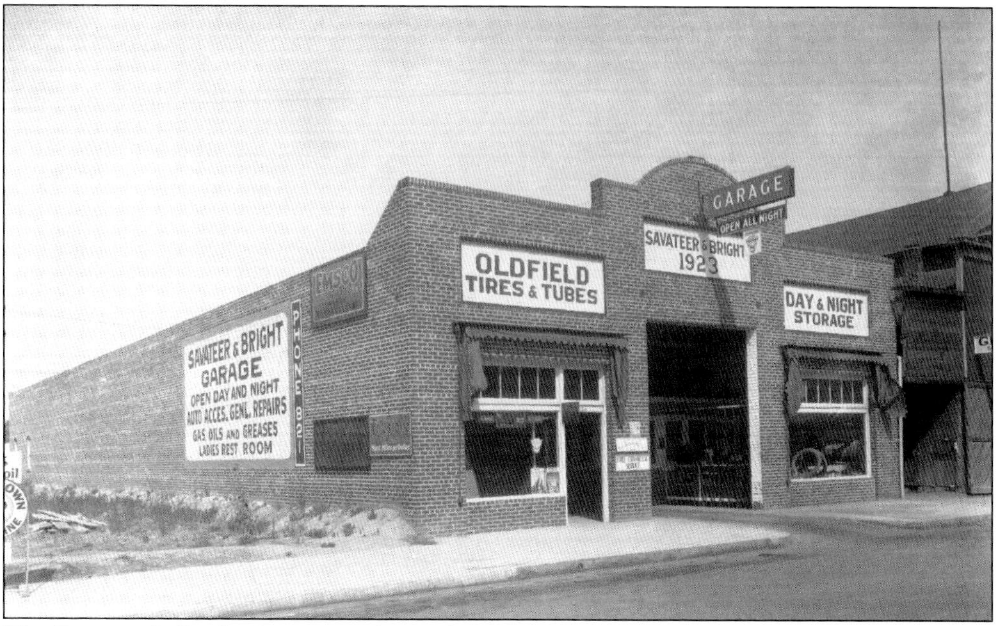

The Savateer & Bright Garage was located at 936 G Street. Jesse Savateer came to Reedley in 1913 and went into the livery stable business. He wisely decided to make the transition to motor vehicles. He is said to have been the first in town to buy a flatbed truck, which he used to develop a hauling business. (Photograph by Nelson Studio.)

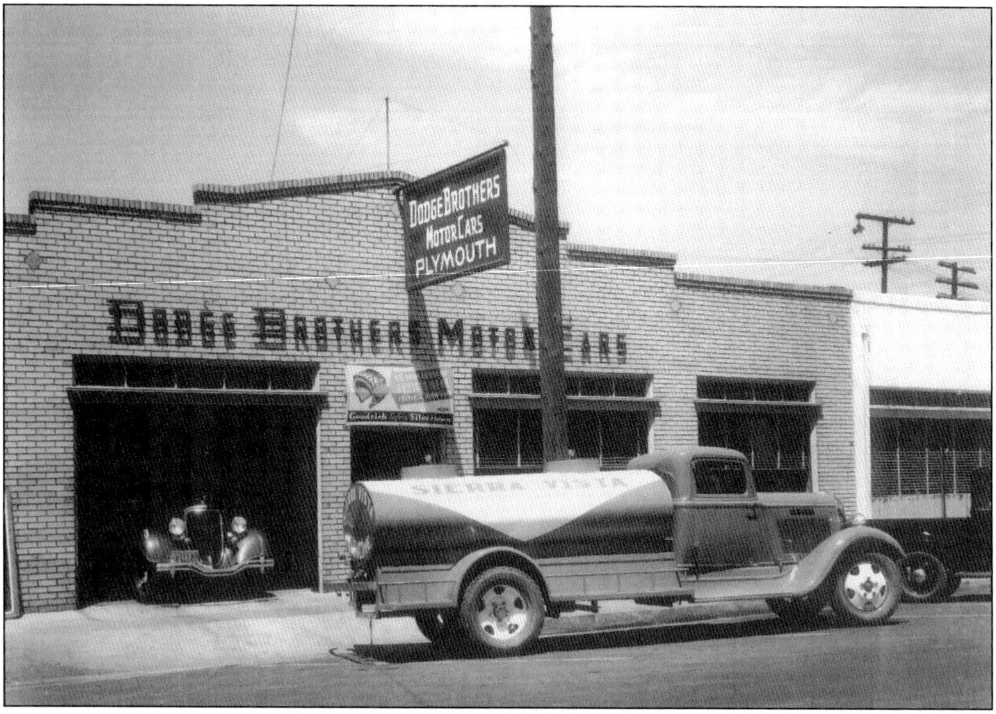

The Dodge Brothers automobile dealership was located at 1765 Eleventh Street. A Sierra Vista gasoline truck is parked out front. Note the drag chain hanging from the back of the truck. This was used to dissipate static electricity. The building now houses Powell's Custom Upholstery.

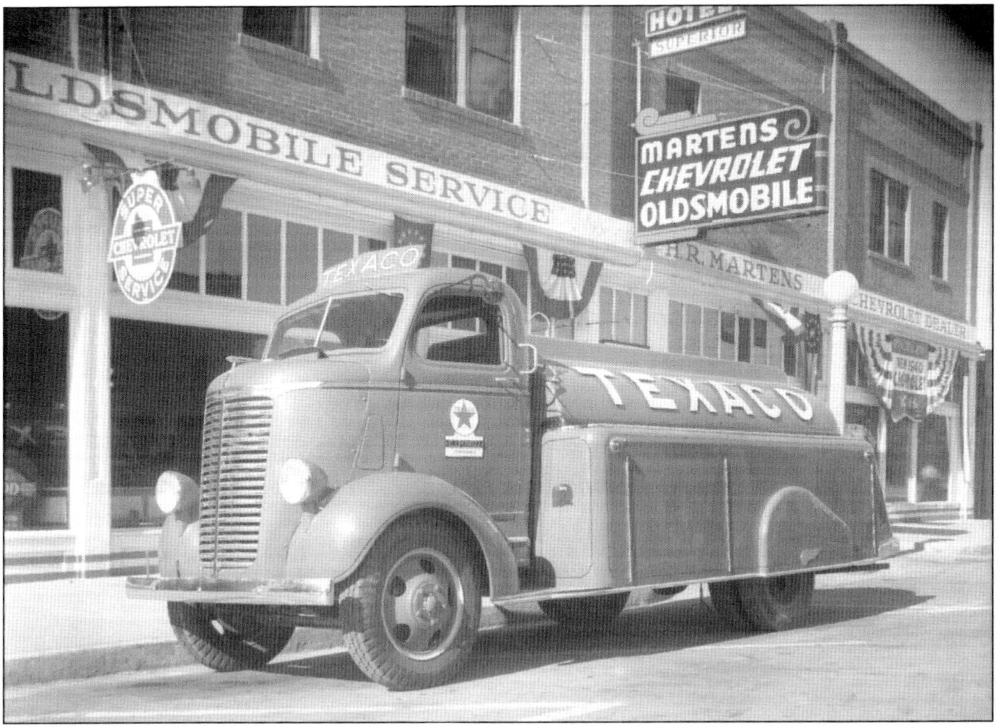

Texaco gasoline distributor E.J. Powell purchased a sleek, new tanker truck from Martens Chevrolet in 1939. Henry Martens had bought the Chevrolet dealership in 1930 and later expanded his business to include Oldsmobiles. The business was located at 939 G Street, on the ground floor of the Superior Hotel building. The Martens family still sells Chevys, but at a new location. (Photograph by Nelson Studio.)

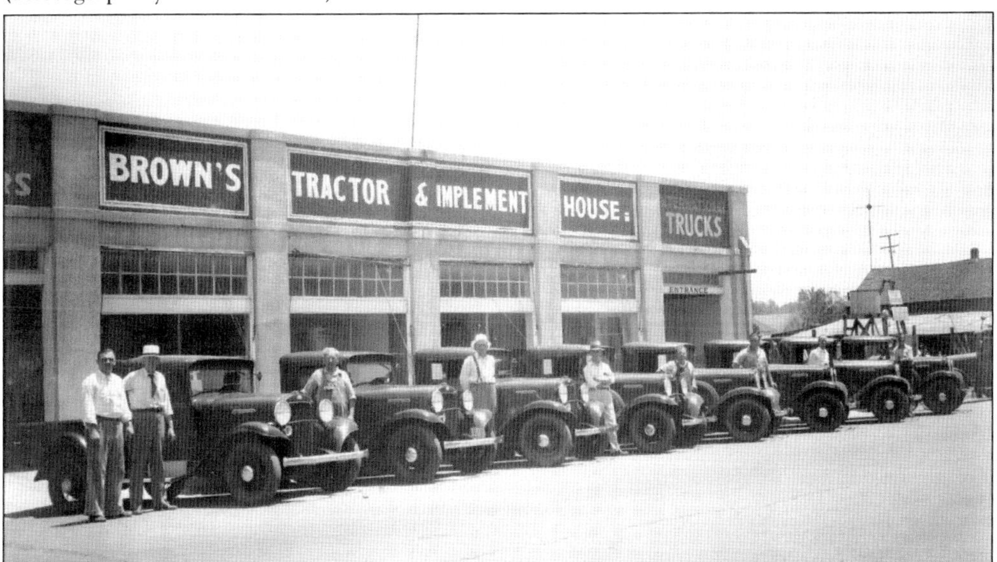

Brown's Tractor & Implement House, a later division of Brown's Hardware, sold International trucks from its location at 1230 G Street. This photograph dates from June 1931. Kings River Tractor now occupies this building. (Photograph by Nelson Studio.)

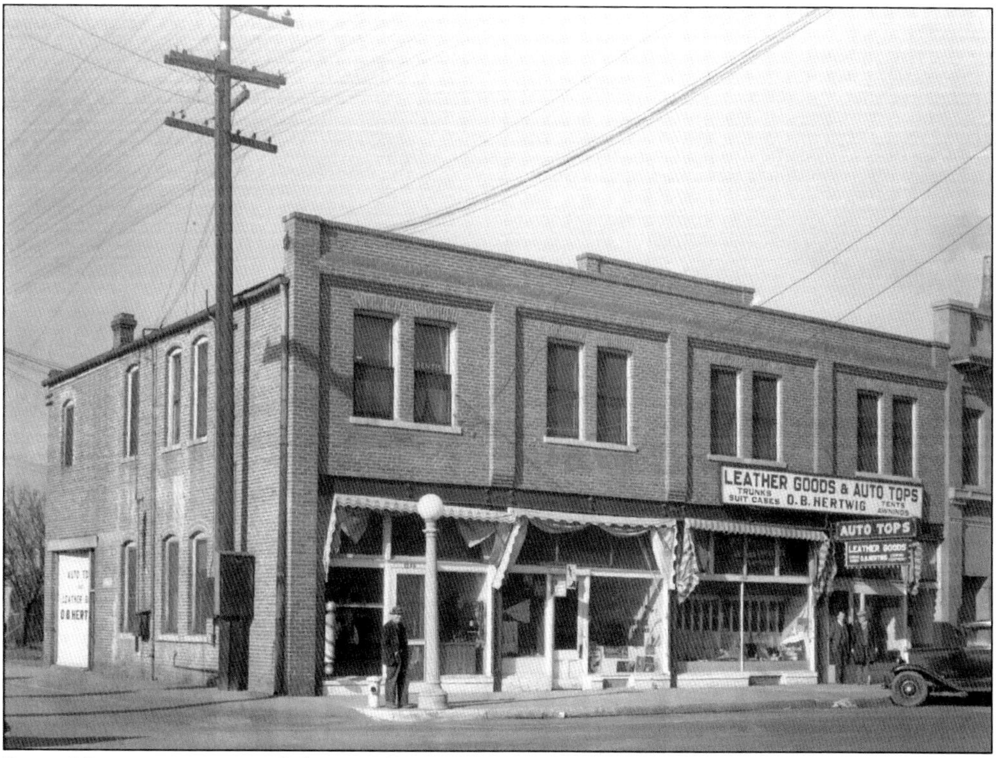

Several businesses occupied the storefronts on the north side of Eleventh Street between G and H Streets. In this January 1931 photograph are, from left to right, a barbershop, Yale's Electric Shoe Repair Shop, and O.B. Hertwig's Leather Goods & Auto Tops store. (Photograph by Nelson Studio.)

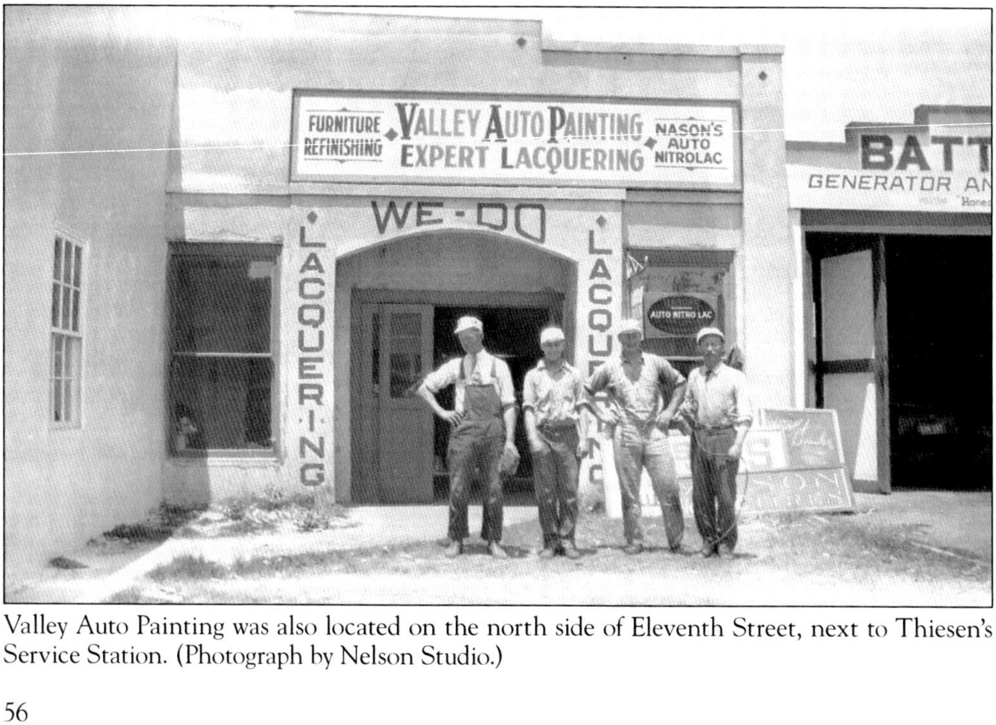

Valley Auto Painting was also located on the north side of Eleventh Street, next to Thiesen's Service Station. (Photograph by Nelson Studio.)

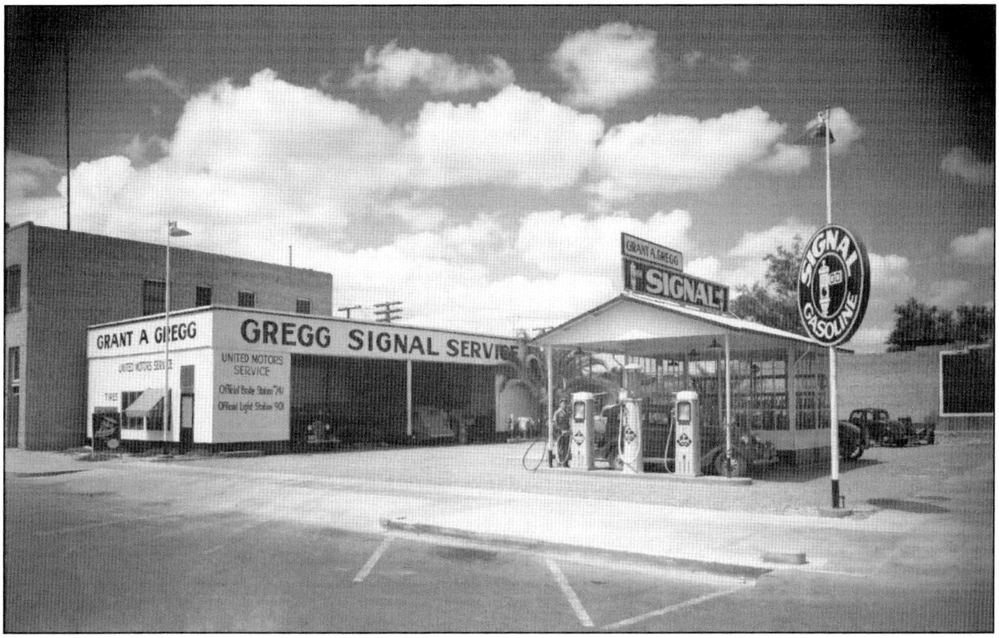

Grant Gregg's Signal Service Station was located on the corner of Eleventh and F Streets, where Wells Fargo Bank now stands. The 1920s and 1930s saw a proliferation of service stations in downtown Reedley. It was the rise of the automobile age. (Photograph by Nelson Studio.)

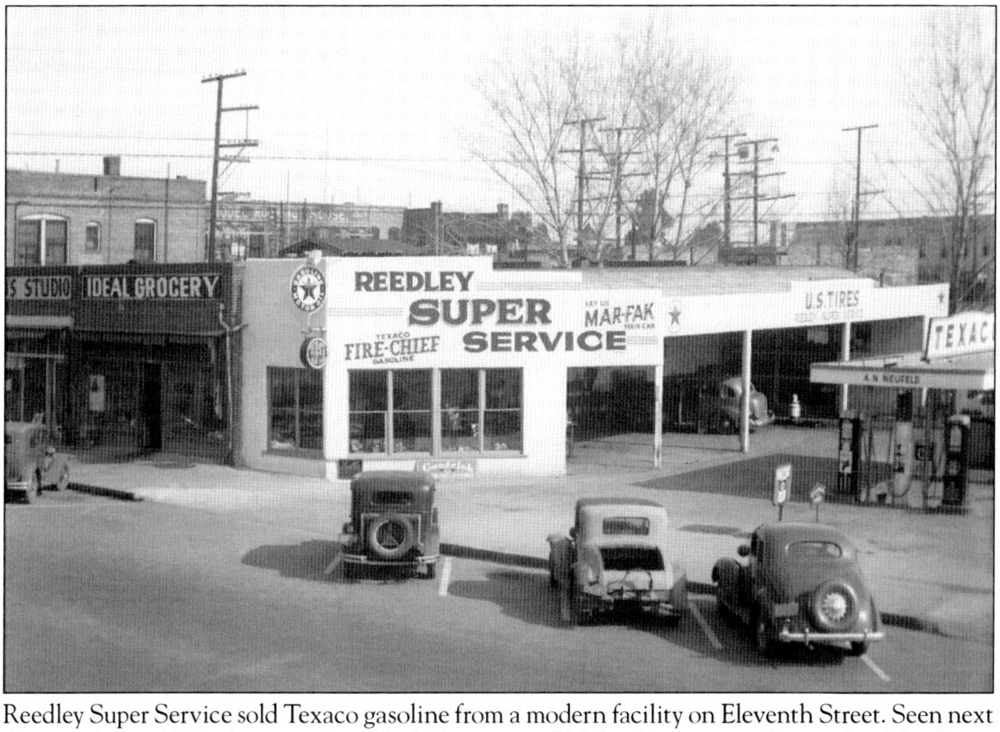

Reedley Super Service sold Texaco gasoline from a modern facility on Eleventh Street. Seen next door in this c. 1934 photograph is Ideal Grocery and Nelson's photographic studio. The Super Service building later became home to Martens Chevrolet and Oldsmobile. Today, it is the Bike Trax store. (Photograph by Nelson Studio.)

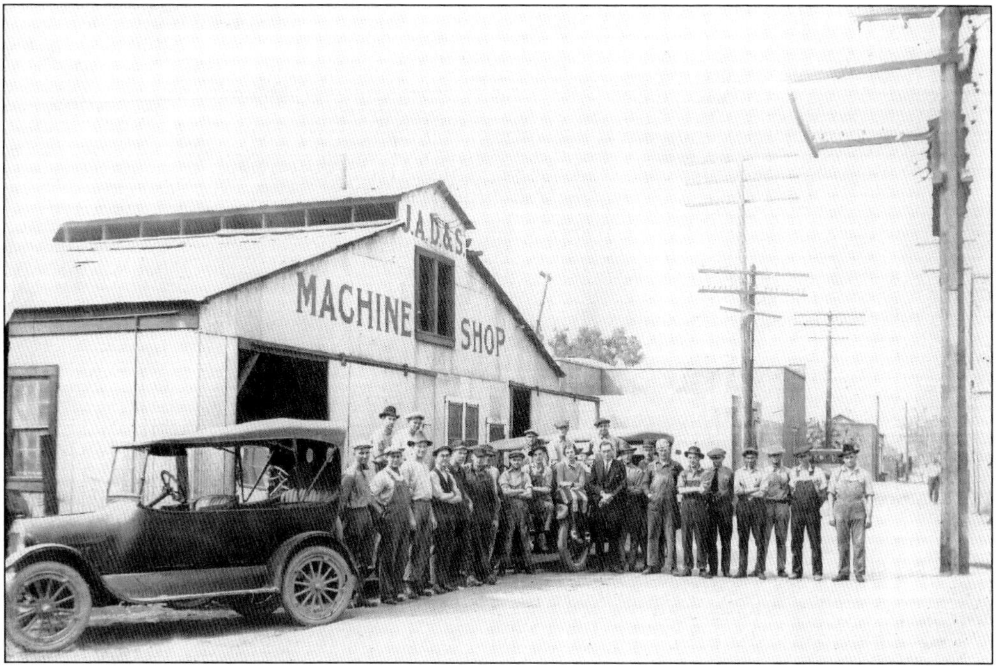

John A. Drake relocated from Traver to Reedley in 1897 to open a machine shop and foundry. Drake's large family of sons joined the business. The firm's development of the popular Jadson valve resulted in its becoming one of Reedley's biggest employers. The business moved to Southern California in 1928. This photograph dates from when the shop was located off the alley behind what is now the Reedley Museum.

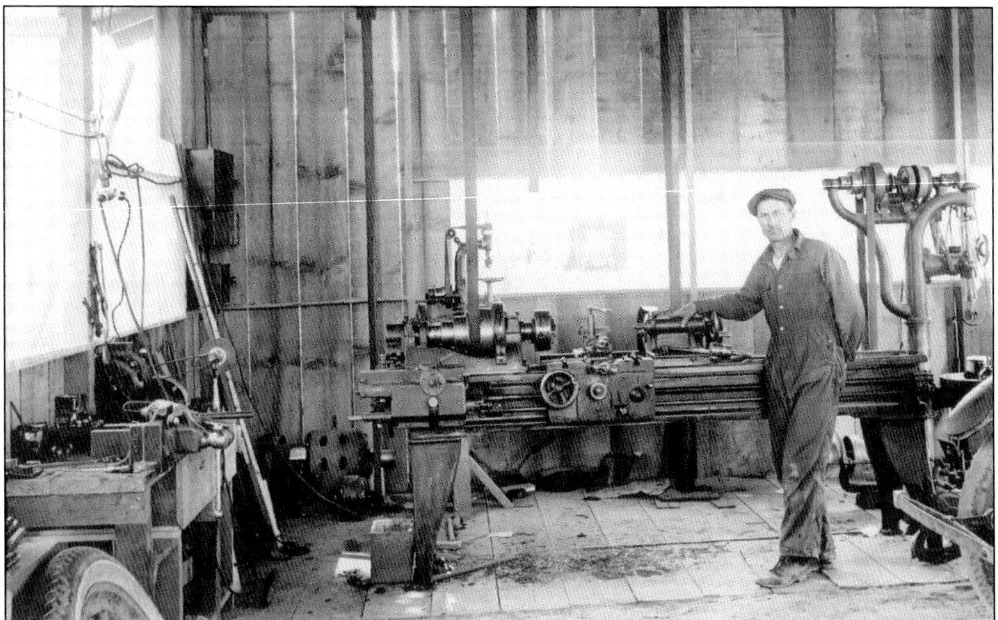

Master machinist Sylvester "Tib" Smith is seen in his shop in downtown Reedley. This photograph was made into a postcard, which Smith probably used in advertising. The always resilient Smith had lost a previous business to fire.

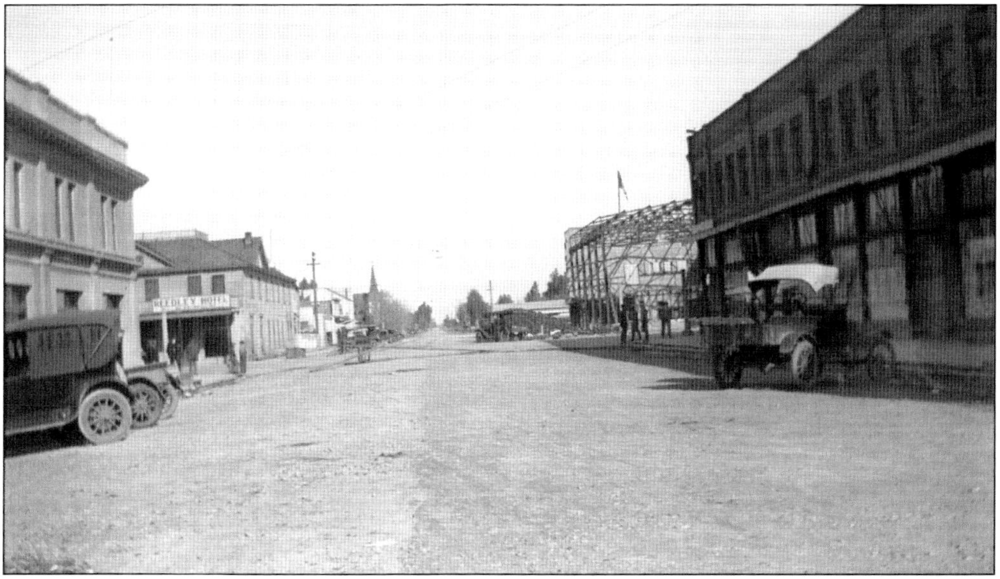

This photograph, looking east on Eleventh Street, dates from 1920. The new Reedley National Bank building, later a Bank of America branch, is seen during its construction at the corner of G and Eleventh Streets. During this period, the post office was located in the corner storefront of the Winnes Hotel building at right. (Photograph by Nelson Studio.)

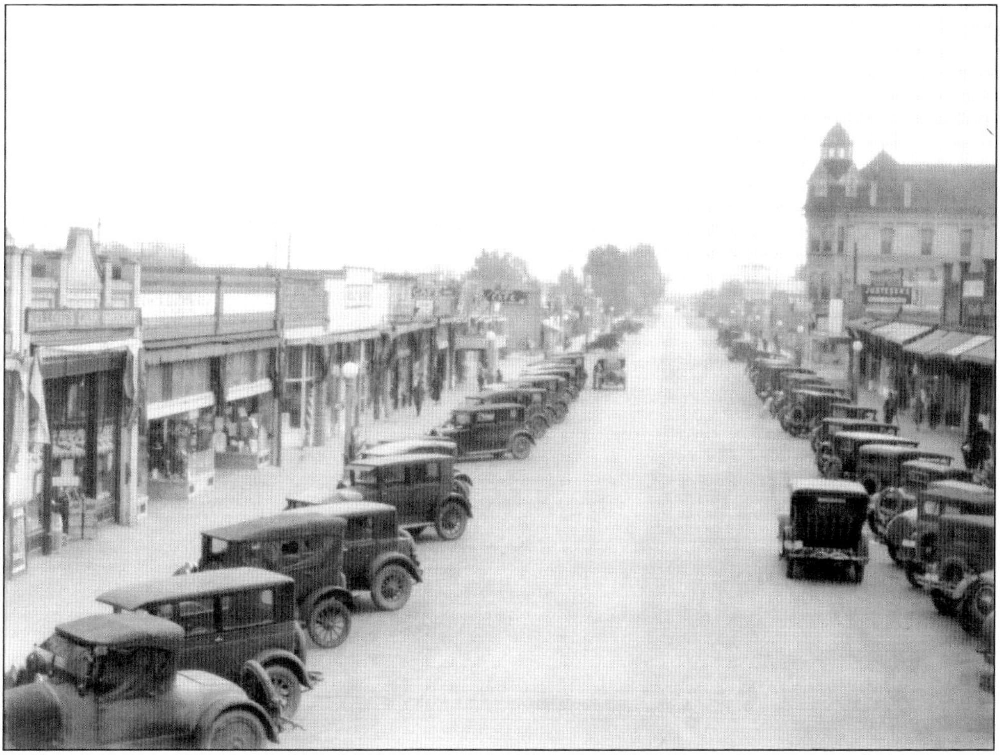

Automobiles line the 1100 block of G Street in this photograph from the mid-1920s. Among the businesses seen here are Kellogg's Cash Grocery, I and A Clothing Co., the *Exponent*, Anderson's Café, Valley Café, Justesen's Grocery, and Reedley Hardware.

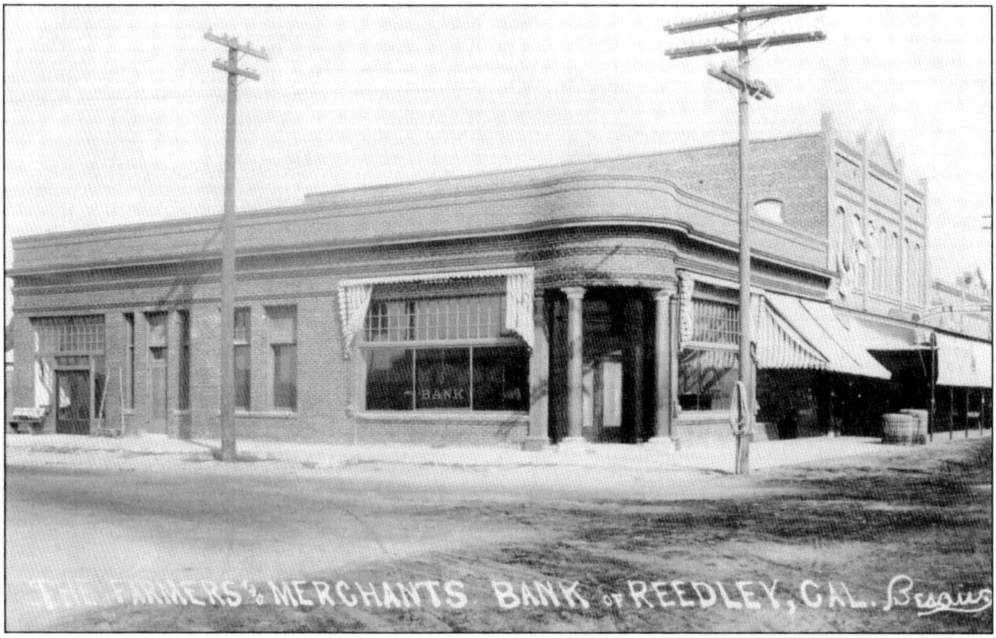

Reedley's second local bank, the Farmers & Merchants Bank, was founded in 1907. The bank erected this new building at G and Tenth Streets in 1908. Then, in 1910, the name was changed to the Reedley National Bank. Chase Bank is now the occupant of this historic building. (Photograph by George Besaw; courtesy of Michael J. Semas.)

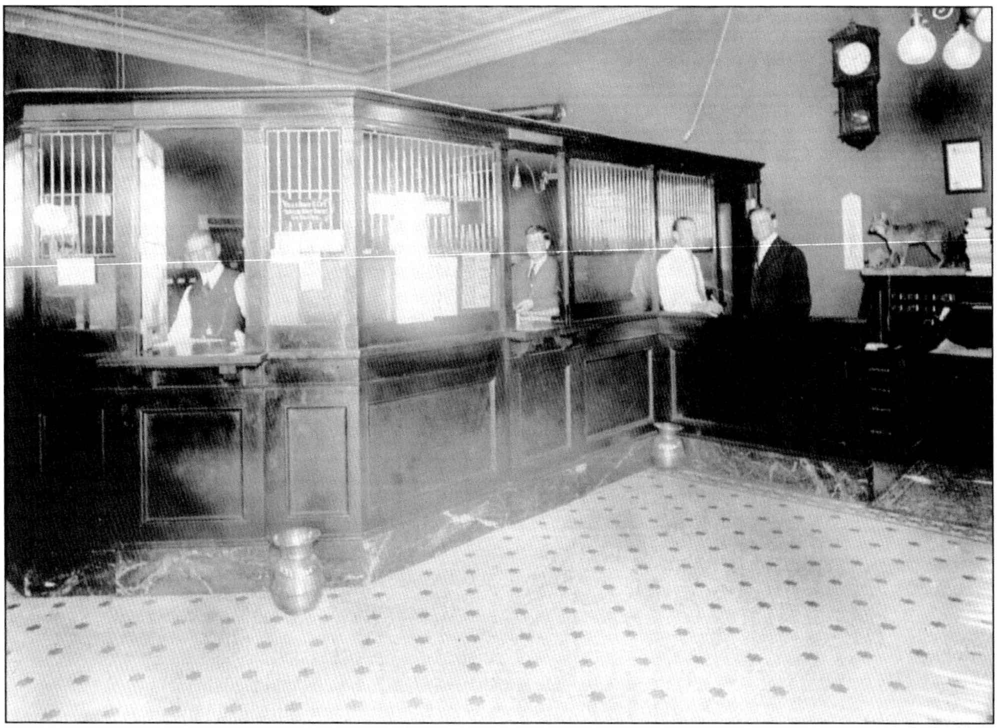

The interior of the Reedley National Bank building is shown in this c. 1915 photograph. John Danielson is on the far right. Next to him is Hank Rasmussen.

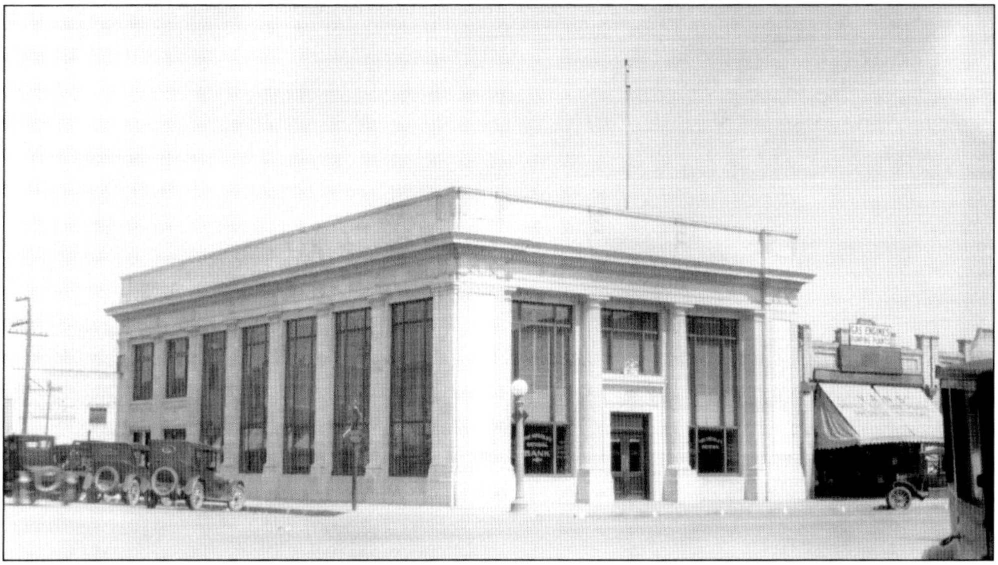

The Reedley National Bank commissioned prominent Fresno architect Ernest J. Kump Sr. to design a new, and much larger, bank for the corner of G and Eleventh Streets. The bank moved into the Classical structure in 1920. Many will recognize the bank from its days as a branch of the Bank of America. The building is listed in the National Register of Historic Places. (Photograph by Nelson Studio.)

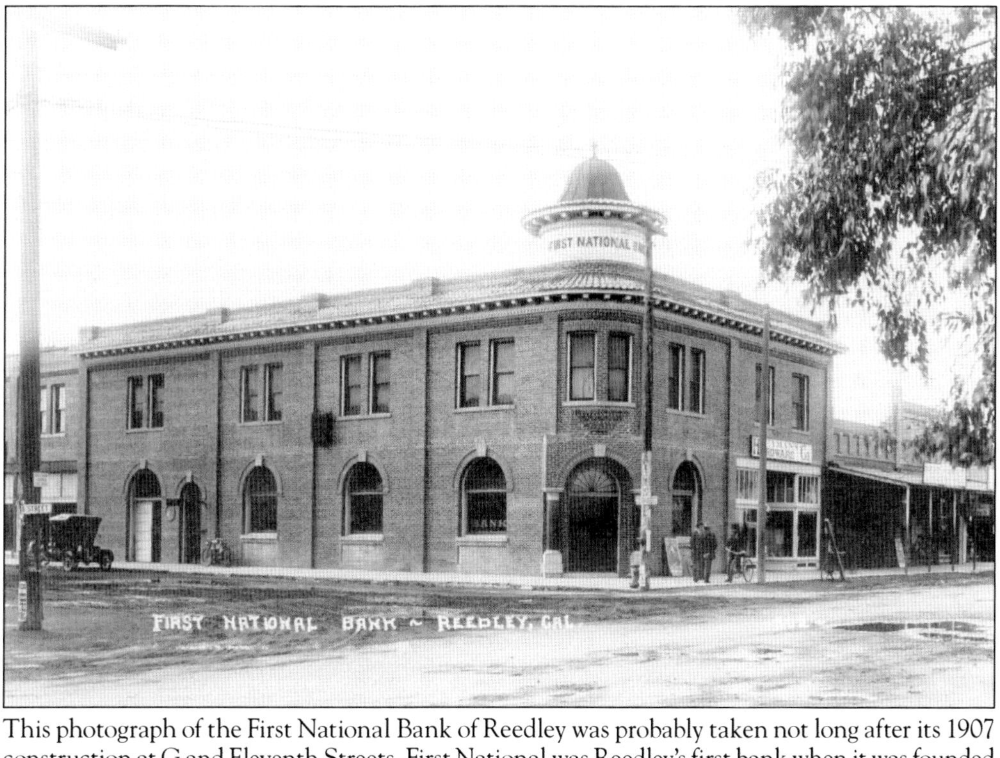

This photograph of the First National Bank of Reedley was probably taken not long after its 1907 construction at G and Eleventh Streets. First National was Reedley's first bank when it was founded in 1903. Originally, the bank had been known as Reedley State Bank. It merged with Valley Bank of Fresno in 1921, and the Bank of Italy acquired it in 1924. (Photograph by George Besaw.)

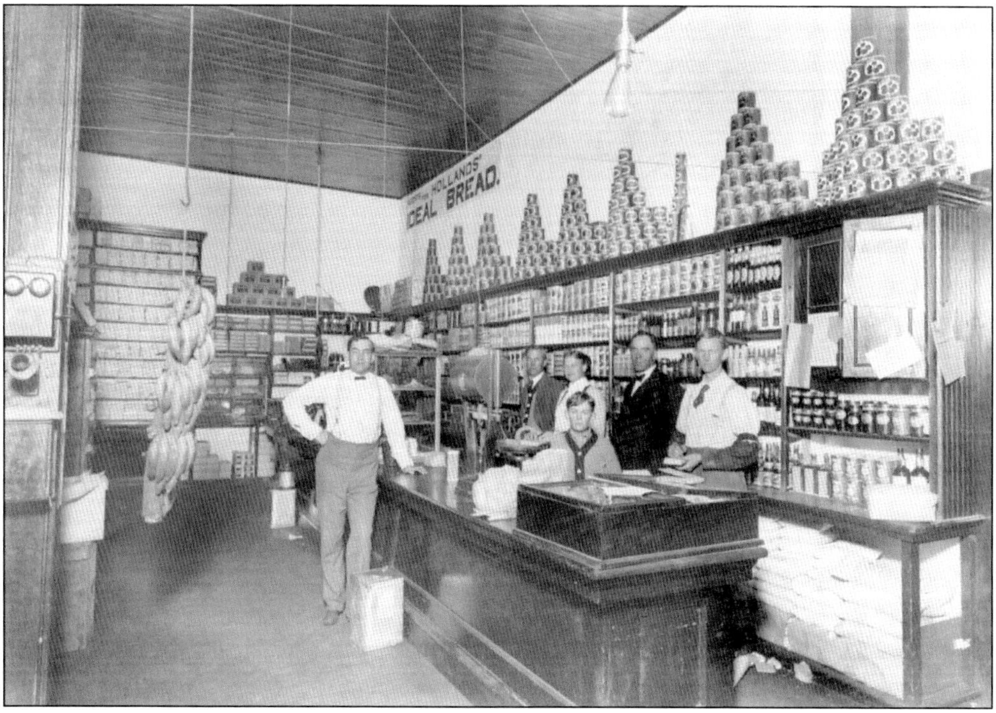

The Crosby store was a fixture in downtown Reedley for many years. The company operated a grocery business on one side of the store and offered general merchandise on the other side. The grocery department is seen here around 1910.

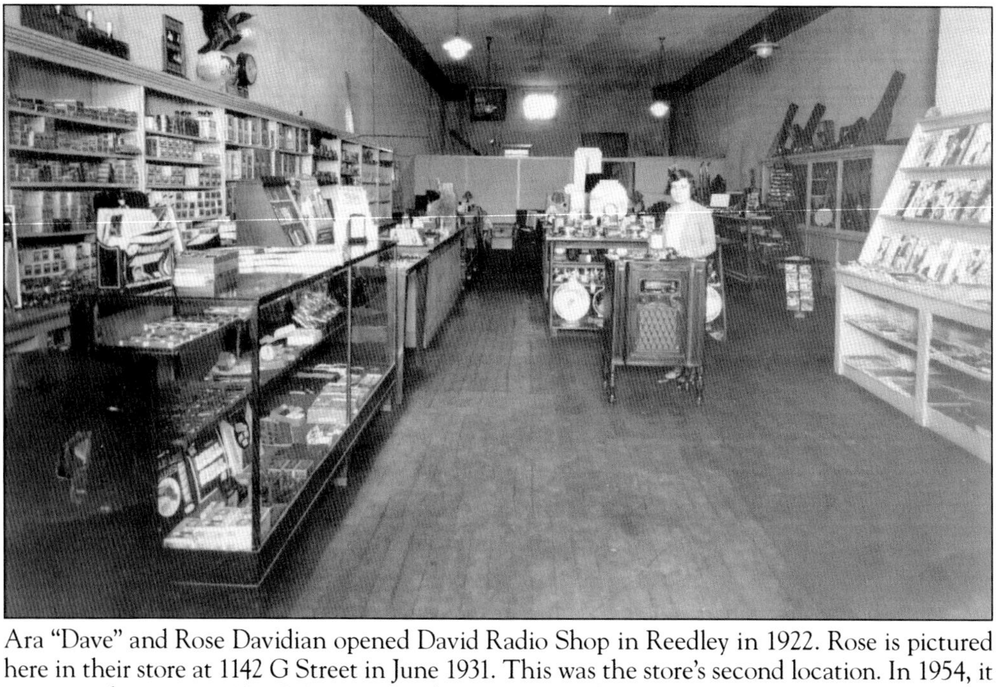

Ara "Dave" and Rose Davidian opened David Radio Shop in Reedley in 1922. Rose is pictured here in their store at 1142 G Street in June 1931. This was the store's second location. In 1954, it was moved again, to 1034 G Street. Now known as David's, a gift shop, the business remains in the family. (Courtesy of Pamela Melville.)

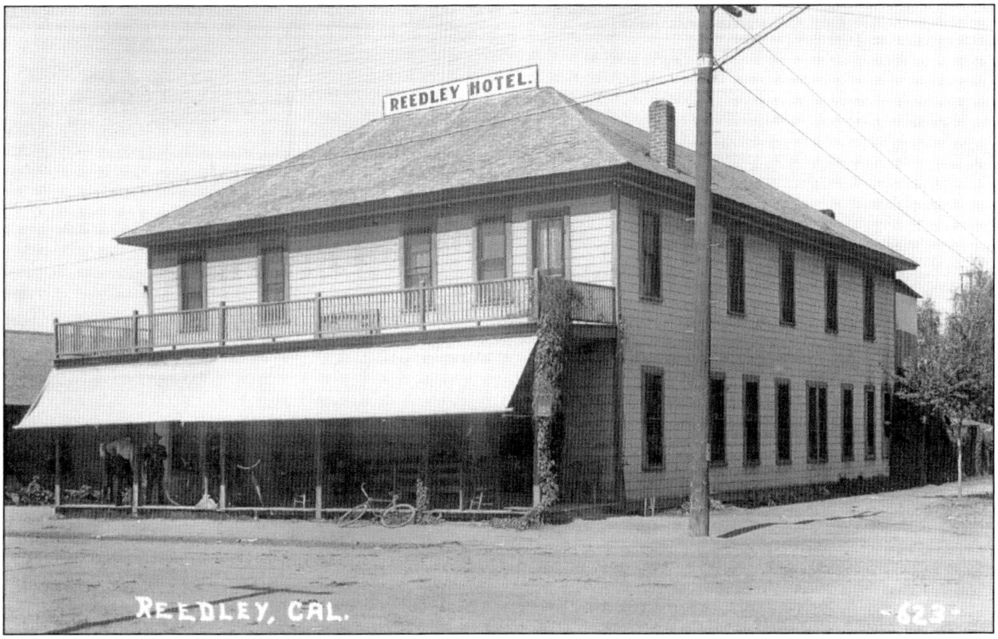

Photographs of the second Reedley Hotel are rare, as the building did not last very long. The first hotel was lost to a fire in 1902. This second hotel building stood for only eight years before it, too, was destroyed by a fire. The third Reedley Hotel still stands on the original site, at G and Eleventh Streets. (Photograph by George Besaw.)

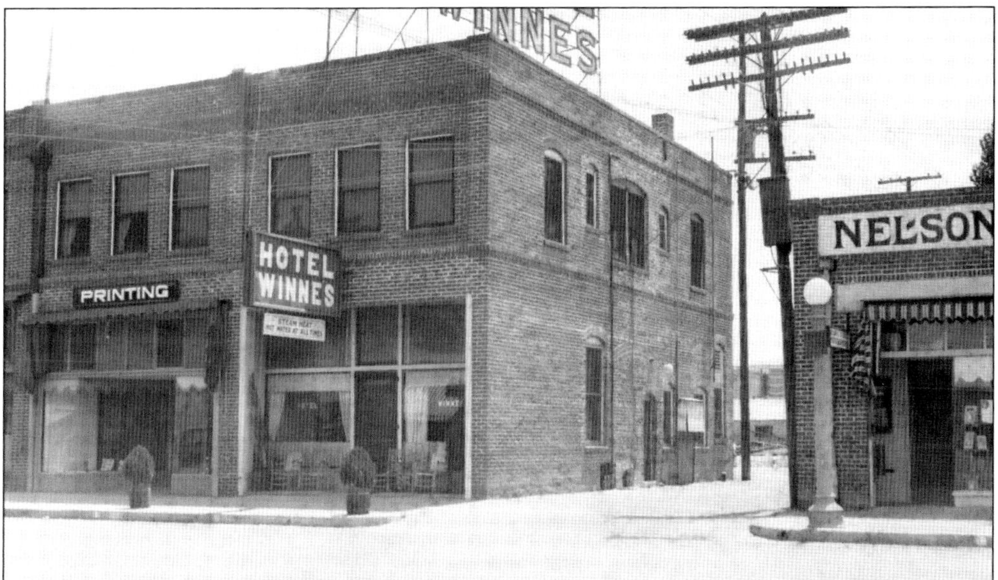

Shown here is the entrance to the Winnes Hotel on the Eleventh Street side of the building. Guest rooms were located on the second floor. According to the sign, a feature of the hotel was "hot water at all times." The Nelson photographic studio is just across the alley. (Photograph by Nelson Studio.)

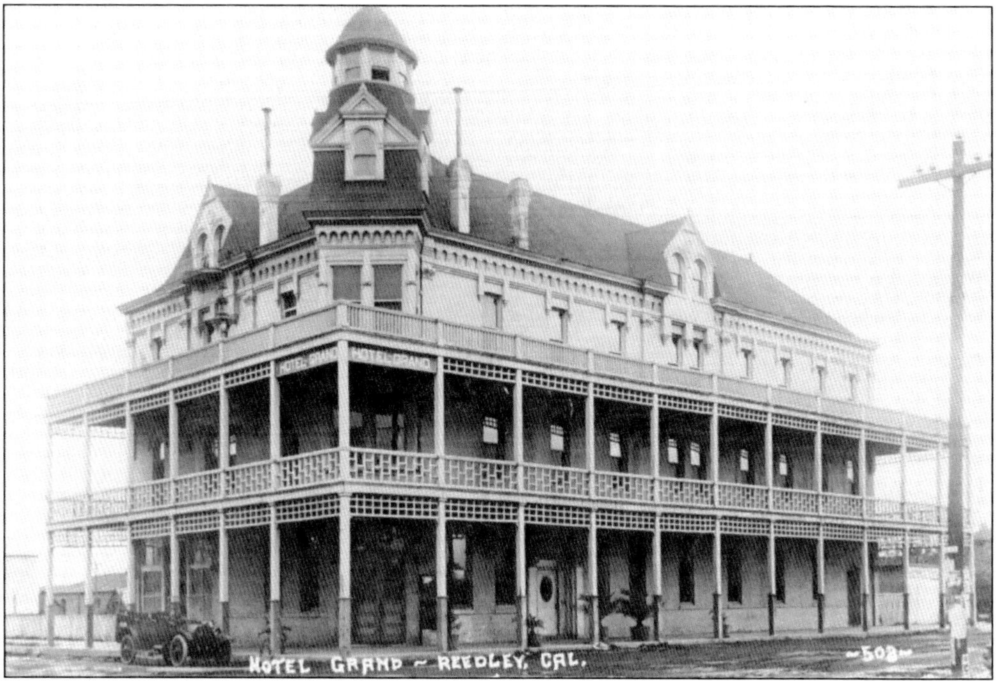

Taken about 1910, this widely reproduced photograph of the Hotel Grand shows the establishment in its heyday. Nothing on Reedley's main street of that era compared to its size and splendor. (Photograph by George Besaw.)

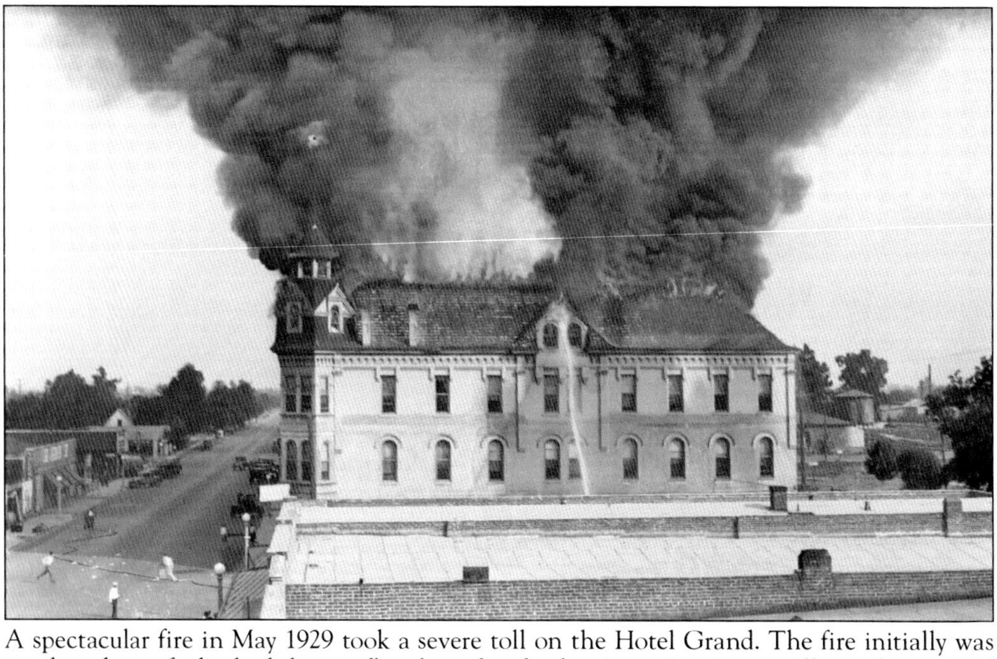

A spectacular fire in May 1929 took a severe toll on the Hotel Grand. The fire initially was attributed to a faulty bath heater flue, but after further investigation, a still was determined to be at fault, as illegal liquor had been cooking upstairs. The hotel owners and manager were found complicit. A federal court ordered the hotel sealed for a period of one year. (Photograph by Nelson Studio.)

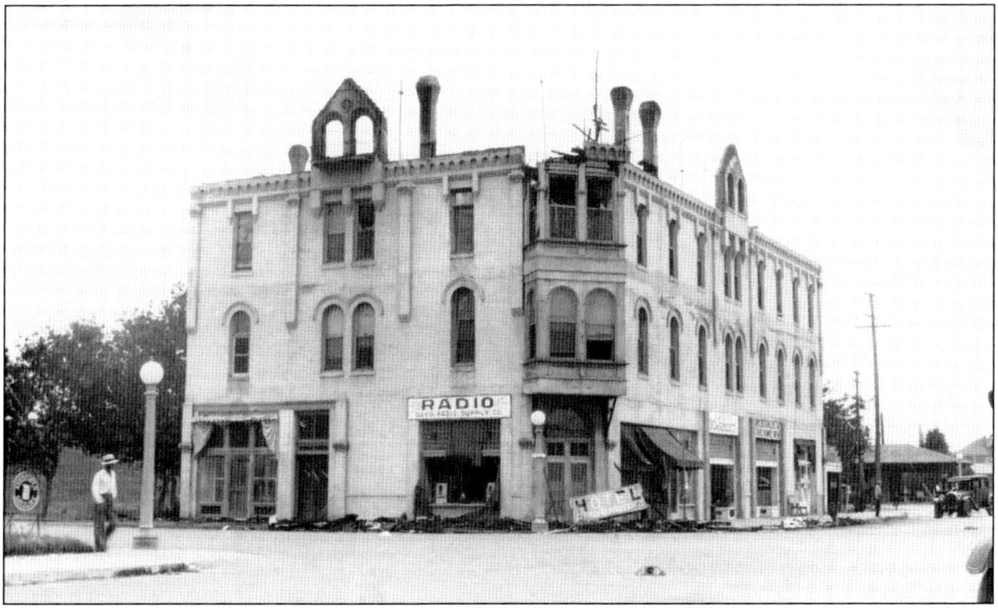

Once the flames had been smothered and the smoke had cleared, only the first and second floors of the Hotel Grand could be salvaged. The peaked roof was gone, and the remnants of the third floor had to be demolished. The balconies that once wrapped around the second and third floors had been removed a few years earlier. (Photograph by Nelson Studio.)

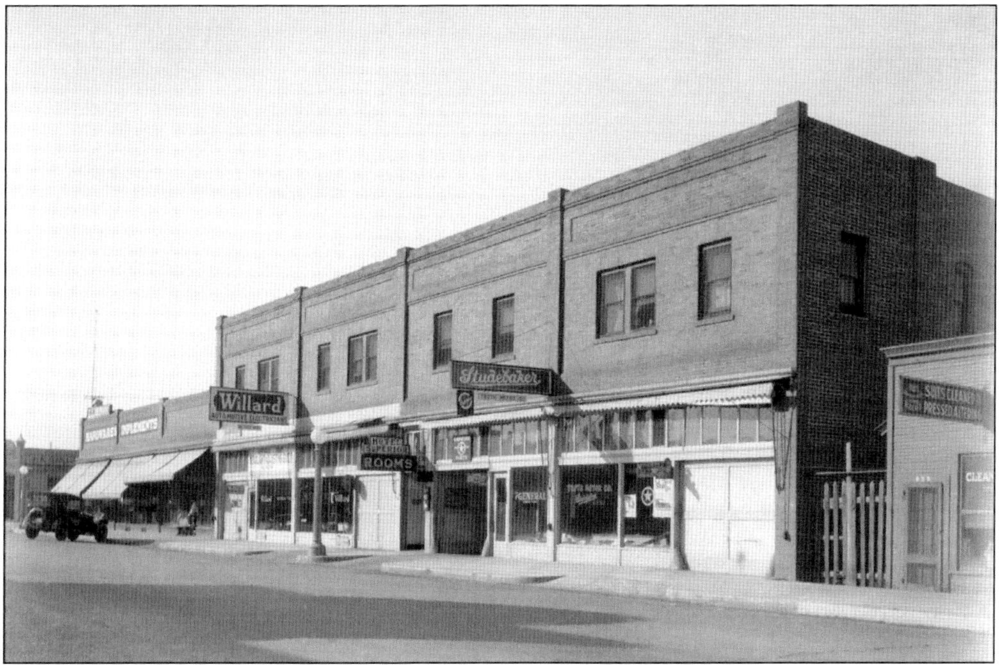

Troth Motor Company's Studebaker dealership occupied the right portion of the Superior Hotel building's ground floor in the 1920s. Next door to the left is Wethey Brothers, an automotive electrical business that sold Willard brand batteries, and in the next adjacent storefront is L.L. Brown's Hardware & Implements store. J.A. Gallaher's general merchandise store was located in the Jansen Building across the street. (Photograph by Nelson Studio.)

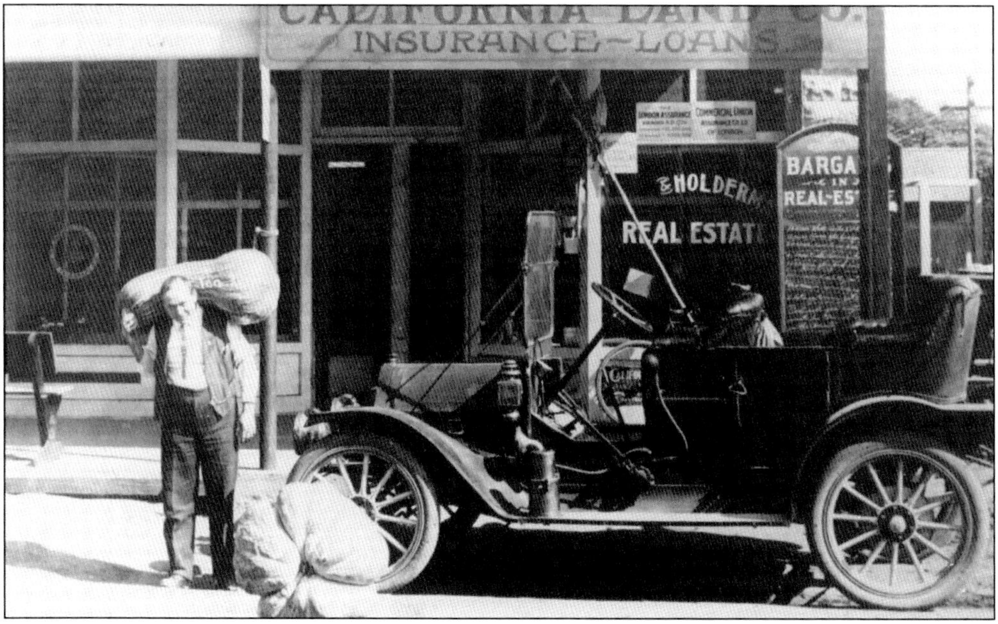

Judge Albert Holderman shows off his oversize pumpkins. The specimen resting heavily on his shoulders weighed in at 100 pounds. Holderman had part-time duties as a justice of the peace. His full-time work was selling real estate and insurance.

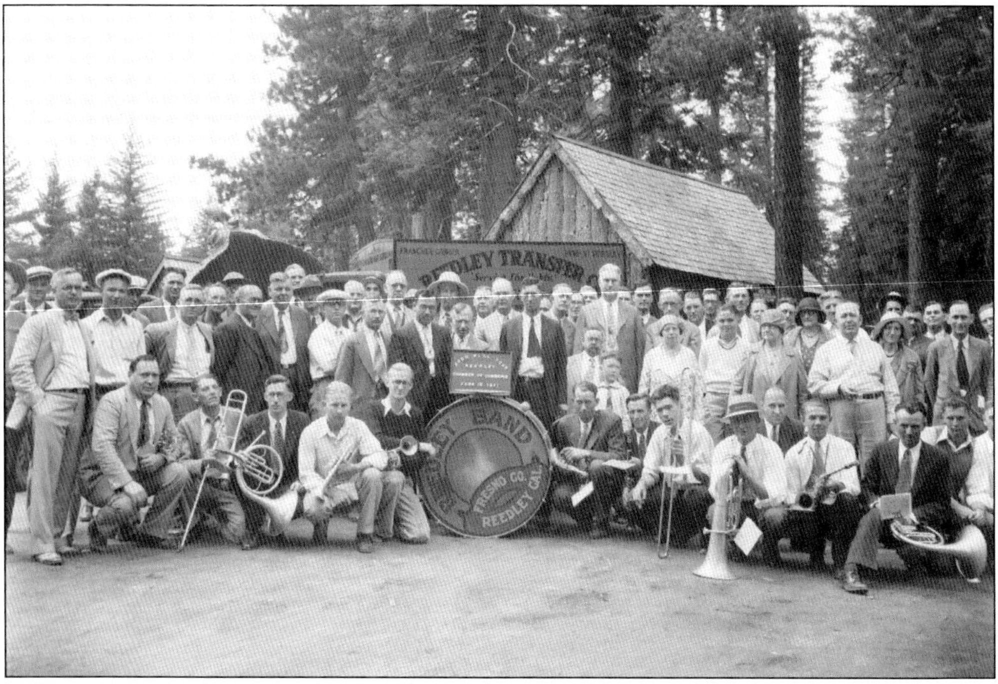

In June 1931, a combination of 94 members and guests of the chamber of commerce hit the road on a goodwill tour. Stops were made in Squaw Valley, Dunlap, Miramonte, Pinehurst, and General Grant Park. The Reedley Band provided music. A highlight was James Fairweather and band director M.T. Garland playing a cornet duet. Garland is squatting on the far left; Fairweather is just left of the bass drum. (Photograph by Nelson Studio.)

The interior of the H.D. Bollin dry goods store is pictured here about 1908.

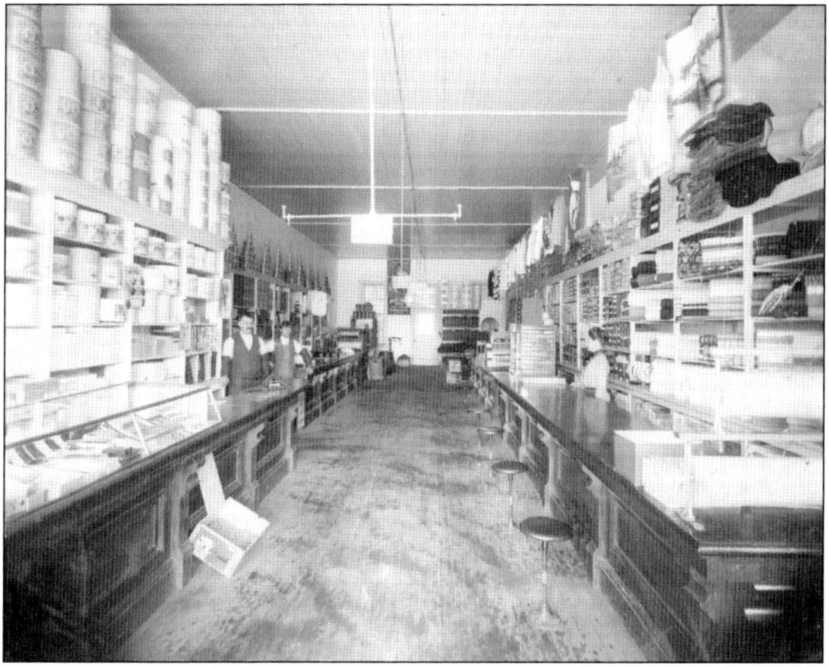

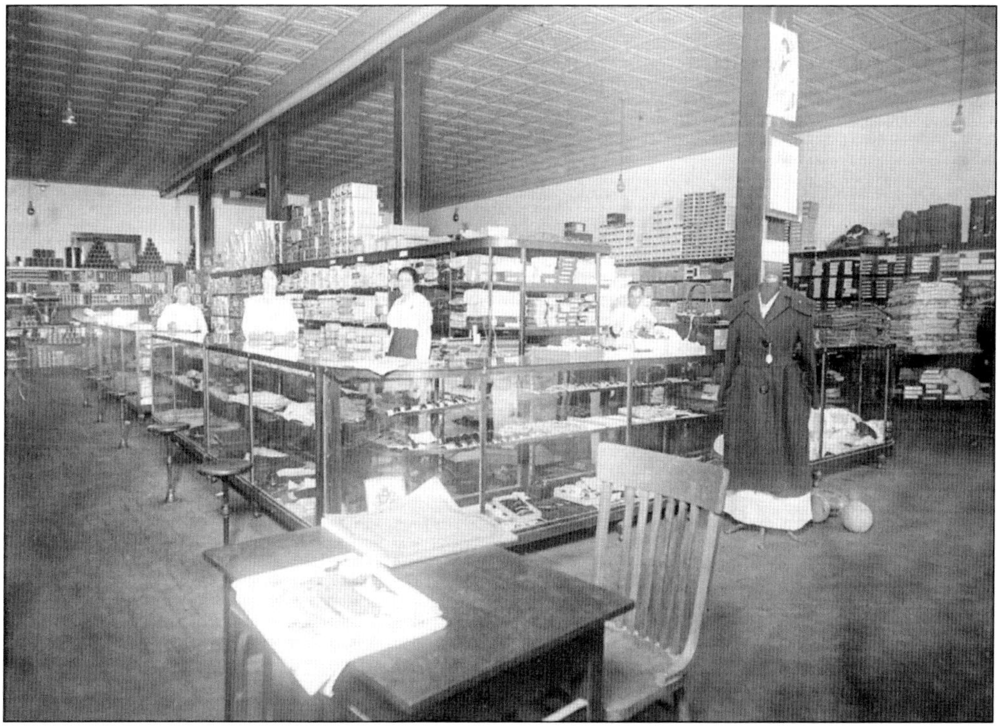

From left to right, J.A. Gallaher, Edna McAmis, Cate Johnston, and Frank Gallaher pose for a photograph in the Gallaher general merchandise store. The store had a tin ceiling—a common feature in Reedley stores of this era. Some downtown stores still have them.

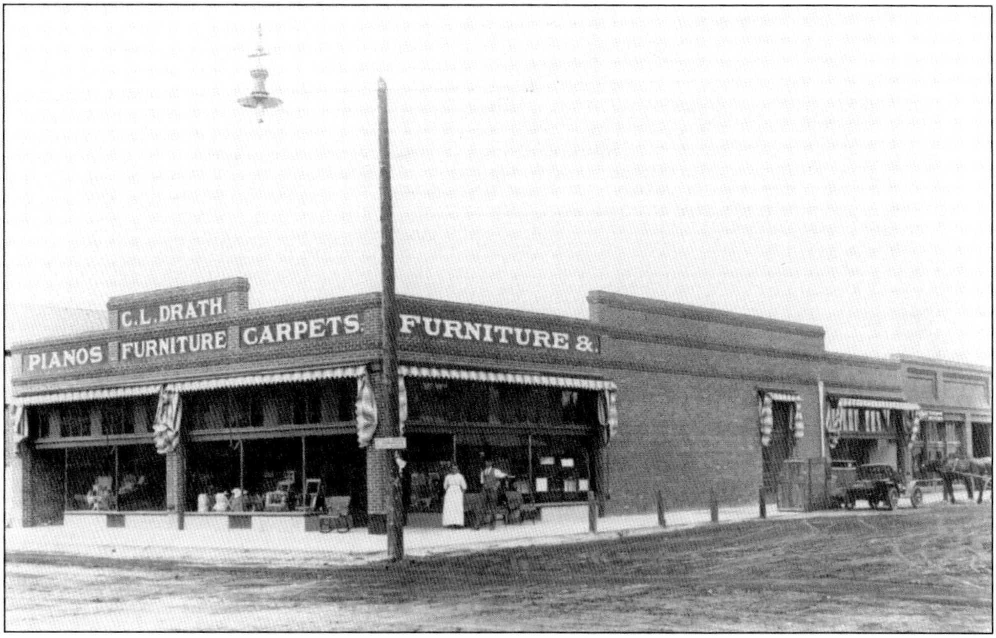

C.L. Drath was among those elected to the first city council when Reedley incorporated in 1913. His furniture store was on the corner of G and Tenth Streets. A succession of other furniture businesses used the building following the Drath era.

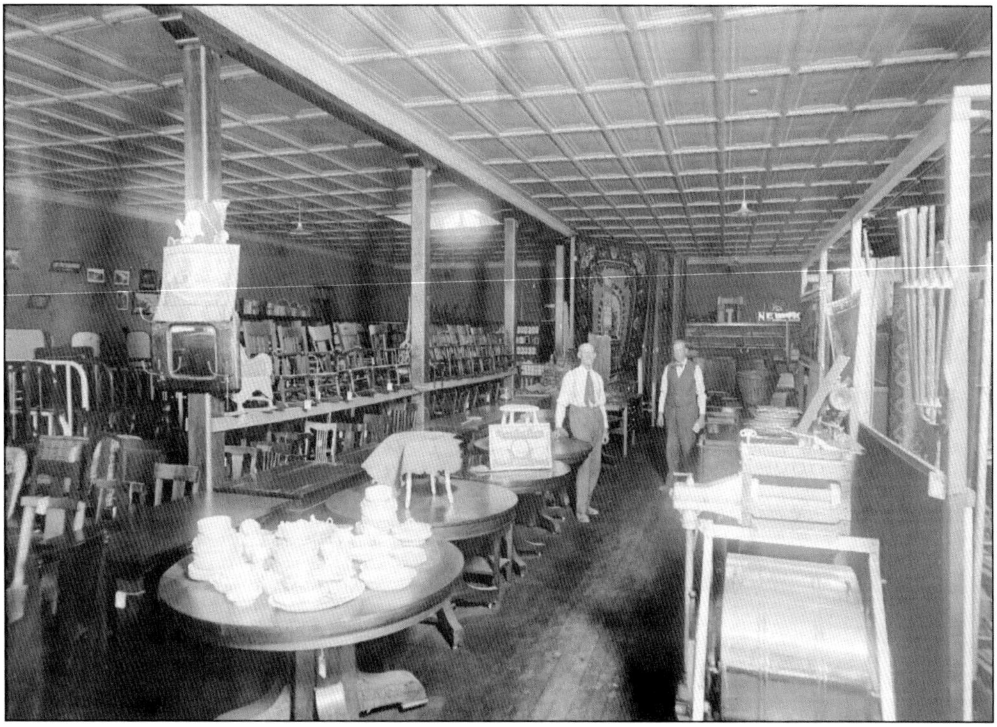

This interior view of the Drath furniture store shows just a small portion of the items available for purchase there. Rocking chairs were obviously a popular item; at least a dozen are on display. The latest in washing machines is shown in the right foreground.

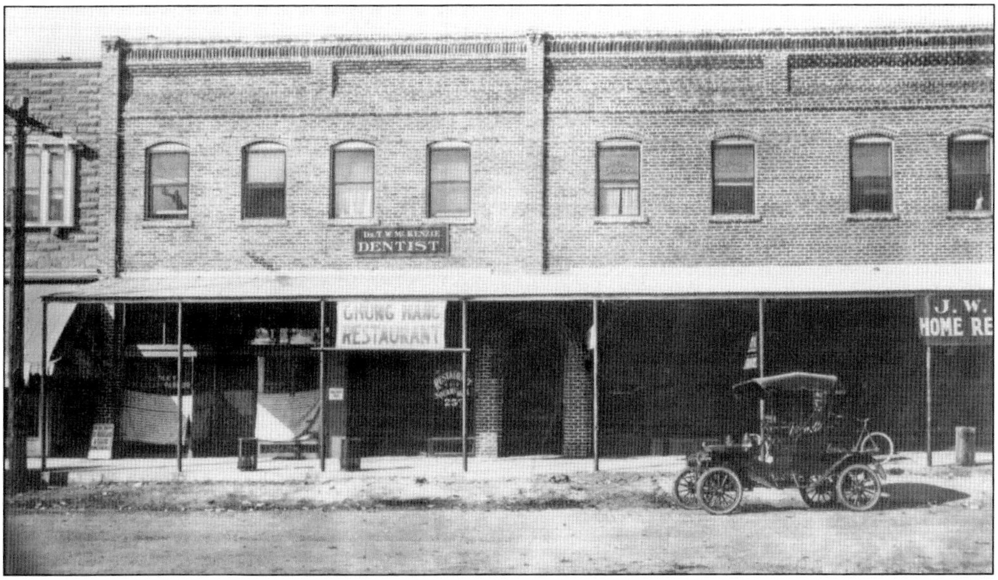

The Chung Hang Restaurant is in business on the ground floor of the Model Rooming House building in this photograph from around 1910. The restaurant advertised a "Big Square Meal 25¢." Next door to the left is the Reedley Ice Cream Parlor. Drs. McKenzie and Shaffer had their offices upstairs.

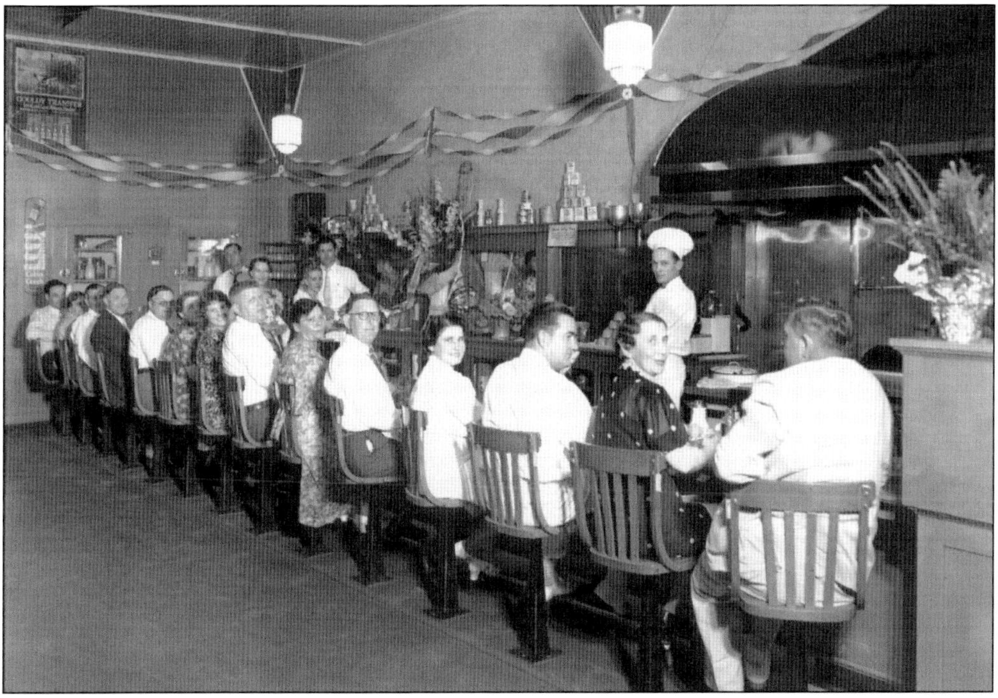

The Gouldy brothers purchased the Reedley Coffee Shop at 1041 G Street and hosted a grand opening in July 1938. This drew a crowd of prominent Reedleyites. In the nearest four seats at the counter are, from left to right, Minnie Carlisle, Mayor Walker Carlisle, Elizabeth Tackaberry, and city attorney Chester Tackaberry. The Saturday-night "Chef's Dinner" cost 50¢. (Photograph by Nelson Studio.)

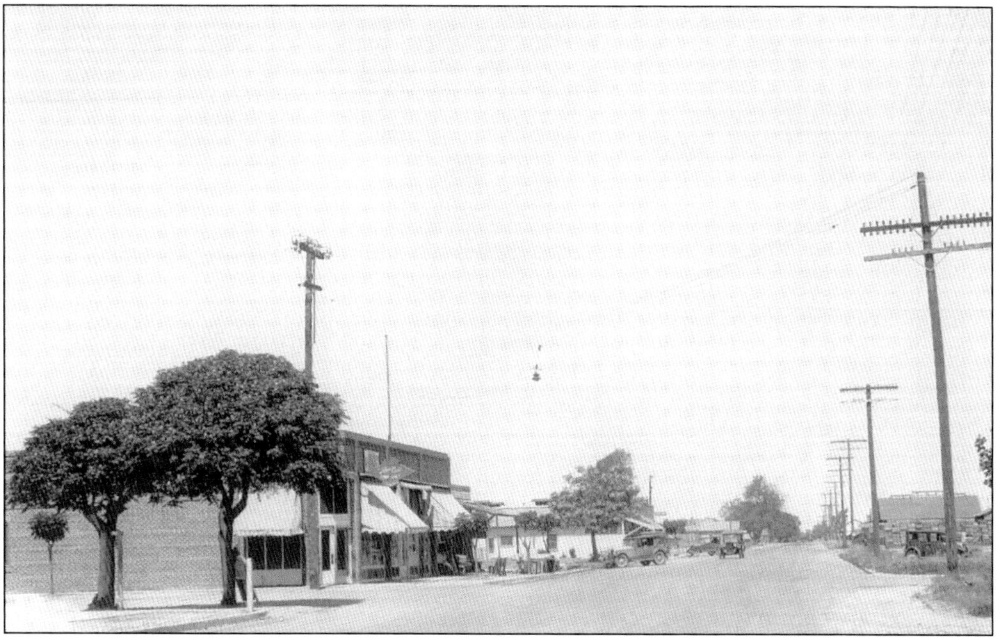

The restaurant at the corner of I and Fourteenth Streets, in Reedley's Chinatown, has been serving Chinese food since at least 1922. This photograph likely dates from the late 1920s, when it was known as the Rose Café. After a change in ownership, the restaurant became the New China Café in 1942. The historic New China remains a popular dining destination for Reedley-area residents.

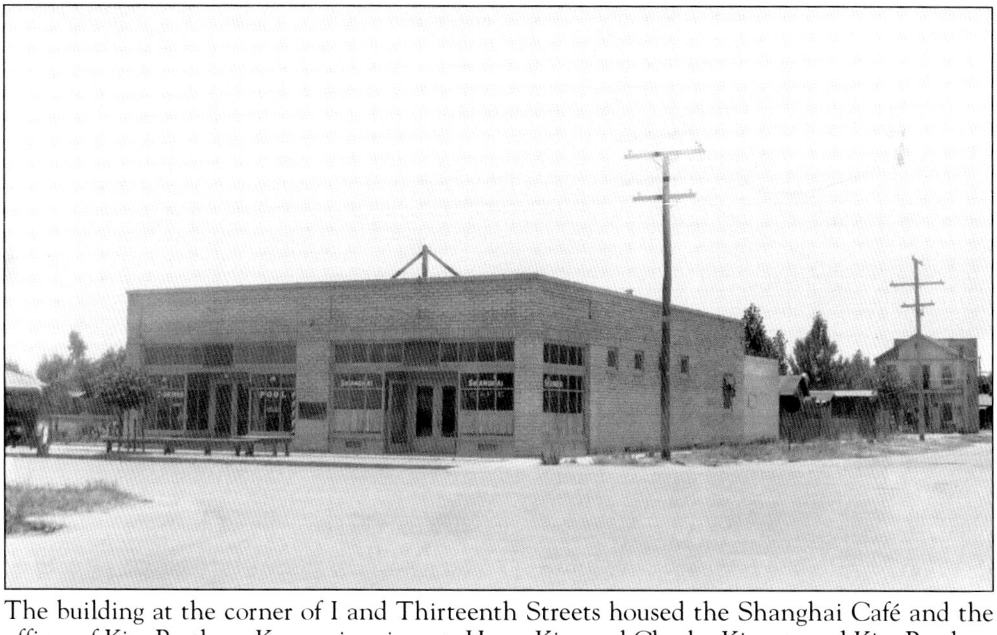

The building at the corner of I and Thirteenth Streets housed the Shanghai Café and the offices of Kim Brothers. Korean immigrants Harry Kim and Charles Kim started Kim Brothers in Reedley in 1921. Their company grew to become a large farming, fruit-packing, and nursery business. The nursery gained prominence in later years for marketing the industry-changing Le Grand nectarine. (Photograph by Nelson Studio.)

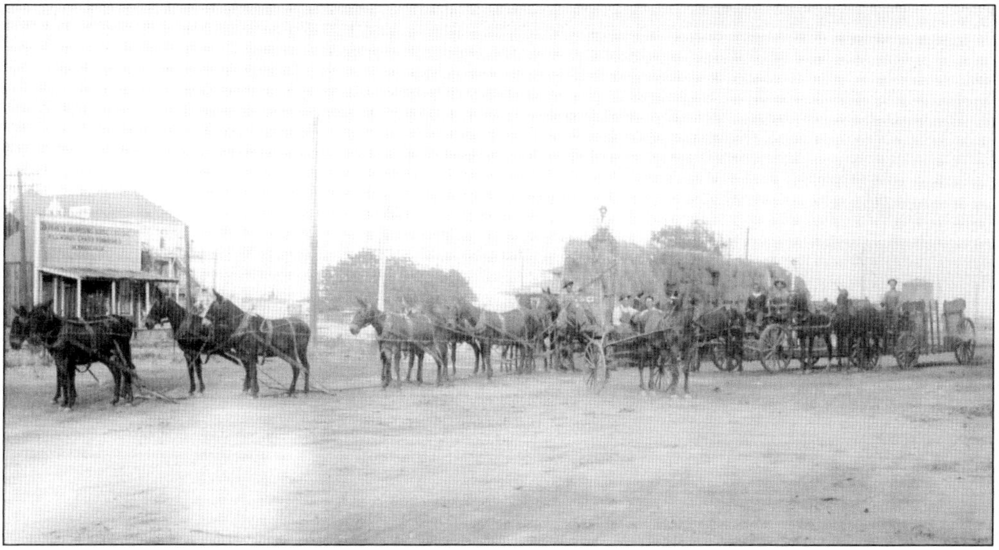

The wagons of the Reedley Transfer Company are seen in the vicinity of H and Twelfth Streets. H. Yasui operated a Japanese boardinghouse, store, and labor bureau in the small building on the left, beyond which is the Hotel Grand. Behind the hay wagon is the Santa Fe Railway depot.

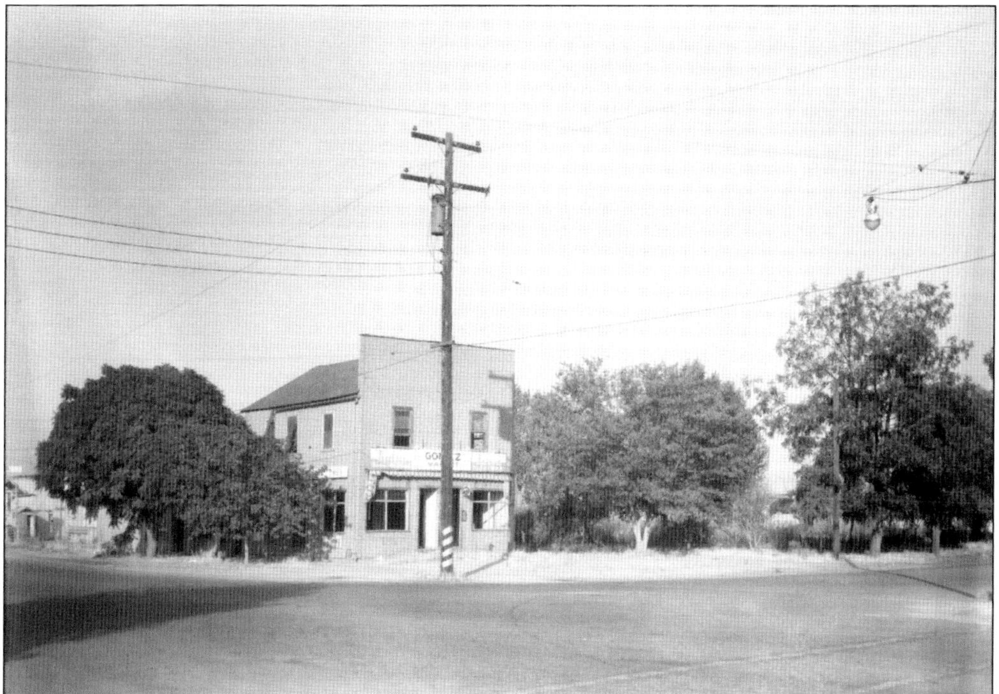

The Gomez Market, at J and Thirteenth Streets, looks abandoned in this photograph. The building should look familiar; this was the former Knauer house and post office that used to stand on F Street at Eleventh Street. It is believed that the building was moved to this site in the 1920s. (Photograph by Nelson Studio.)

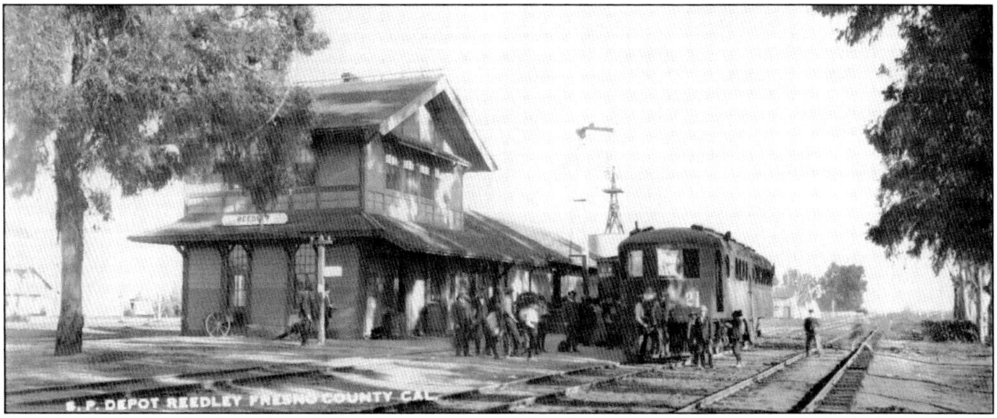

Passengers wait to board a McKeen motor car at the Southern Pacific depot. Travelers could catch a train out of Reedley several times a day in 1909. The Southern Pacific had two northbound and two southbound trains stop each day. The Santa Fe had three northbound and three southbound trains arrive and depart at its depot each day. Before Parlier had a secondary school, students would commute by train to attend Reedley High School.

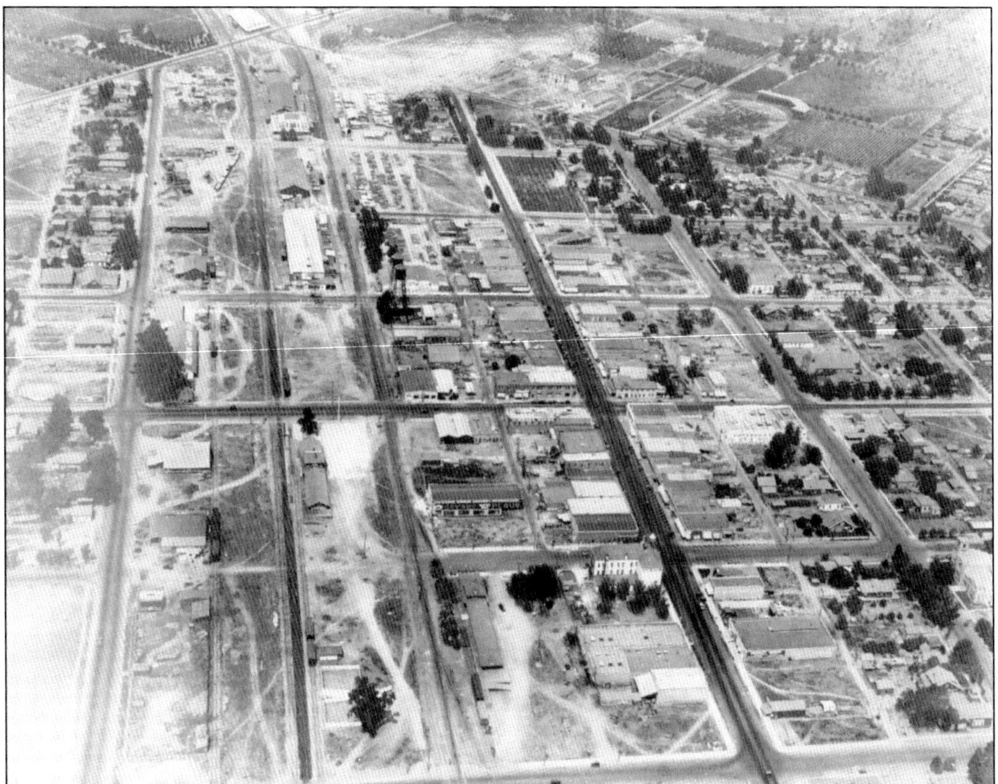

This aerial view of Reedley from the mid- to late 1920s shows the growth of the town in its first 40 years.

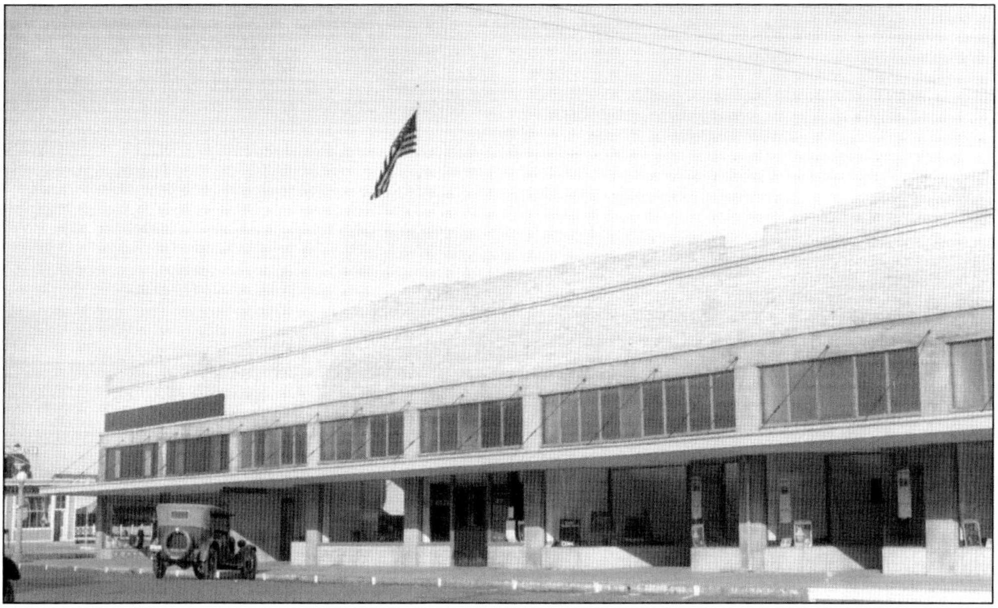

This building still stands on the south side of Eleventh Street at F Street. It was known as the "post office block," because from 1923 to 1940, the US Post Office occupied the center storefront at 1612 Eleventh Street, directly below the flagpole. The J.C. Penney store occupies the space on the far left. (Photograph by Nelson Studio.)

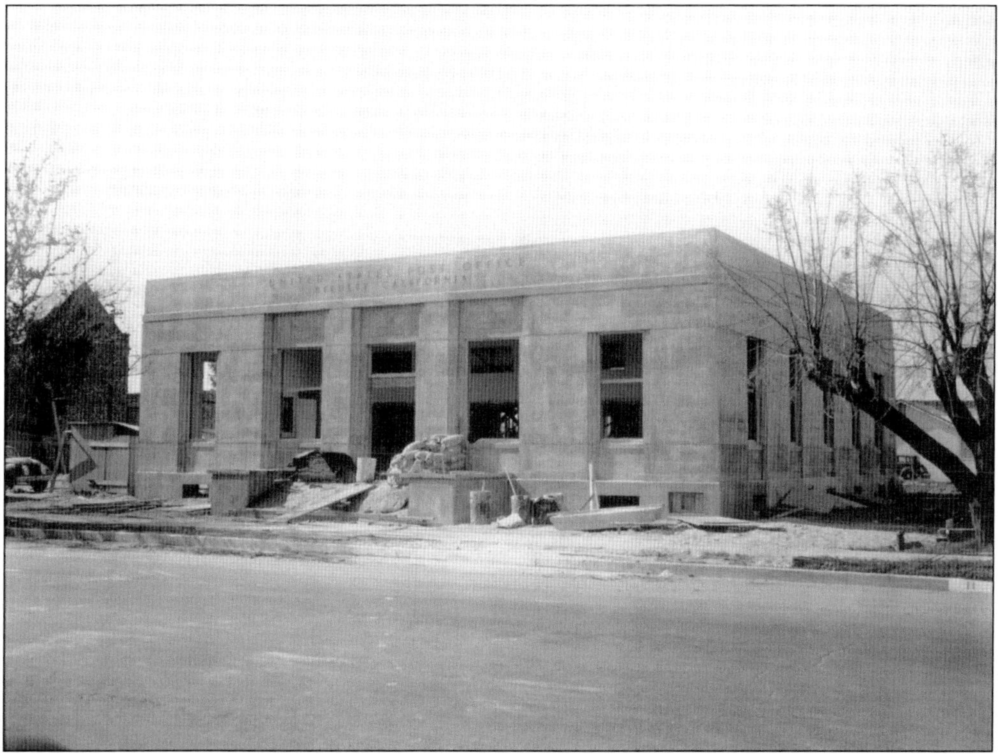

Reedley's new post office is under construction at Eleventh and E Streets in early 1940. It was dedicated on April 26, 1940.

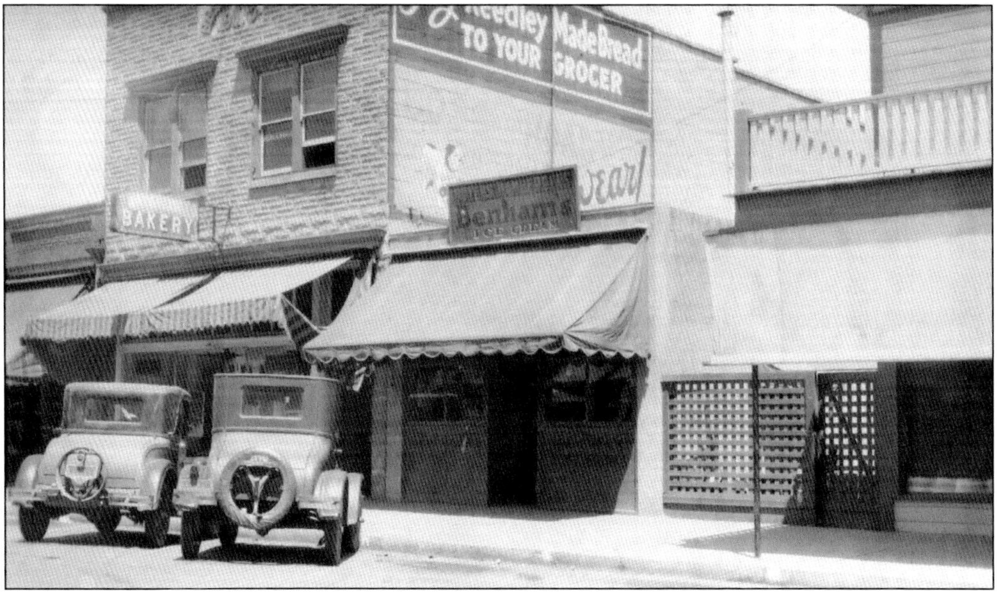

Boyers Hamburgers, with Benham's Ice Cream, is next door to the Reedley Hotel (right) in this c. 1929 photograph. To the left is the two-story Besaw Brothers building, which housed the Reedley Bakery. A real estate office was located upstairs at the time of this image.

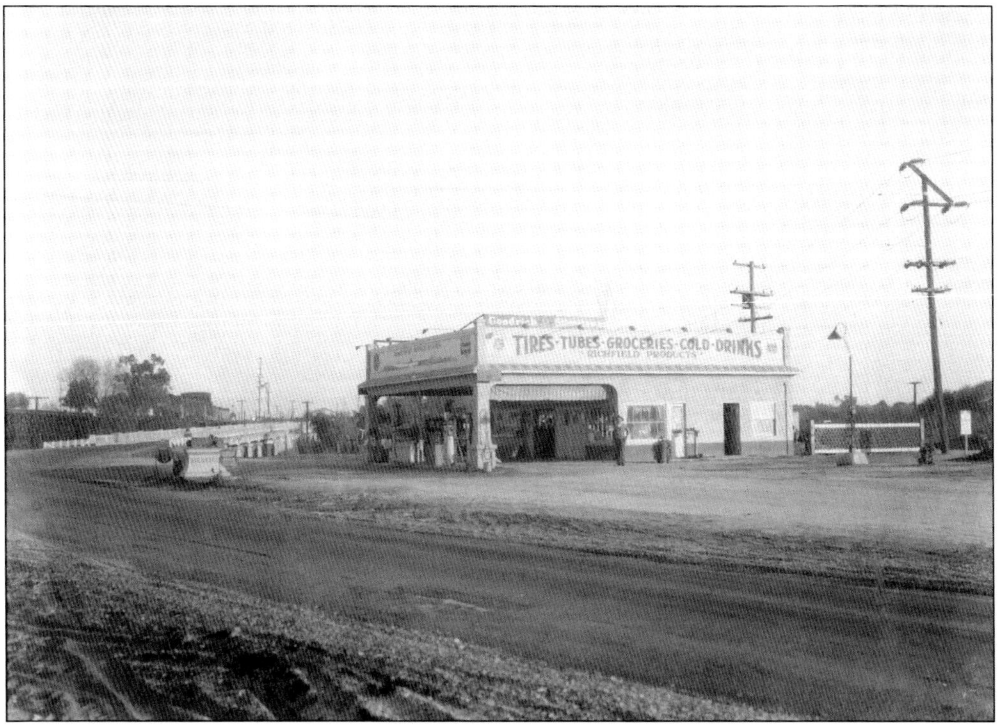

The Kings River Service Station was located just west of the Manning Avenue bridge. An interesting feature is the Richfield race car on the pedestal at the roadside. At left, in the distance, is the old winery that once stood between the Southern Pacific and Santa Fe railroad tracks. (Photograph by Nelson Studio.)

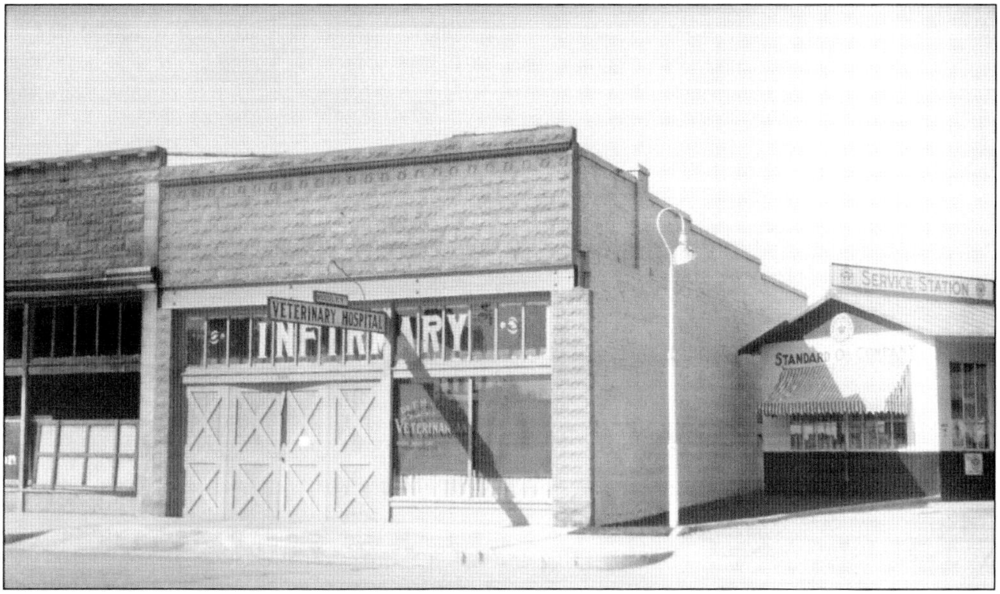

Dr. F.M. Norris had his practice at the Reedley Veterinary Hospital at 909 G Street. A Standard Oil Service Station was located next door, on the corner. (Photograph by Nelson Studio.)

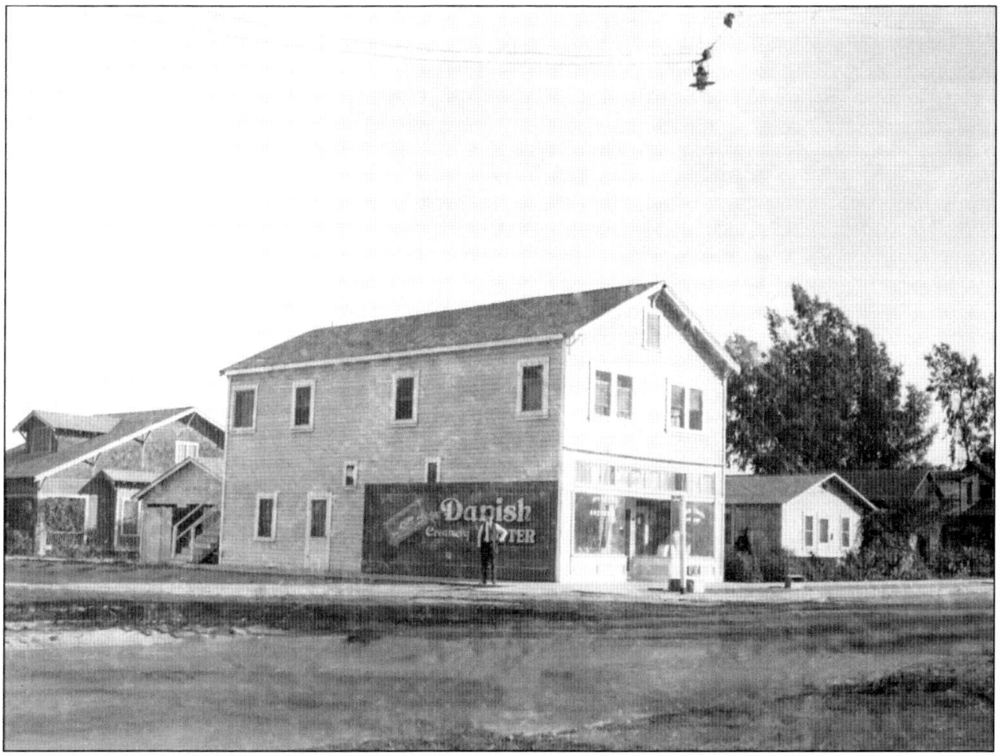

Ayoob's Grocery was a longtime business at Eleventh and C Streets. Solomon Ayoob, a Lebanese immigrant, opened his business about 1923. Many current Reedley residents will remember this as the location of a successor business, George's Market. (Photograph by Nelson Studio.)

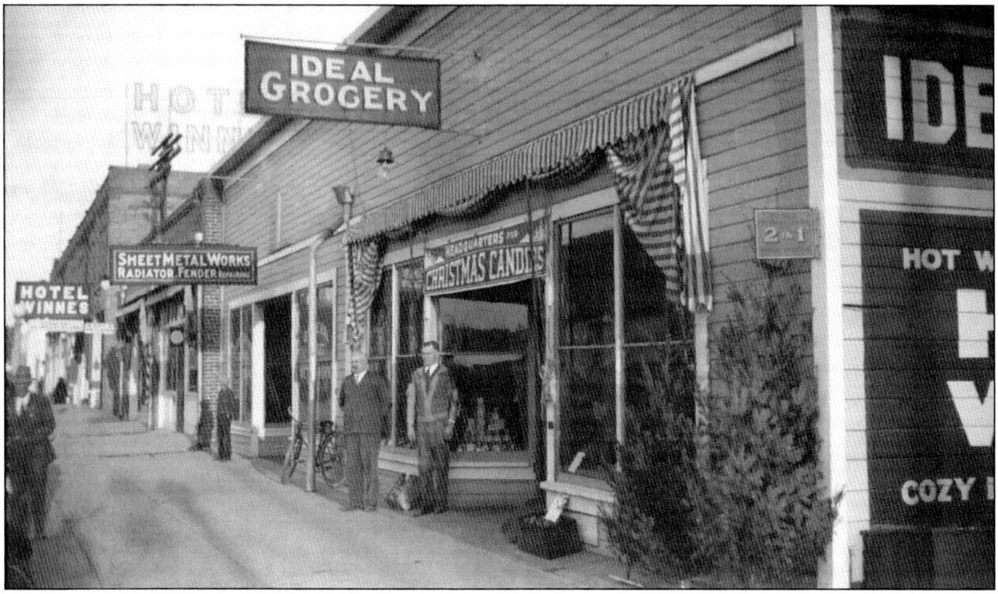

Christmas trees and candies were for sale at Ideal Grocery on Eleventh Street in the 1920s. The store was on the south side of the street, across the alley from the Winnes Hotel. (Photograph by Nelson Studio.)

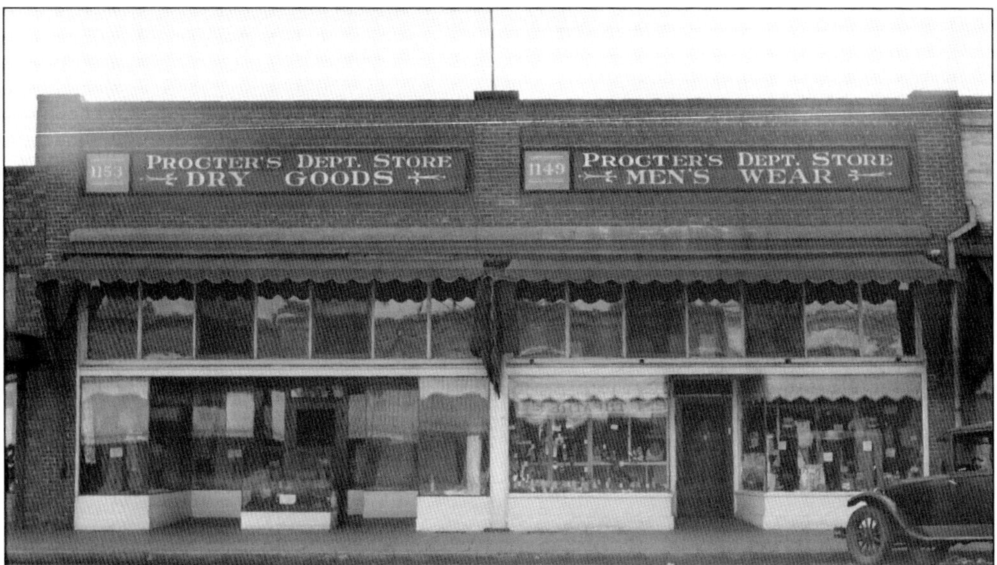

This 1920s photograph shows Procter's Department Store. The large store encompassed two storefronts at 1149 and 1153 G Street. (Photograph by Nelson Studio.)

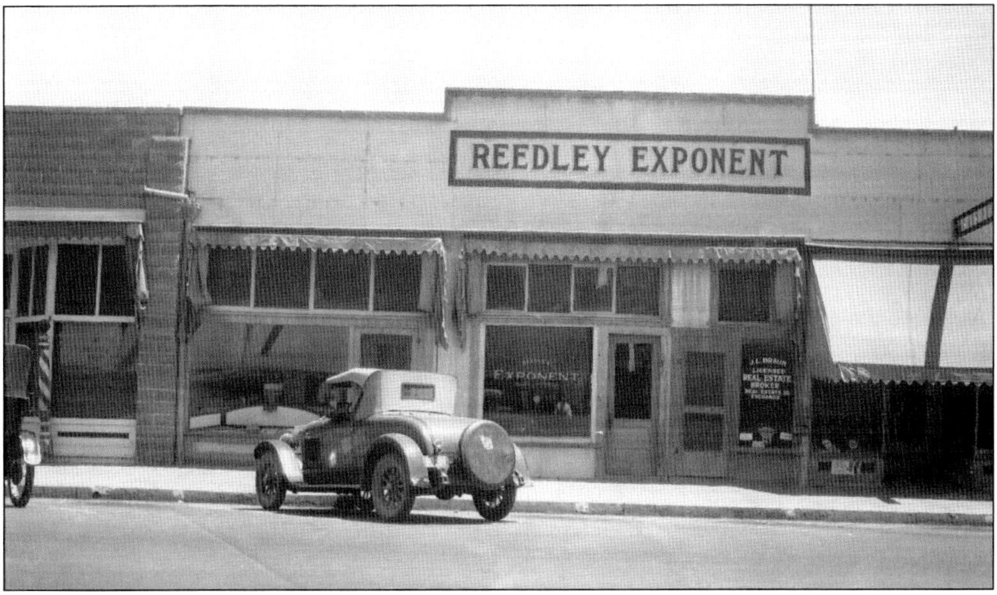

The *Reedley Exponent* newspaper was founded in 1891 and printed its first edition in a room at the Knauer home and post office building at F and Eleventh Streets. It moved to G Street the following year. The office burned down later in the year, then was rebuilt where it has stood ever since. This 1927 photograph shows the *Exponent* sharing a storefront with J.L. Braun's real estate office. (Photograph by Nelson Studio.)

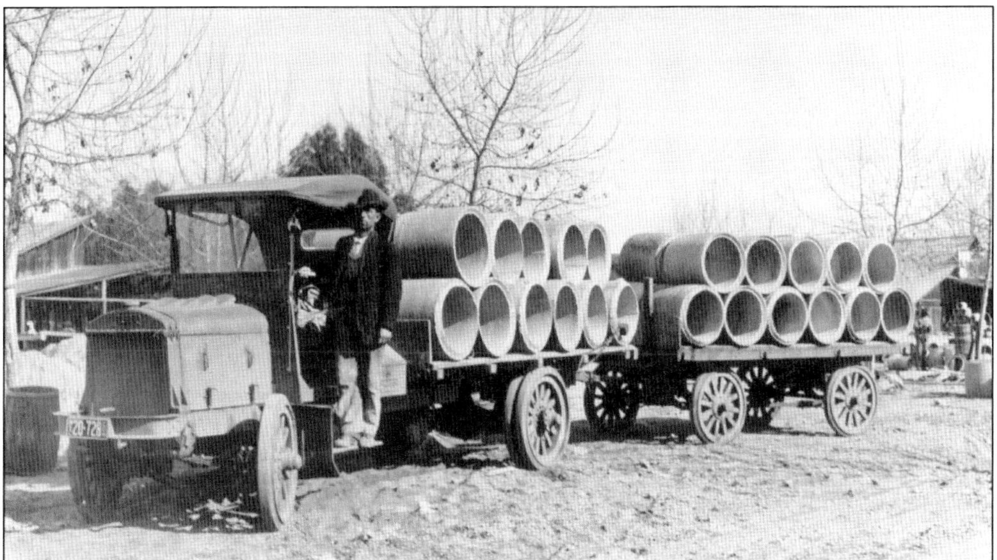

Floyd Ramsey stands on the running board of a truck, ready to deliver pipe to a customer of the Reedley Cement Pipe Company. Based on documented information about the company's location at that time, this photograph likely was taken when the company's operations were at G and Fourteenth Streets.

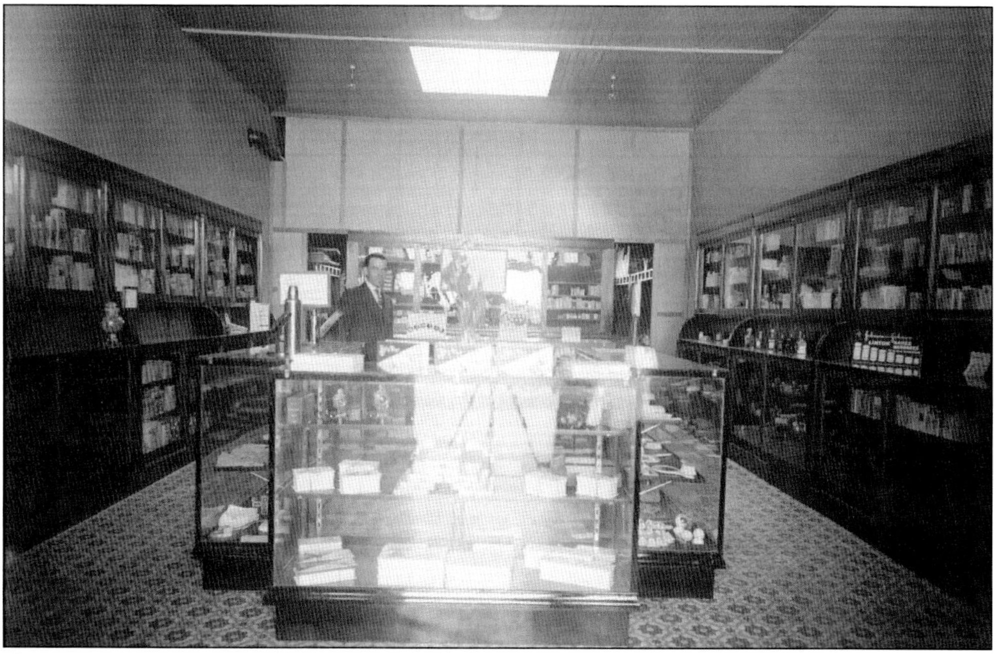

Pharmacist Max Hare poses for a photograph in his drugstore at 1045 G Street. Kodak and other camera supplies were a specialty. Hare opened his business at this location in December 1919, and it closed in the mid-1960s. Upon Hare's retirement, Charles Taguchi opened his Reedley Camera Shop here.

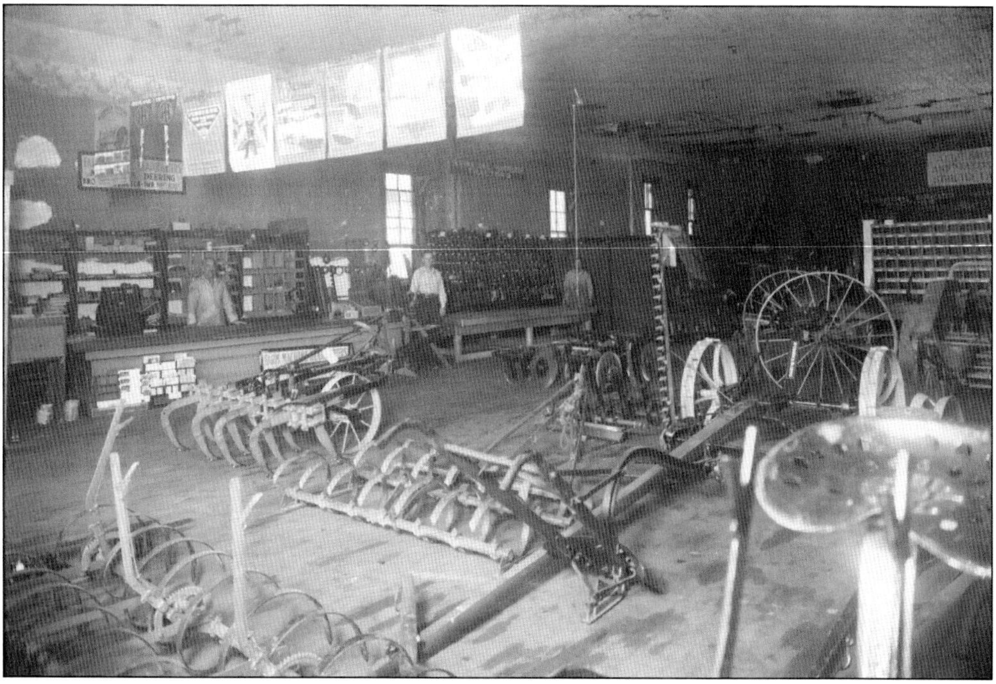

Recent visitors to the elegant Reedley Opera House may be astonished to learn that the building once served as Brown's Tractor & Implements House, as this June 1930 photograph attests. (Photograph by Nelson Studio.)

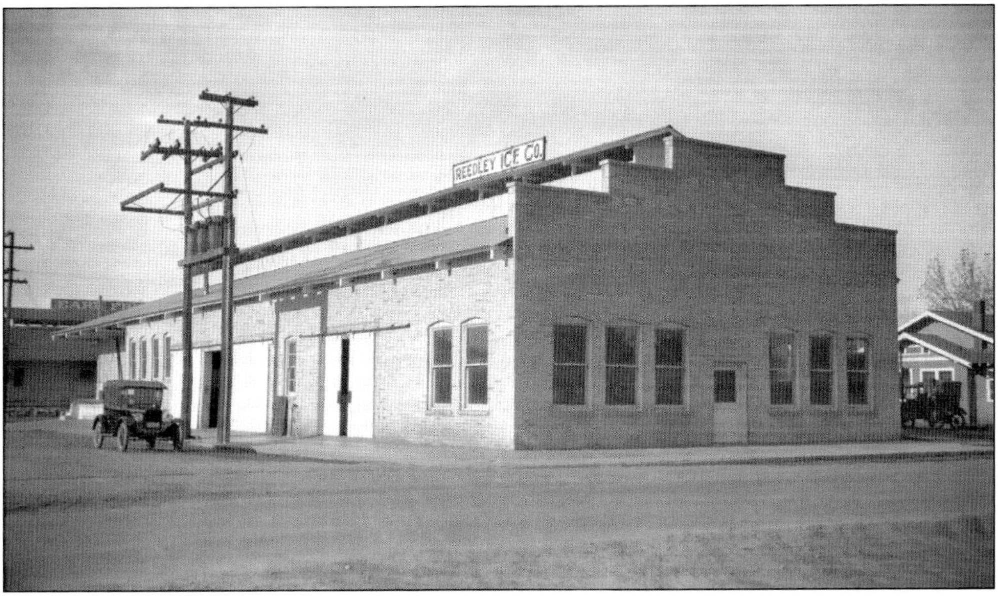

Reedley's new, modern icehouse was located at G and Fifteenth Streets. The railroads were among the biggest customers for the ice manufactured in this facility. Ice-cooled refrigerated railcars, or "reefers," allowed Reedley-grown perishable fruit to safely reach distant markets.

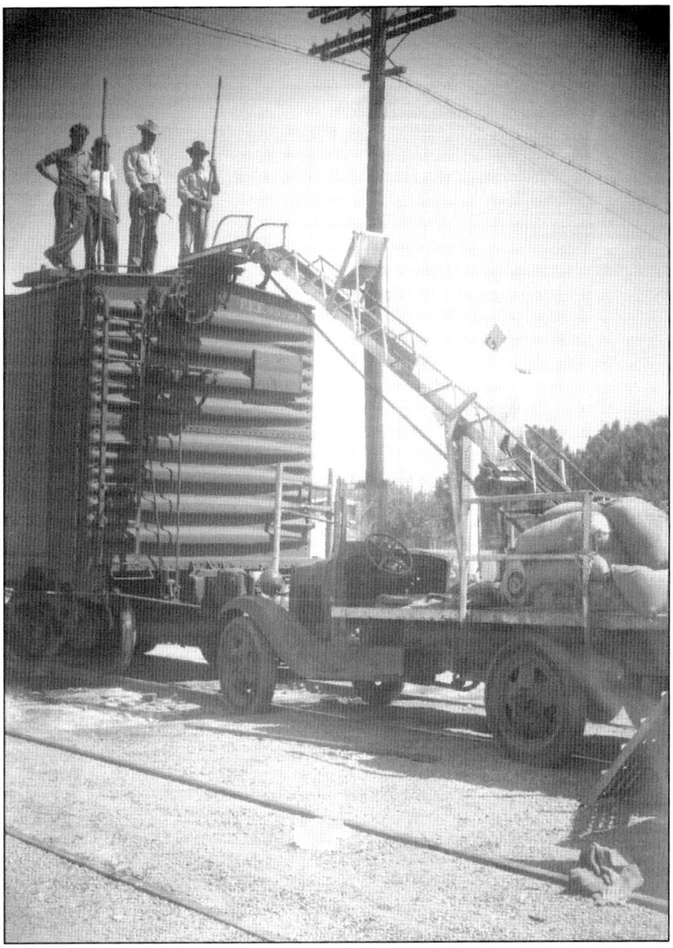

A large block of ice is on its way up the conveyor, from where workers would send it down into the ice bunker of this Pacific Fruit Express refrigerated boxcar. (Photograph by Nelson Studio.)

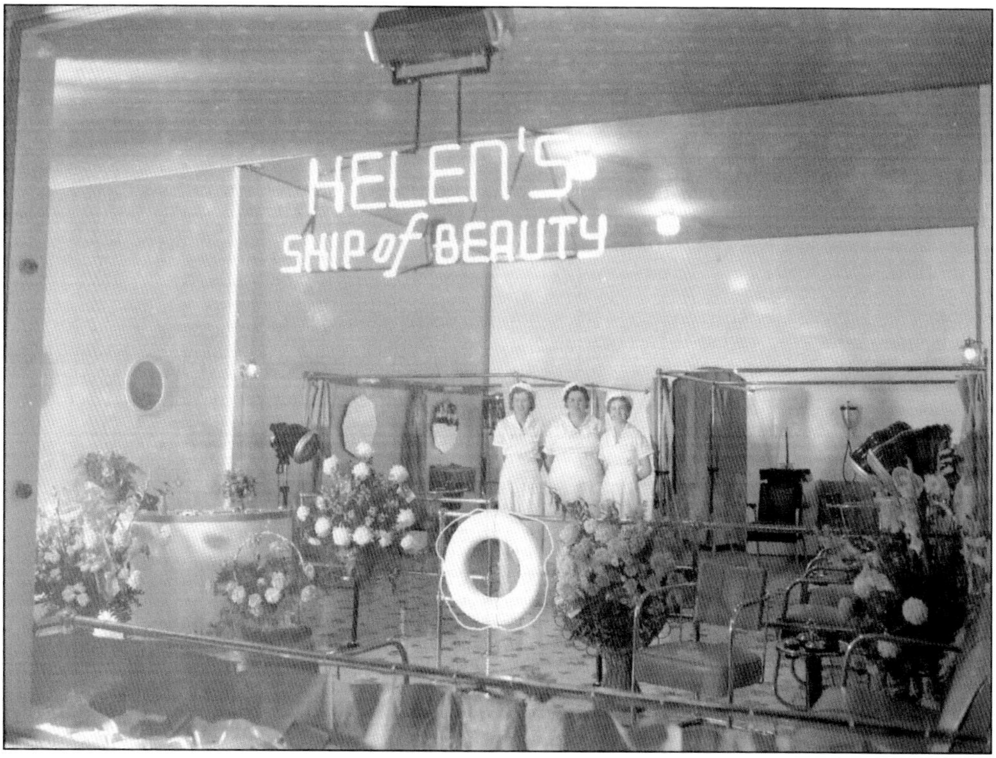

Helen's Ship of Beauty, located at 1722 Eleventh Street, employed a unique nautical theme for its interior decor. The 1939 city directory reveals that the proprietors were Mrs. H.M. Buller and Mrs. Agnes Patt. (Photograph by Nelson Studio.)

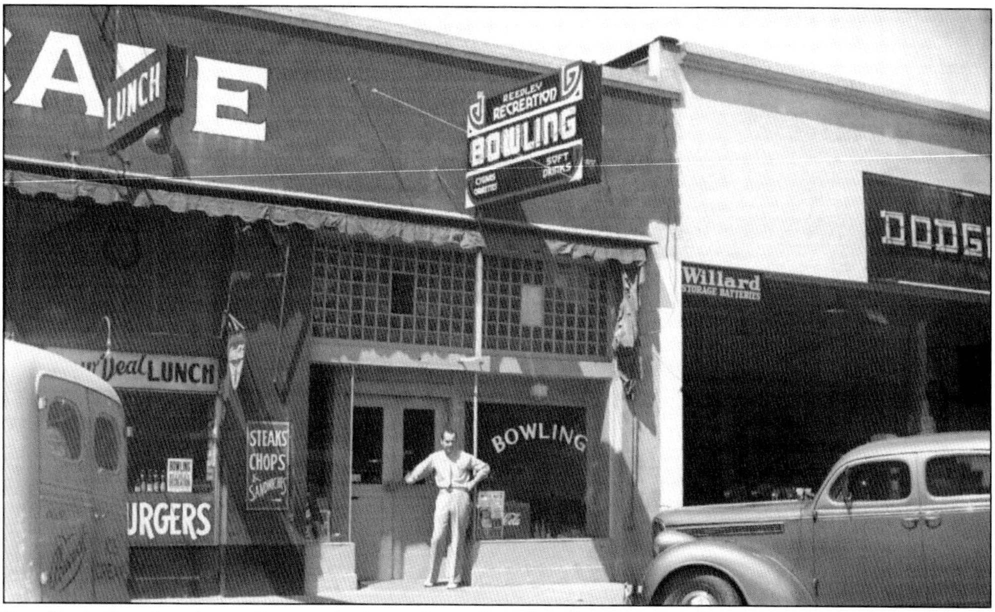

Reedley's first bowling alley might have been Reedley Recreation, located at 1017 G Street. In this 1938 photograph, the Dodge dealership is visible next door, along with a new model parked out front. (Photograph by Nelson Studio.)

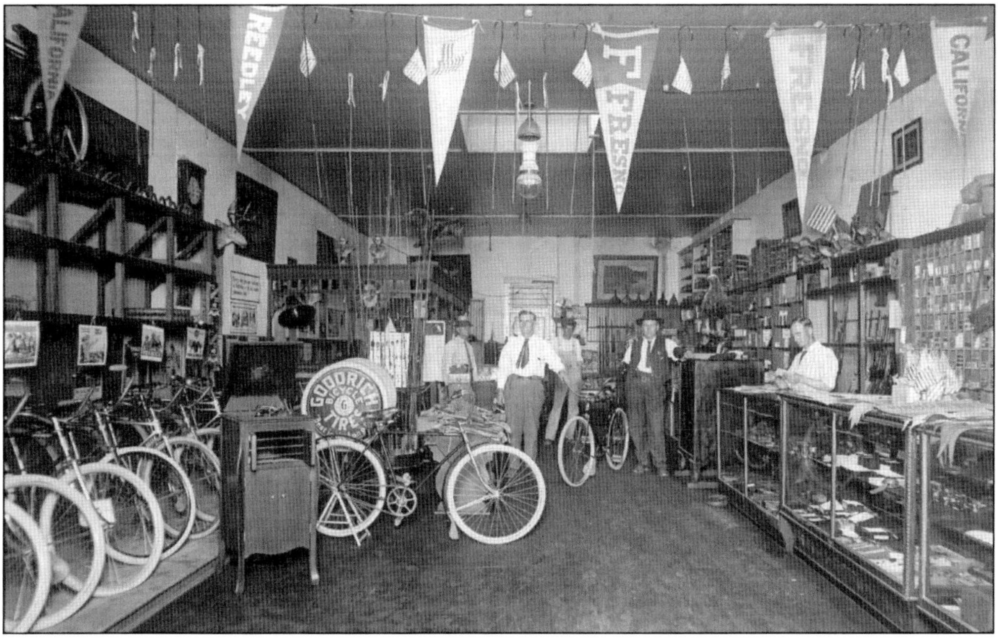

This shot is likely the interior of the Sheibley bicycle and sporting goods store in the 1910s. The marshal is resting his right hand on a Pierce bicycle. Shotguns, fishing rods, and a Victrola phonograph record player are among the many items available here.

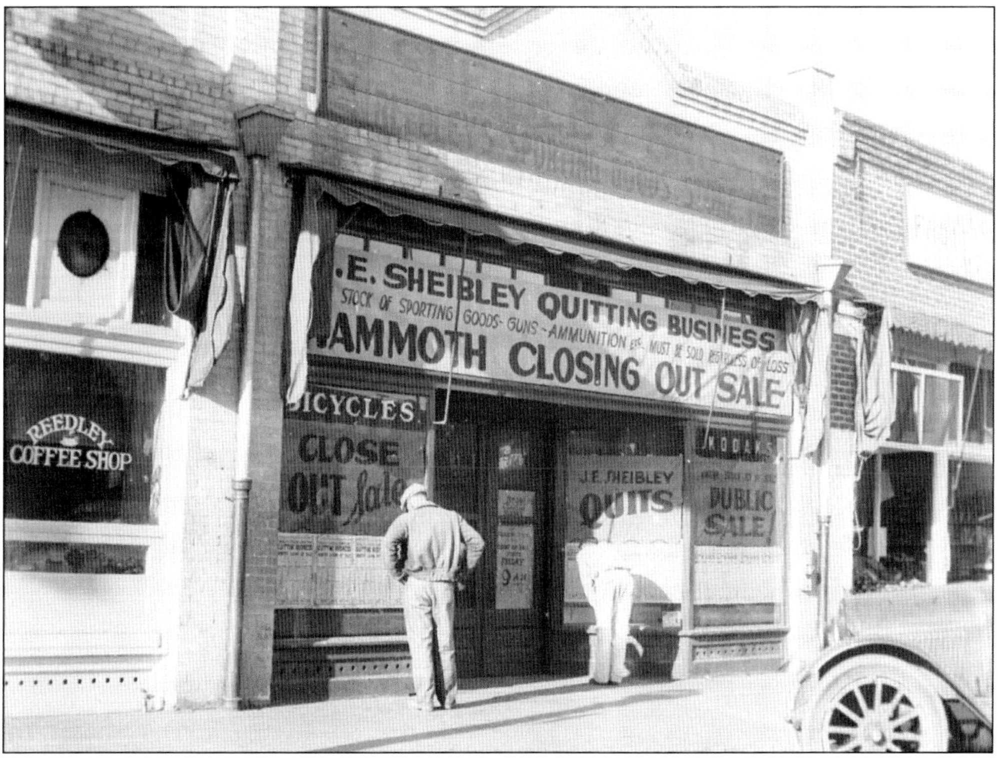

Sheibley's had a good run, with 29 years in Reedley, but in October 1930, the business closed. (Photograph by Nelson Studio.)

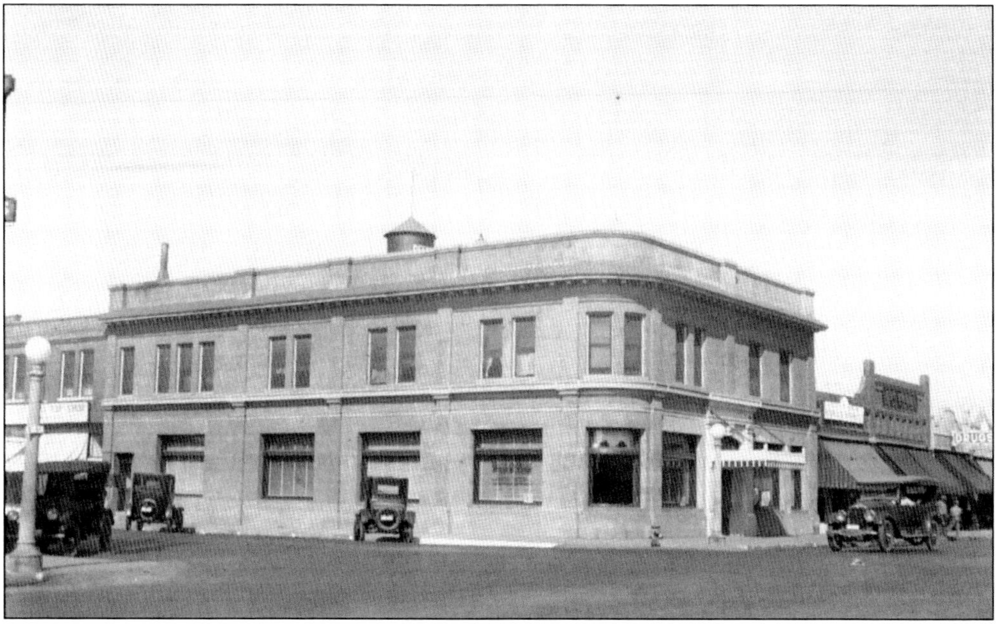

This photograph was taken around 1925, when the Bank of Italy was located in the former First National Bank building. Keen observers will note that something has changed. The building's brick exterior has been covered with a concrete finish to simulate stone tiles. Also, the cupola and corner entrance have vanished. The remodeling occurred in 1919. The corner entrance would reappear after yet another renovation. (Photograph by Nelson Studio.)

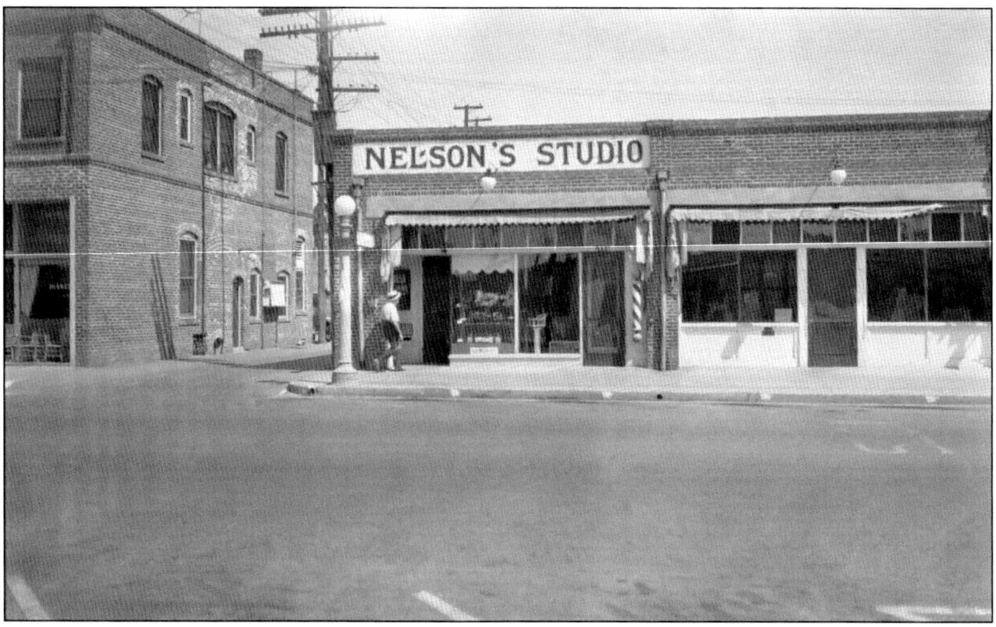

Many of the photographs in this book are the work of August and Arthur Nelson, who had their studio on Eleventh Street, across the alley from the Winnes Hotel. This photograph is estimated to have been taken in 1927 because the studio is selling "Postcards of Lindy." This is likely in commemoration of Charles Lindbergh's nonstop flight across the Atlantic that year. Mr. Entz's Oak Barber Shop is next door. (Photograph by Nelson Studio.)

Four

EDUCATION

The education of the young was a high priority for the area's early settlers. Smith's Ferry School was established in 1886. When Reedley was founded in 1888, plans were made to move the building to the townsite. Unfortunately, a fire of unknown origin destroyed the school the night before its relocation. Classes were held in temporary quarters at the United Brethren Church.

Voters went to the polls to pass a bond measure to build a new grammar school. But this was not to be another simple wood schoolhouse. Something more fitting a community on the move was required. A massive two-story brick building was constructed west of the railroad tracks. The school had a bell tower that rose grandly above the second floor. Visitors to the top of the lofty perch could see for miles.

A high school district was formed in 1898. Classes were initially held at the grammar school, but rapid enrollment necessitated a separate high school, which opened in 1905.

Just six years later, voters again went to the polls to approve bonds for a second grammar school, today's Lincoln School. And, in 1924, a junior high school was erected at yet another site. In these early years, the rural areas surrounding Reedley were establishing schools just as quickly. There was Riverbend, Riverside, Mount Campbell, Citrus Cove, Mount Olive, Wahtoke, Fink, Frankwood, Windsor, Alta, Wahtoke, and several others.

Higher education was also on the agenda. There was a junior college in Fresno. Reedley's high school principal thought there should be one in Reedley, too. His board agreed, and so did the people of Reedley. Reedley Junior College opened its doors in 1926 with an offering of six classes taught on the high school campus. A decade later, the college had grown sufficiently, justifying the construction of a two-story building to house classrooms, offices, and a large multipurpose room.

Reedley was committing itself to education.

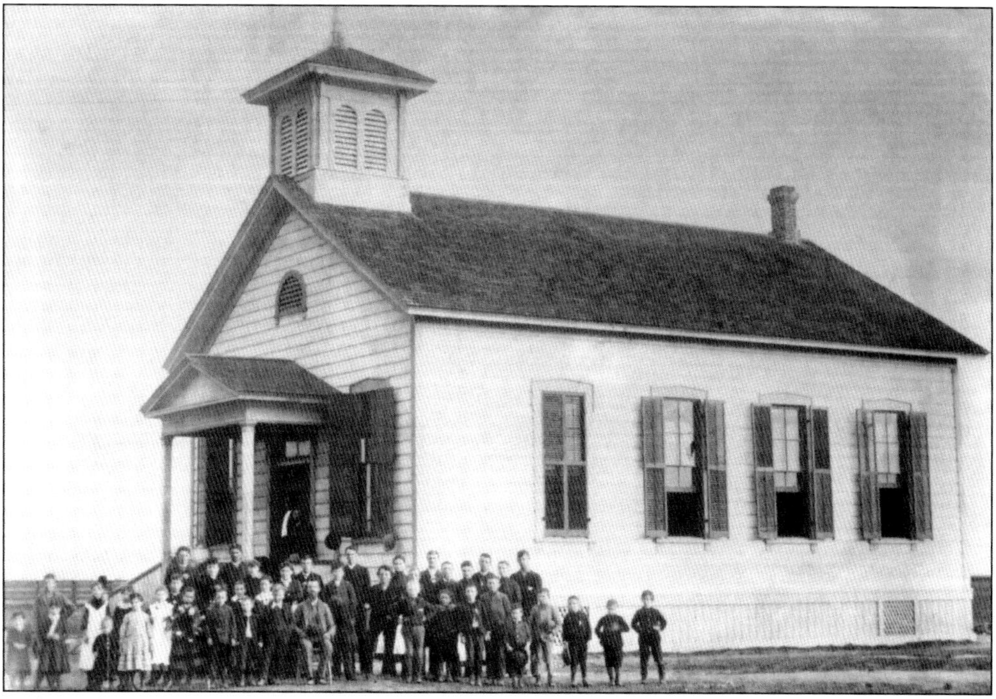

Early settlers established Smith's Ferry School in 1886, two years before Reedley was founded. The school was built near the corner of Frankwood and South Avenues on land donated by T.L. Reed. This photograph was taken at Christmastime in 1888. Teacher Frank Knauer is seated in front.

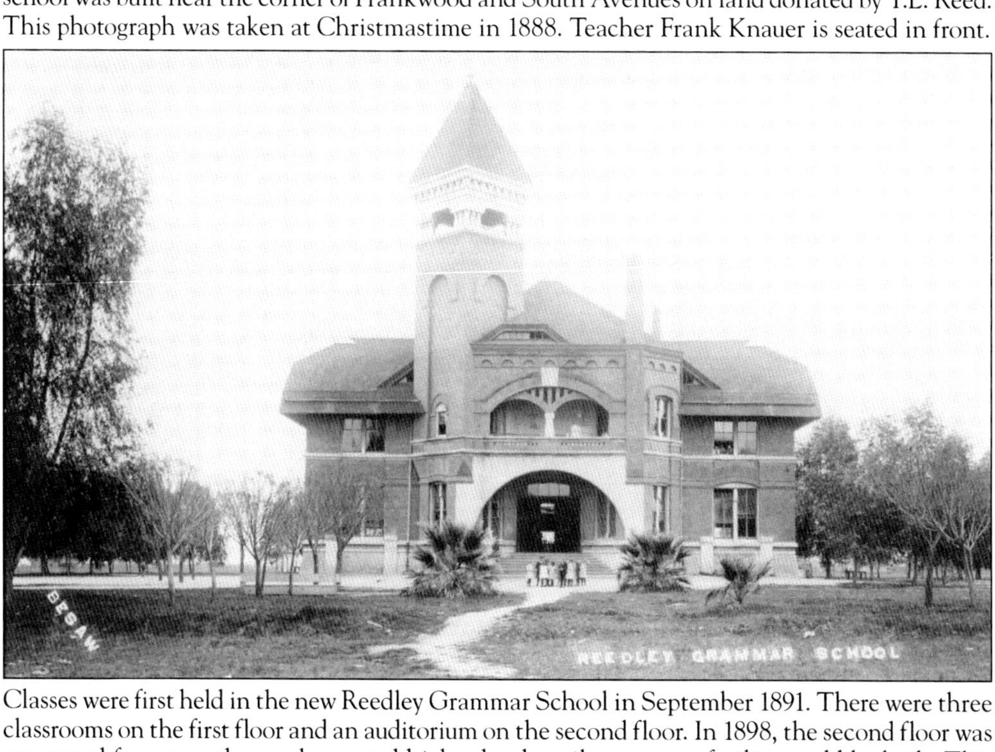

Classes were first held in the new Reedley Grammar School in September 1891. There were three classrooms on the first floor and an auditorium on the second floor. In 1898, the second floor was converted for use as the newly created high school until a separate facility could be built. This photograph was taken around 1908. (Photograph by George Besaw.)

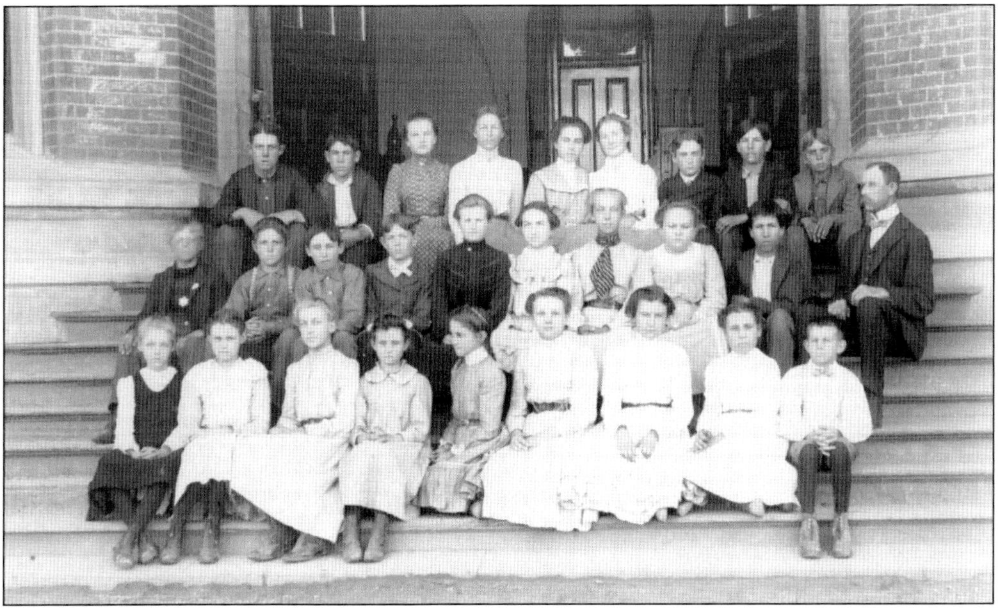

The Reedley Grammar School class of 1902–1903 poses for a photograph on the steps of the school.

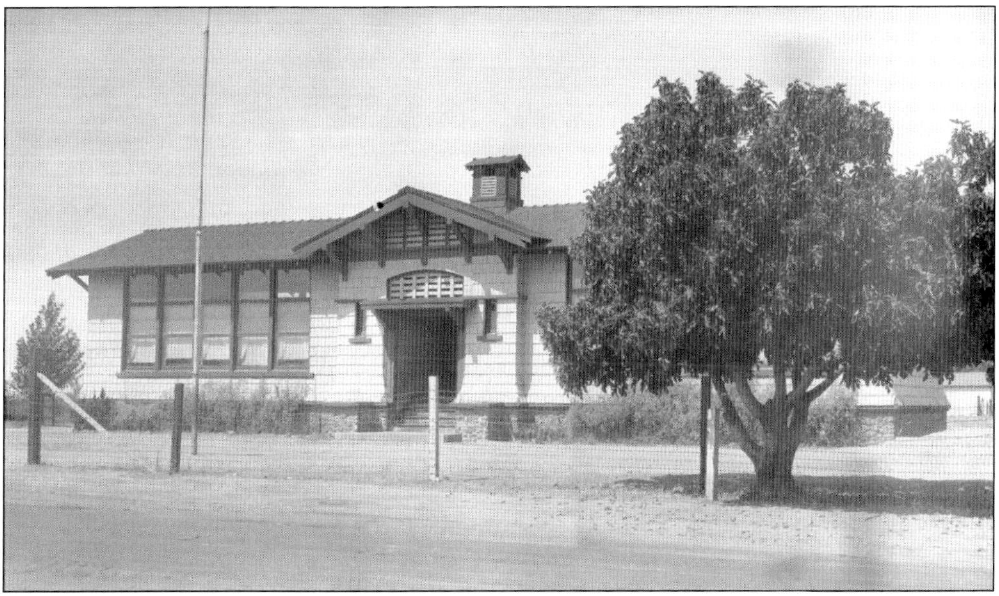

Before the formation of the unified school district, numerous rural districts served the area surrounding Reedley. In 1916, the original Alta School, shown here, was built east of town, at the corner of Dinuba and Englehart Avenues. The attractive building was constructed in the Craftsman style. (Photograph by Nelson Studio.)

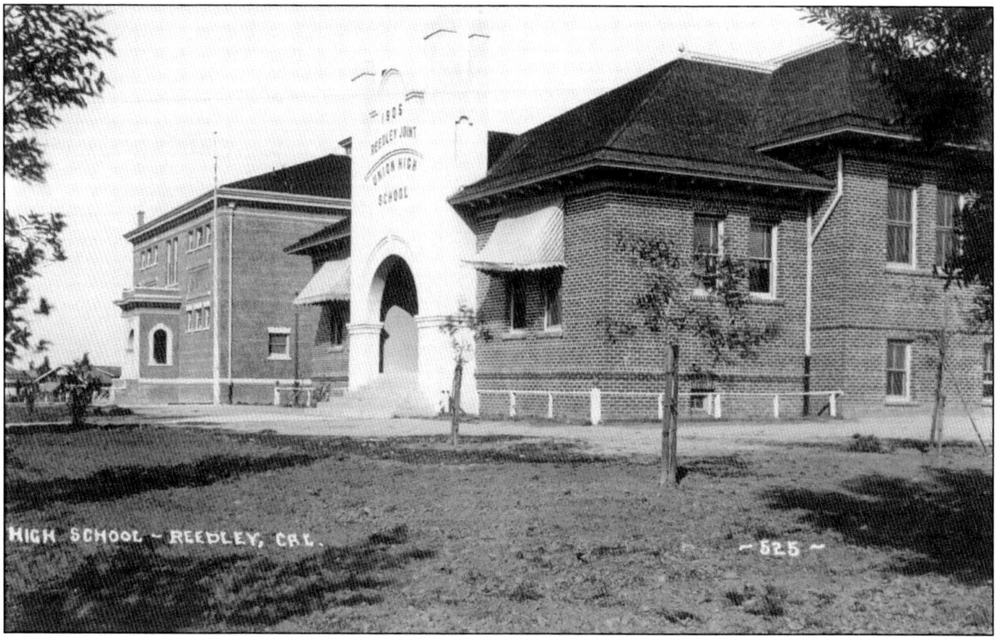

In 1905, the high school moved to a new building (right) on a new campus at the corner of West (now Reed) and Dinuba Avenues. The science building (left) was added in 1912. The high school remained here for just 21 years before relocating to its current site on North Avenue. In 1939, the old high school building became Reedley Hospital. (Photograph by George Besaw.)

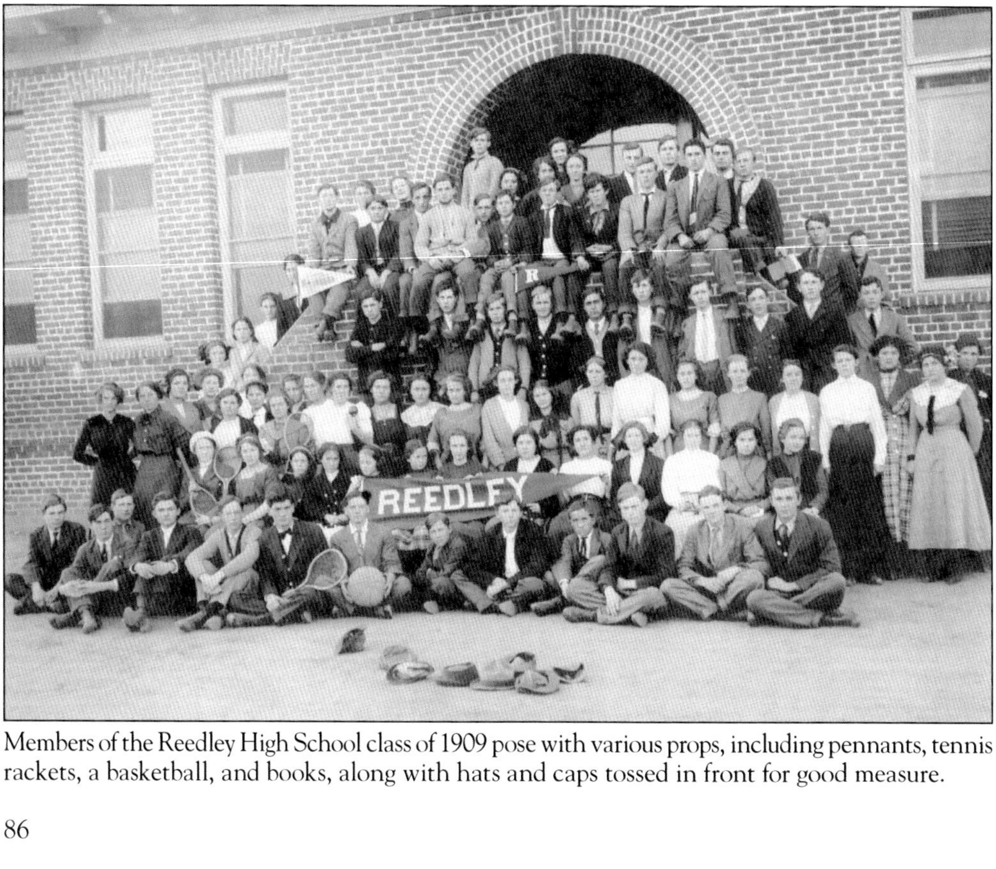

Members of the Reedley High School class of 1909 pose with various props, including pennants, tennis rackets, a basketball, and books, along with hats and caps tossed in front for good measure.

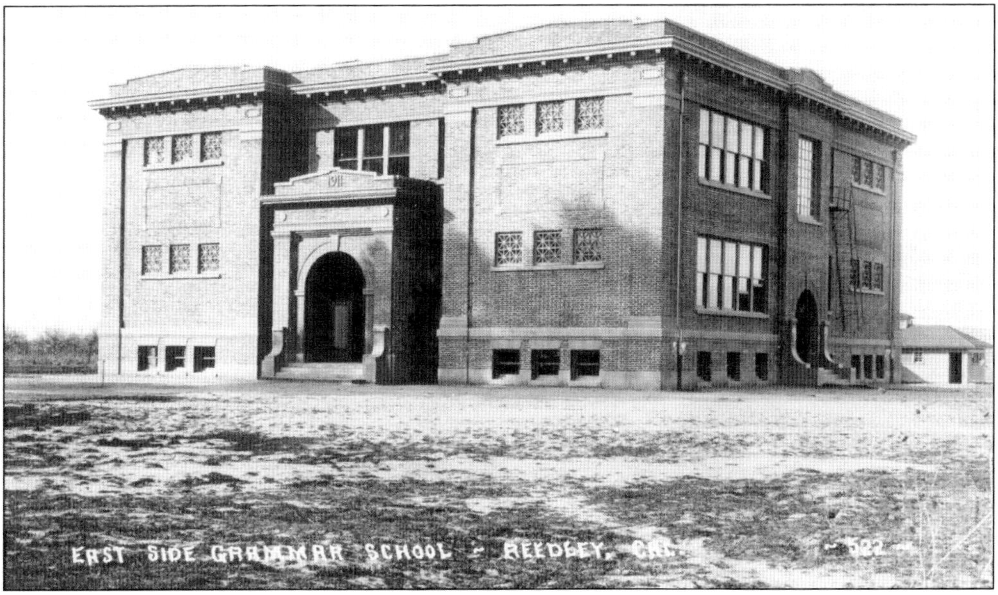

A bond measure to build a second grammar school was passed with a 129-10 vote in May 1911. An additional school was needed to accommodate enrollment, which now exceeded 400 students. East Side School was located on what is now the playground west of the present-day Lincoln School. The original building was demolished in 1952 for failing to meet modern earthquake standards. (Photograph by George Besaw.)

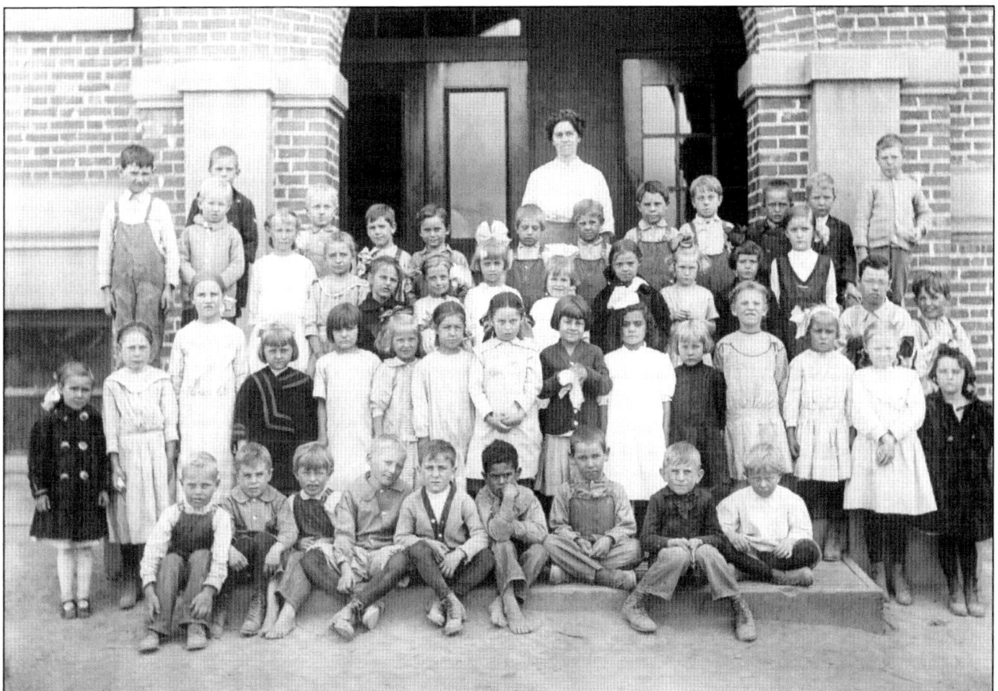

The custom of posing students on the school steps for their annual class portrait was observed at East Side as well. Miss Lyon's first grade class of 1913 is pictured here. (Photograph by Unmuth and Miller.)

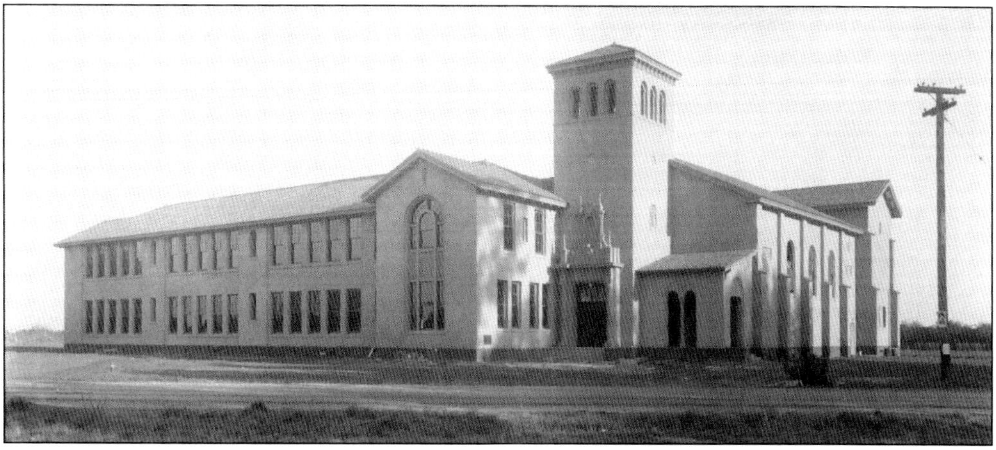

A decade after building what had become the Lincoln School, rising enrollment caused officials to propose construction of a separate school for the district's seventh and eighth grades. A bond passed in 1923, and construction immediately began on General Grant Departmental School (pictured). A new earthquake-safe Grant school was built on adjacent property in 1953. The old school building is now home to the Full Gospel Tabernacle. (Photograph by Nelson Studio.)

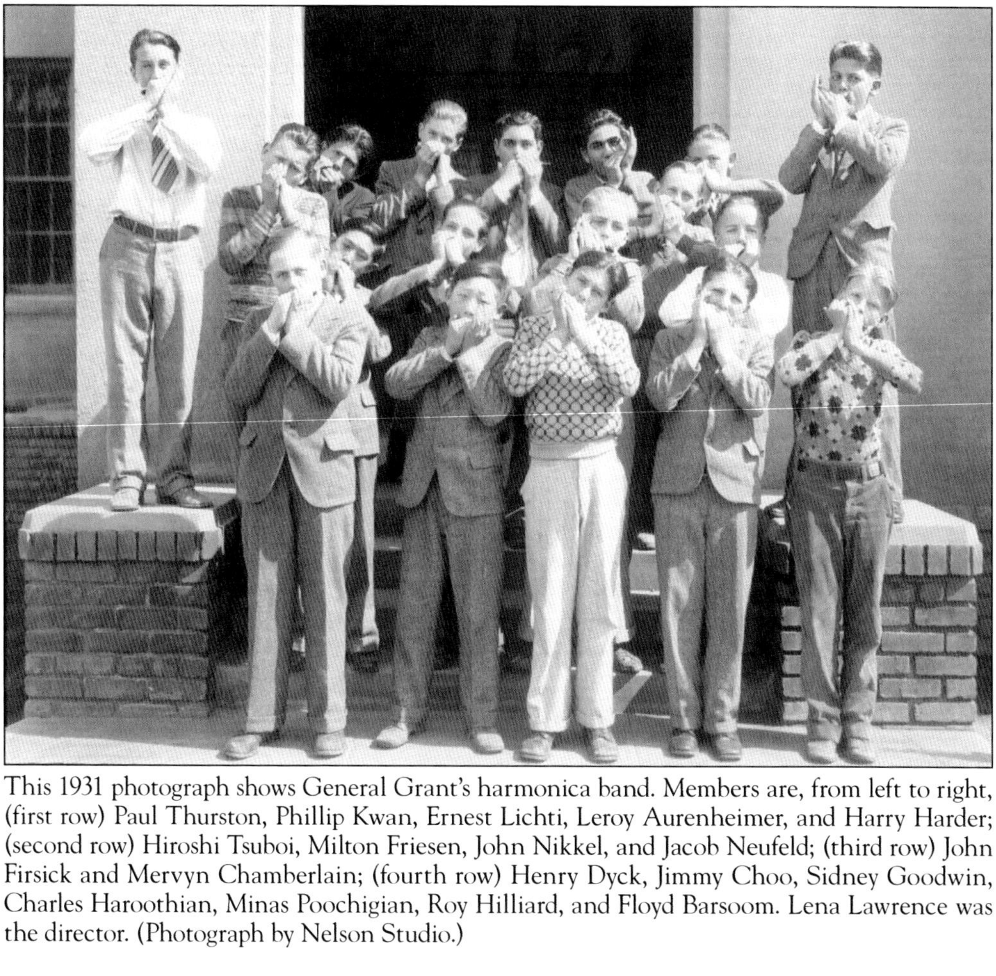

This 1931 photograph shows General Grant's harmonica band. Members are, from left to right, (first row) Paul Thurston, Phillip Kwan, Ernest Lichti, Leroy Aurenheimer, and Harry Harder; (second row) Hiroshi Tsuboi, Milton Friesen, John Nikkel, and Jacob Neufeld; (third row) John Firsick and Mervyn Chamberlain; (fourth row) Henry Dyck, Jimmy Choo, Sidney Goodwin, Charles Haroothian, Minas Poochigian, Roy Hilliard, and Floyd Barsoom. Lena Lawrence was the director. (Photograph by Nelson Studio.)

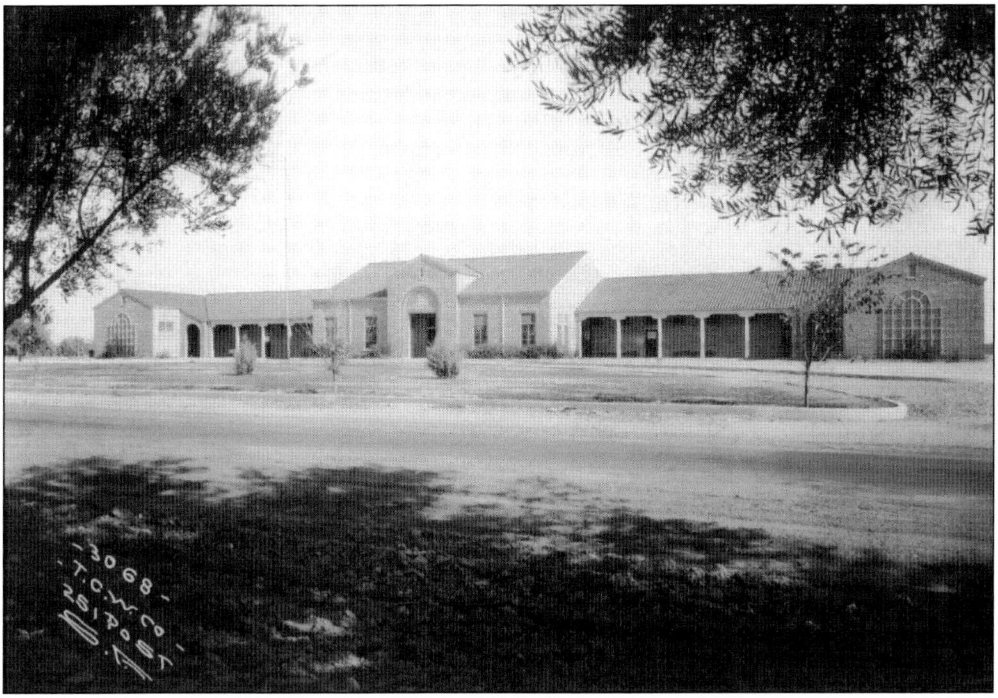

Riverview was another of the rural schools in the Reedley area. The Riverview district was formed from the consolidation of the old Riverbend and Riverside school districts. These rural districts served families living west of the river. Riverview School, shown here in 1925, was built on Lac Jac Avenue, just north of Manning Avenue, in 1921. (Photograph by TCW Company.)

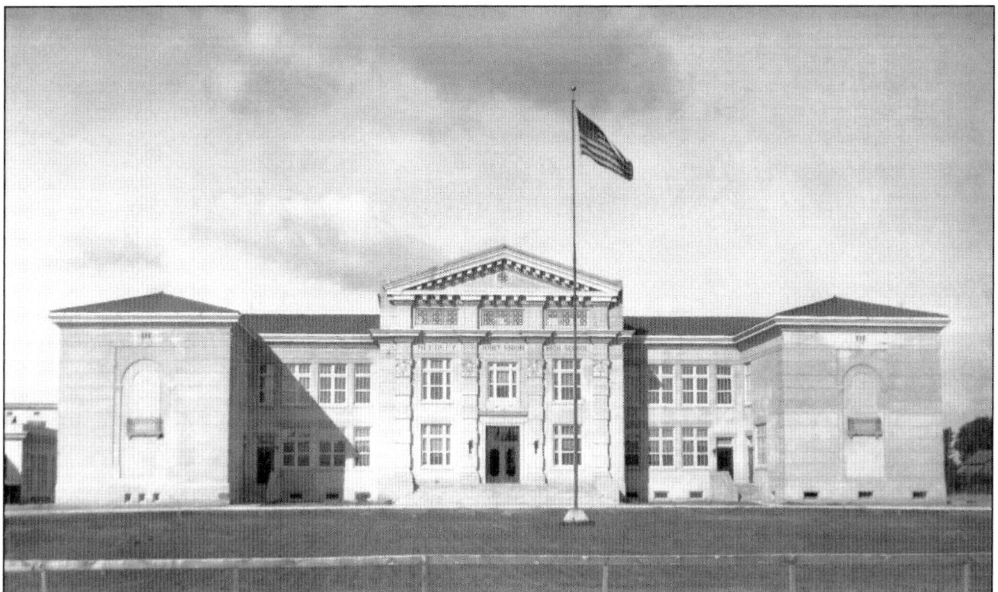

The new North Avenue campus of Reedley High School was dedicated in October 1923. The imposing main building housed classrooms, a library, offices, and a large auditorium. An enormous fire destroyed the building in 1974, just before its scheduled demolition. (Photograph by Nelson Studio.)

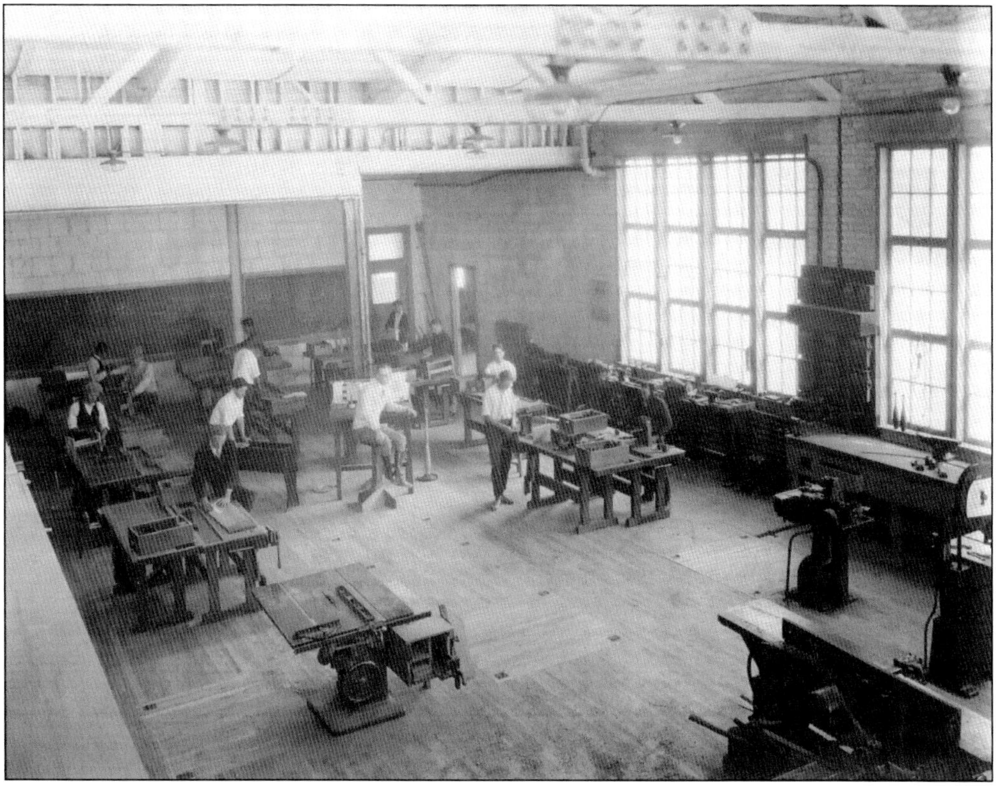

A woodworking class is under way in Reedley High School's new industrial arts building during the 1923–1924 school year. G.A. "Gus" Reimer, sitting on the stool at center, is the teacher.

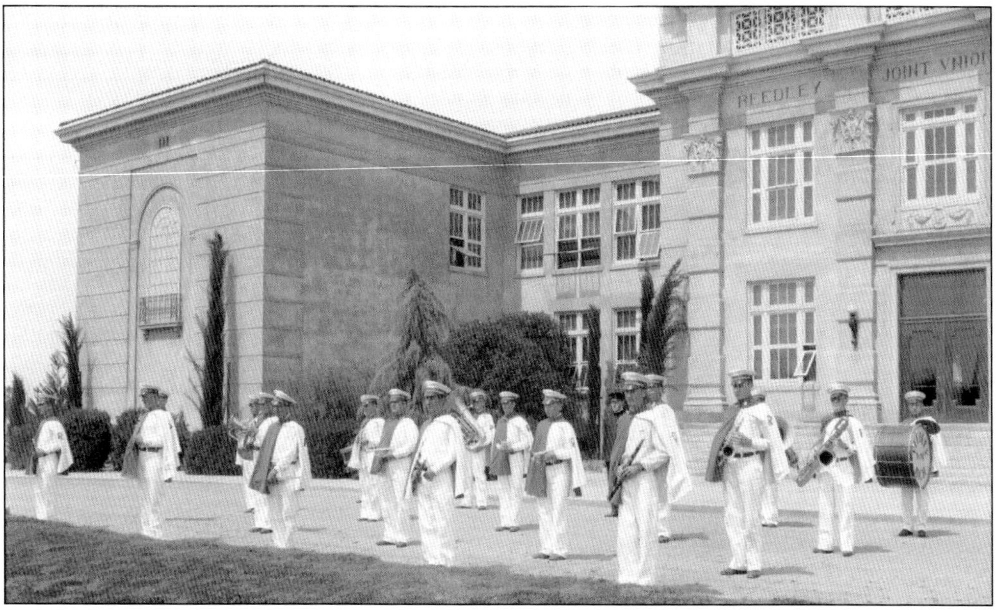

Reedley High School has long had a tradition of superior music instruction. In April 1929, the high school marching band stood in rank-and-file formation for a photograph session in front of the main building. (Photograph by Nelson Studio.)

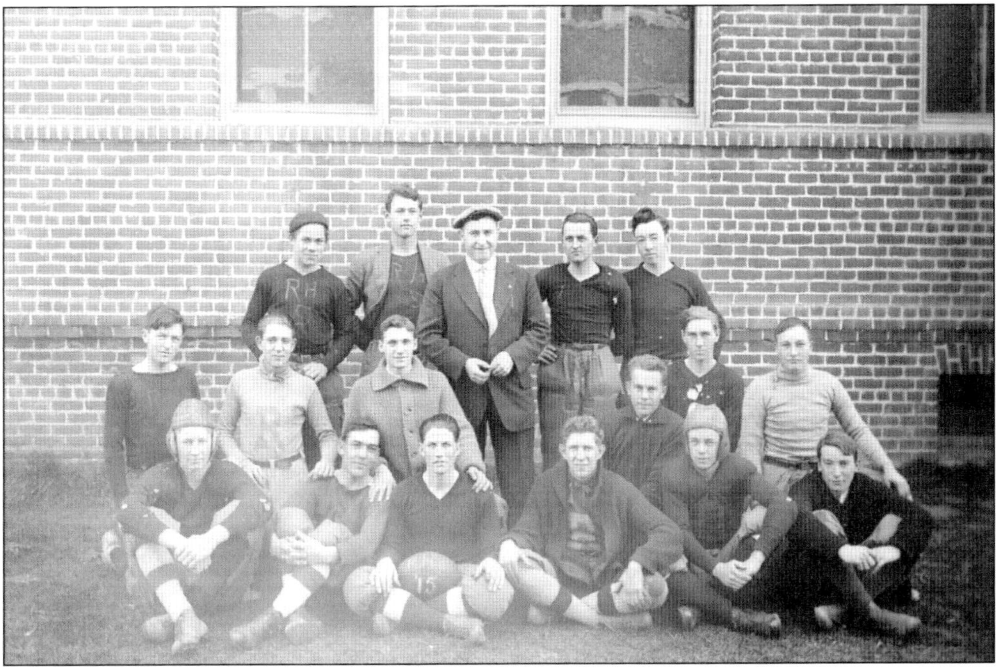

Competitive athletics became an integral part of Reedley High School's activities early in the school's history. The proud members of coach V.A. Dunlavy's 1915 football team are seen here. (Photograph by E.M. Vogt.)

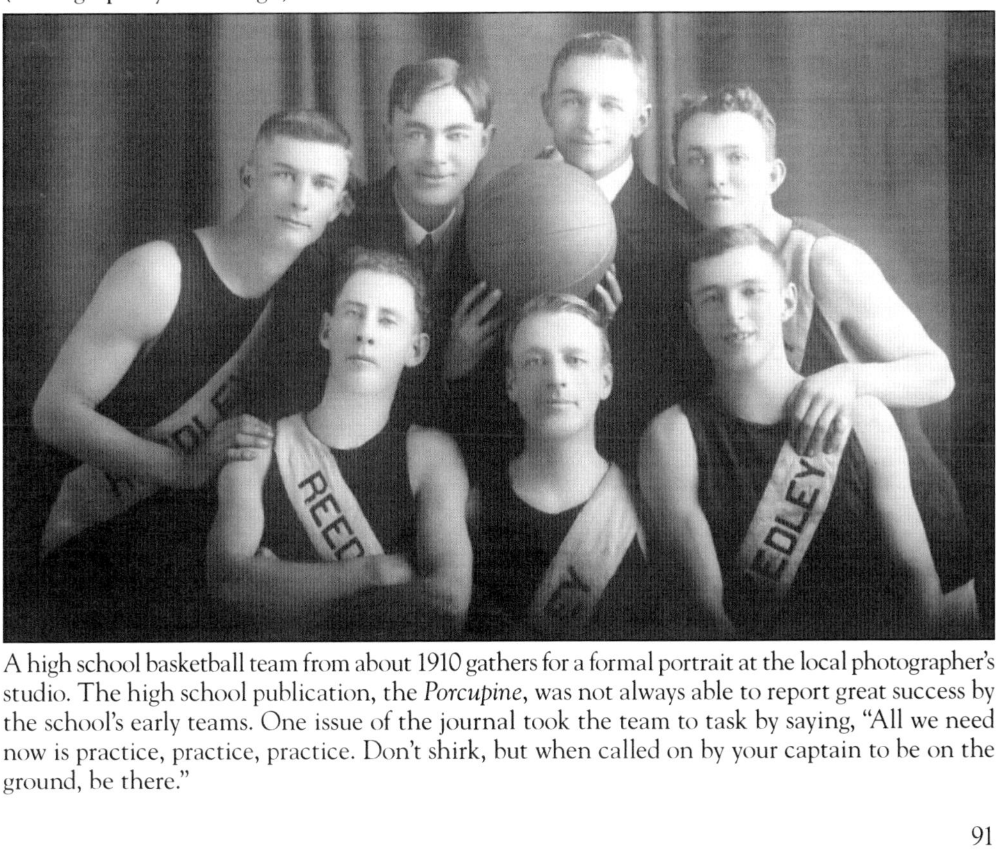

A high school basketball team from about 1910 gathers for a formal portrait at the local photographer's studio. The high school publication, the *Porcupine*, was not always able to report great success by the school's early teams. One issue of the journal took the team to task by saying, "All we need now is practice, practice, practice. Don't shirk, but when called on by your captain to be on the ground, be there."

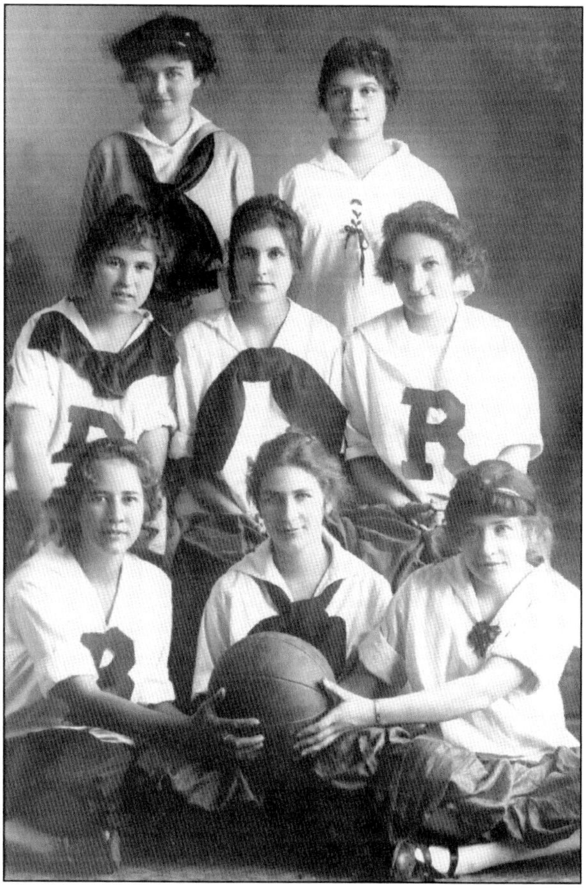

Reedley High School's female students participated in sports in the early years, too. Basketball was particularly popular. The young ladies taking to the court in the 1914–1915 school year were, from left to right, (first row) Estrella Beutler, Edna Erwin, and Eunice Donnell; (second row) Kate Gouldy, Susie Minix, and Inga Smith; (third row) coaches Miss Venard and Edith Swanson.

Reedley High's baseball team is seen posing by the Santa Fe Railway depot in the fall of 1909. Perhaps they were catching a train to an away game. Team members are, from left to right, (first row) Blaine Lyon, Merrill Furlong, Everett Drake, and Tom Bushman; (second row) Bill True, Walter Bozeman, Bill Bloyd, Irwin Frane, and Ben Cress. (Photograph by George Besaw.)

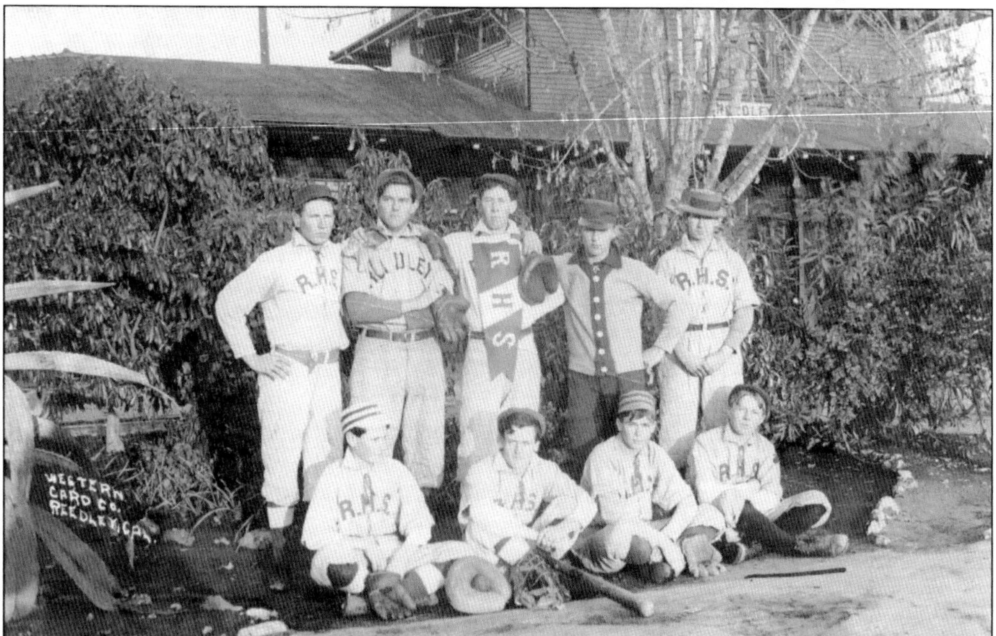

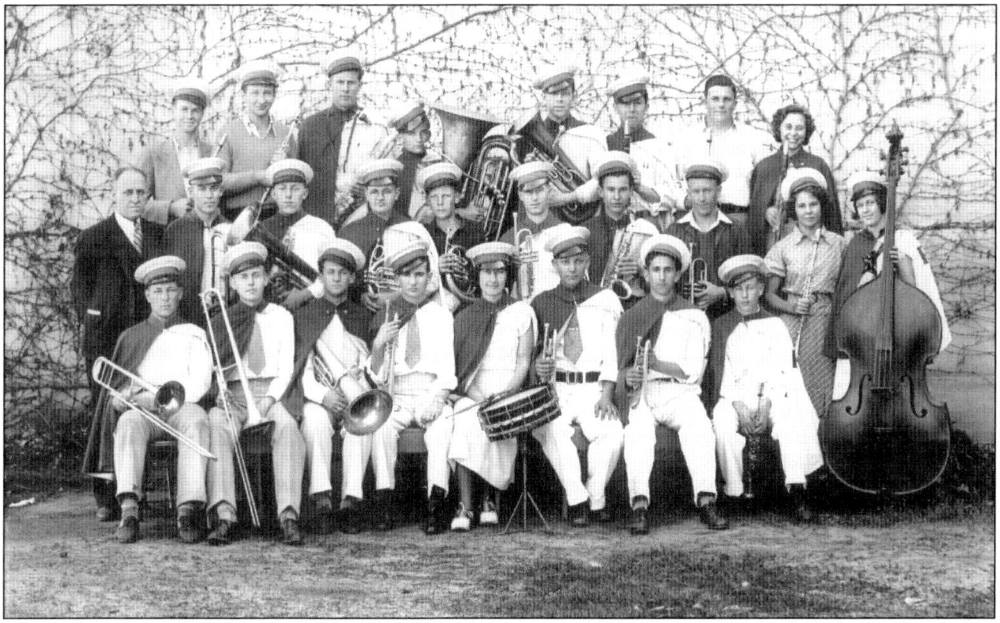

Most of the members of the 1934–1935 Reedley High School concert band remembered to bring their caped uniforms for "picture day." The director, Burton Strock, is seen at left in the second row.

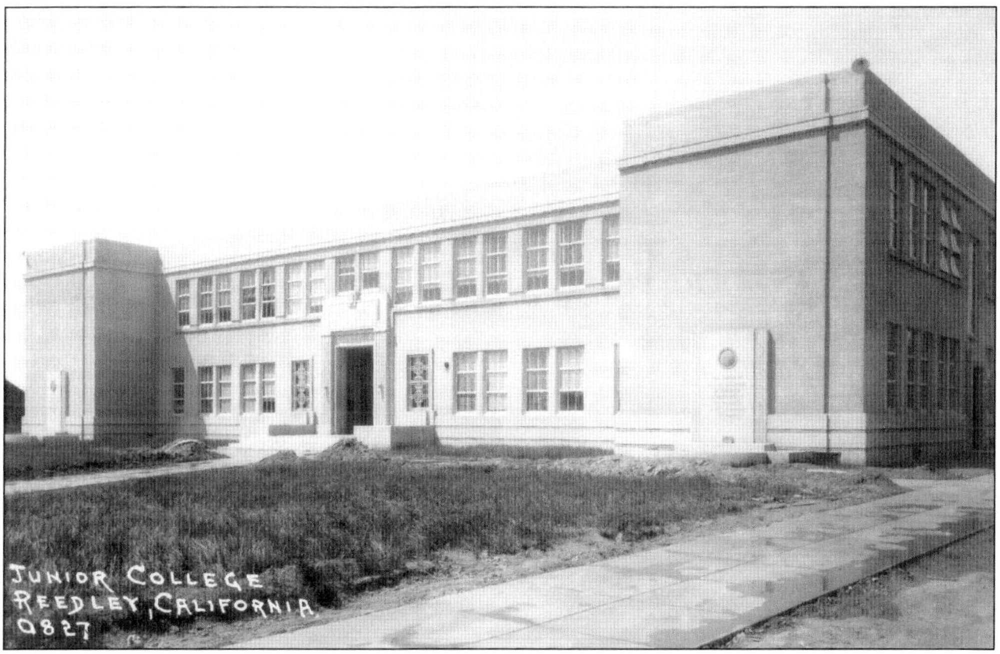

The high school district established Reedley Junior College in 1926. The college moved into its own building on the west side of the high school campus in 1936. When the college relocated to its new campus in 1956, the old college building became known as West Hall, which the high school used for classrooms and administrative offices. (Courtesy of Michael J. Semas.)

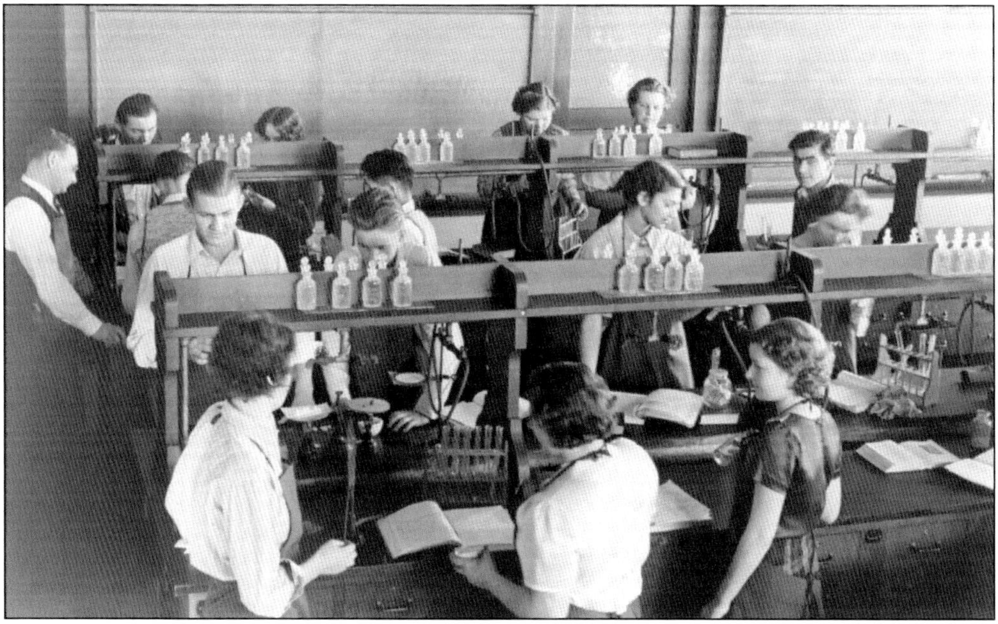

Leo Wolfson (far left) is conducting a chemistry lab at Reedley Junior College in the 1930s. Wolfson would later become director of the college.

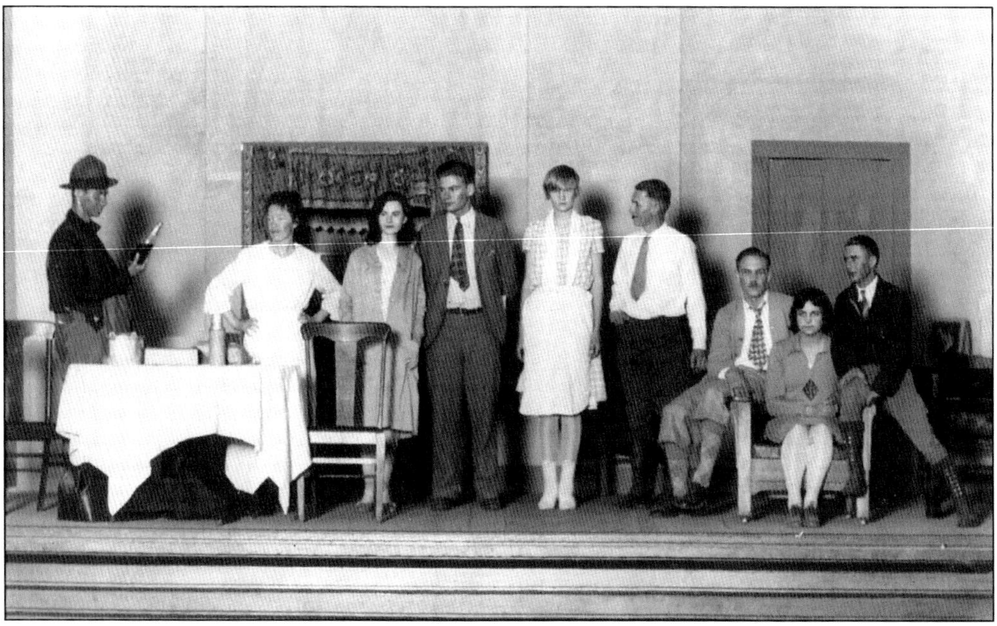

Through the years, countless plays, musicals, and concerts were presented on the large stage in the high school's auditorium of the main building. The Reedley Junior College Players took to the stage in March 1929 to present the comedy *Laff That Off*. Members of the cast were, from left to right, Ellis Chamberlain, Evelyn Beach, Louise Green, Wendell Sheibley, Hilga Bentson, Robert Miller, C. Franklin Howell, Helen Stewart, and Willie Hagen.

Five

LIFE

As soon as the railroad depot was built and the first businesses opened their doors, the residents of Reedley began creating those things that comprise the life and activities of a community. Churches were founded. Kids went to school. Fraternal groups and social organizations were established. A city band was formed. A library was started.

Sports teams were organized, and competition with neighboring towns built community pride. The opera house hosted traveling vaudeville acts and other entertainments. A distinguished lecturer would come and offer his wisdom. And, soon, movies arrived. Politicians passed through town, soliciting support and votes. Relaxation and respite from the summer heat was found at the Kings River or Wahtoke Lake. Those so inclined could seek diversion in one of the saloons or pool halls on G Street, much to the consternation of those who preferred that such places be banished.

The city incorporated in 1913. City trustees were elected and quickly began the task of city building. The privately owned waterworks became a public utility. A public park was created. The city band became taxpayer funded. A marshal was appointed to establish law and order, and a volunteer fire department tried to keep the town from burning down—again.

Reedley may have been a small rural town, but it was not isolated. Fresno was a short train ride away. San Francisco was just seven to eight hours away by rail. Around town, the horse and the buggy took people where they wanted to go. Bicycles were a sensation. Then the automobile appeared. Dr. George Hawkins got one, and so did Fr. George Seubert. The Bollin store got one for deliveries. Harley Davidson and Indian motorcycles cruised down Reedley streets. With all these new forms of transportation, traffic accidents became routine.

Celebrations were many. The Fourth of July was a grand affair, and after World War I, Armistice Day was a time for thanks and the celebration of life. Such things as orations, footraces, bicycle and automobile races, and parades marked these events. The band played and elaborately decorated floats amazed both the young and old.

Reedley was alive.

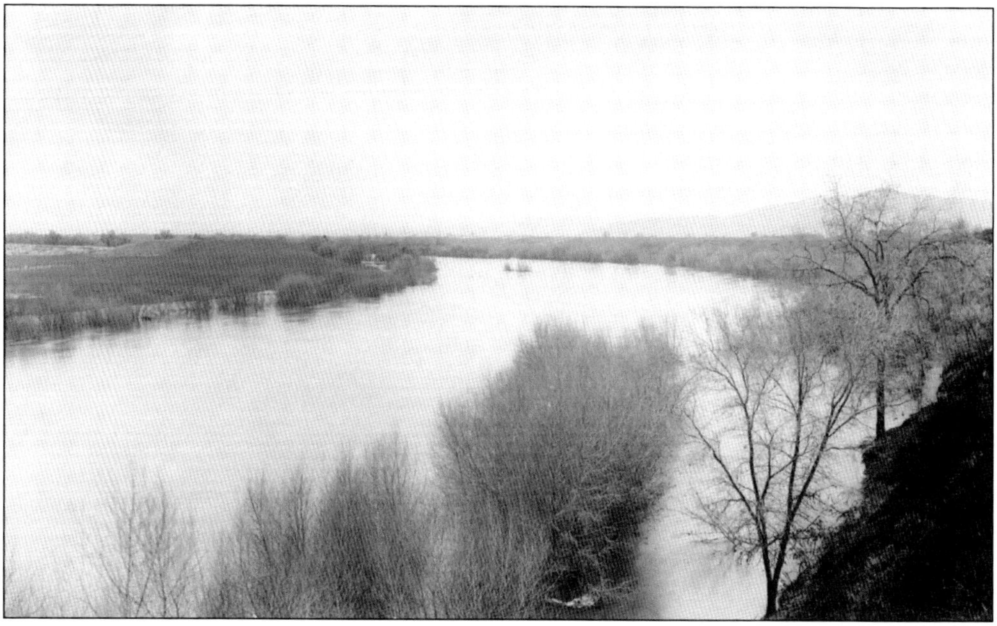

Spanish military officer and explorer Gabriel Moraga gave this river its modern name. He and his men camped on the banks of the river on January 5 during their expedition of 1805. The next day was Epiphany, the commemoration of the arrival of the three kings in Bethlehem. Moraga had his inspiration. He called the river *El Rio de los Santos Reyes*, the River of the Holy Kings. (Photograph by George Besaw.)

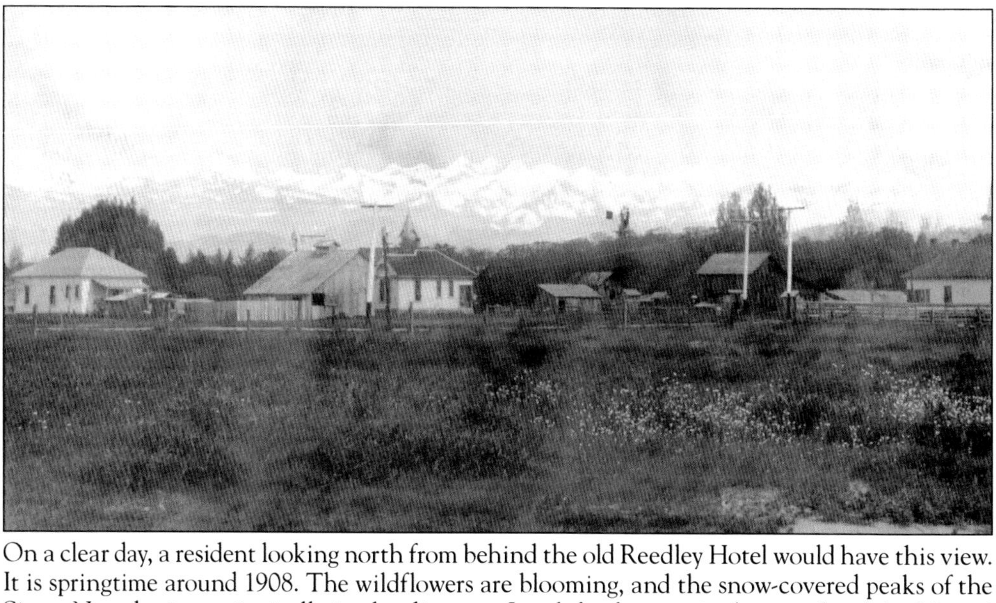

On a clear day, a resident looking north from behind the old Reedley Hotel would have this view. It is springtime around 1908. The wildflowers are blooming, and the snow-covered peaks of the Sierra Nevada rise majestically in the distance. Just left of center is the steeple of the United Brethren Church. (Photograph by George Besaw.)

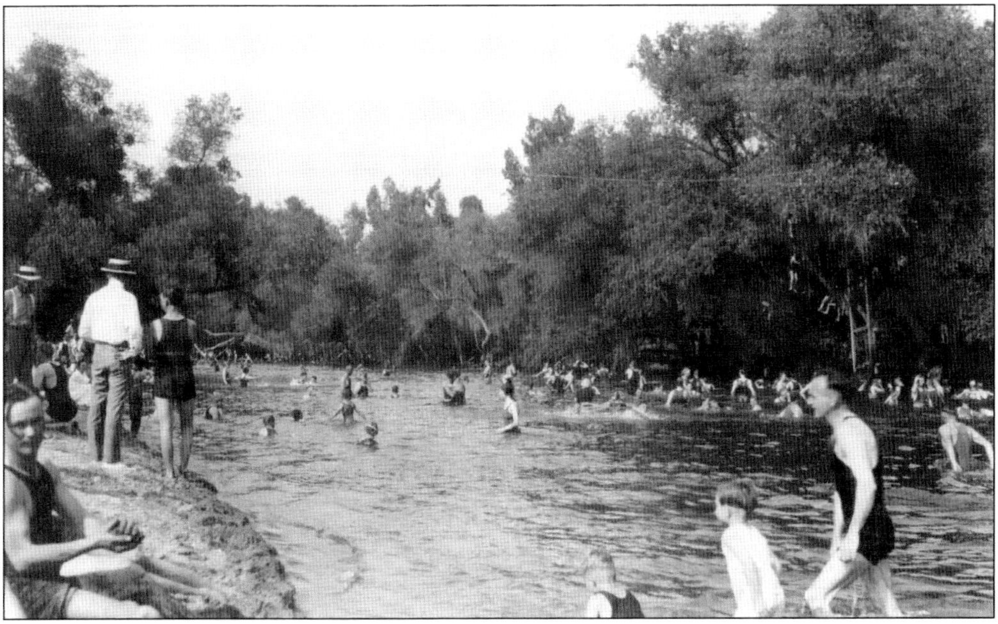

Reedley Beach was a popular place from the beginning of the community. Air-conditioning and backyard swimming pools were unknown to the people pictured here enjoying the cool Kings River in the 1910s. The City purchased the beach property in 1918. In 1921, a citizens committee did the rest. The property was cleaned up, along with the addition of men's and women's bathhouses and a concession stand that would operate throughout the summer.

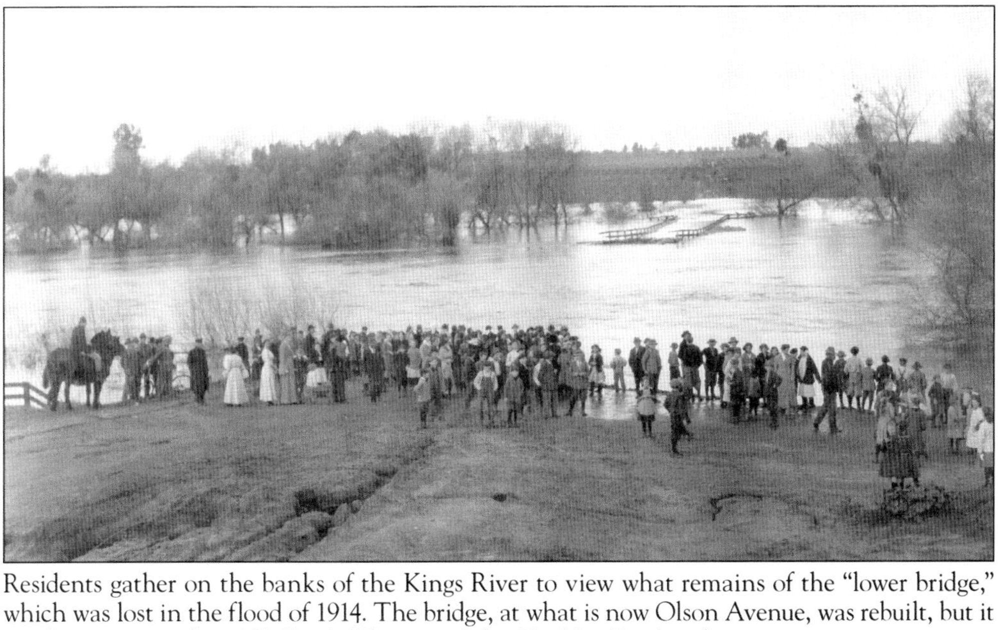

Residents gather on the banks of the Kings River to view what remains of the "lower bridge," which was lost in the flood of 1914. The bridge, at what is now Olson Avenue, was rebuilt, but it was lost again in the 1950 flood. (Photograph by Sheibley Brothers.)

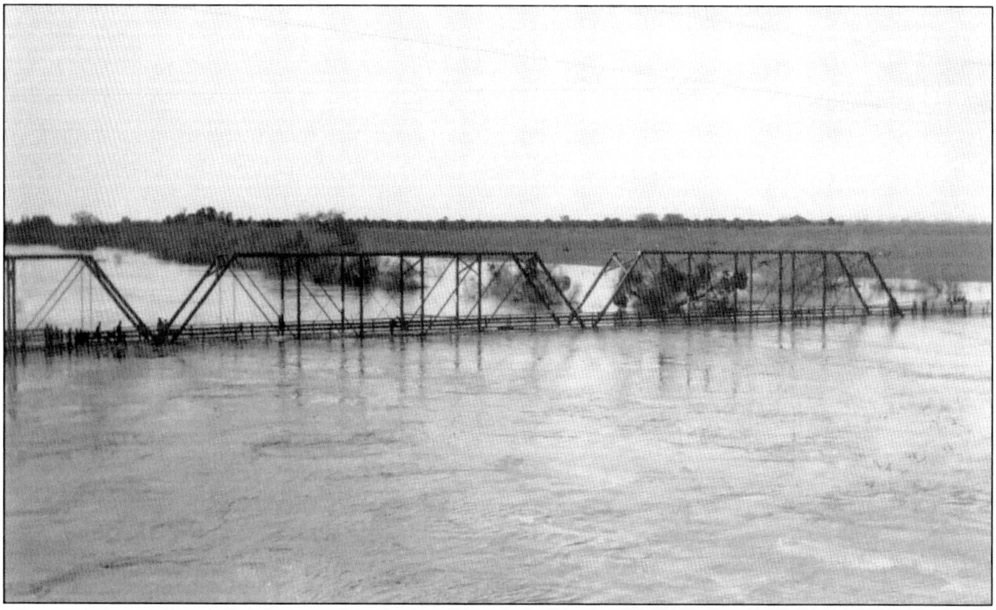

The old wagon bridge at Manning Avenue fared better than the lower bridge in 1914. Water flowed over the roadbed, but the bridge survived. Some of the men seen on the bridge are working to save the structure by clearing accumulated debris. This photograph was taken on the date of high water, January 26.

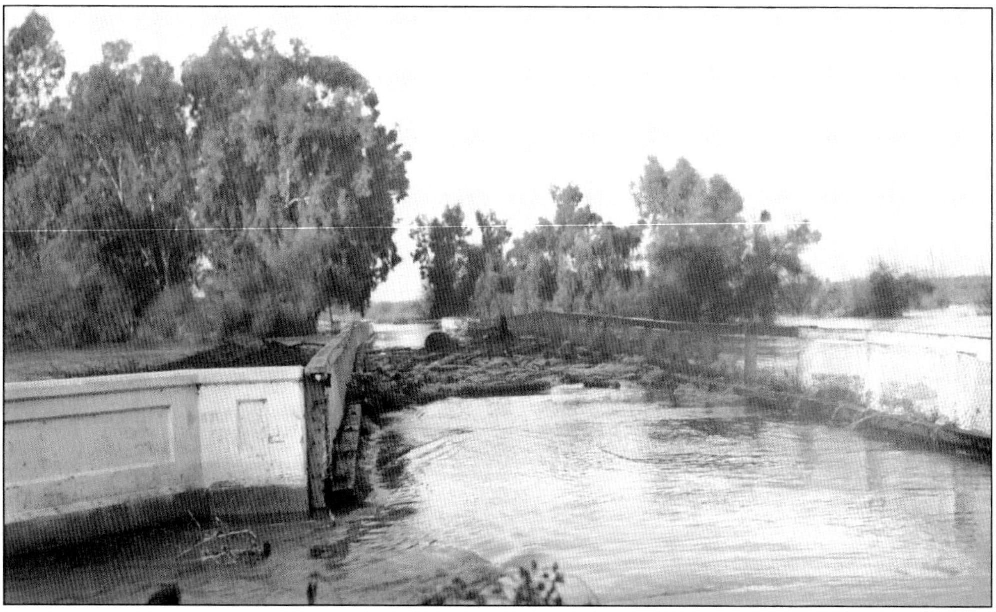

Serious flooding of the Kings River occurred again in December 1937. It was reported that, at its worst, the river was rising three feet per hour. The lower bridge, shown here, was damaged, but it remained standing. Repairs were made but only lasted three years before officials declared the bridge unsafe. Orders were given to build a replacement bridge with an added two feet in height. (Photograph by Nelson Studio.)

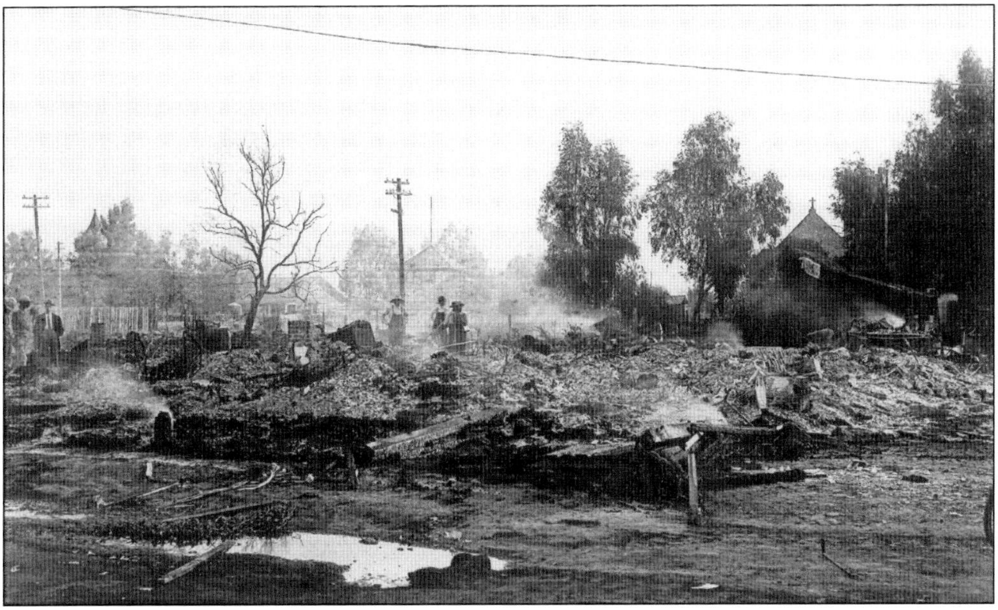

The last of the three fires that devastated sections of Reedley's downtown occurred in 1910. Seen here are the smoldering remains of the Reedley Hotel. An oil-fired cooking stove exploded in the kitchen, resulting in a quick-moving fire that completely destroyed the restaurant and hotel. Also lost was the adjacent Webb real estate office, Green's drugstore, and the telephone office. (Photograph by George Besaw.)

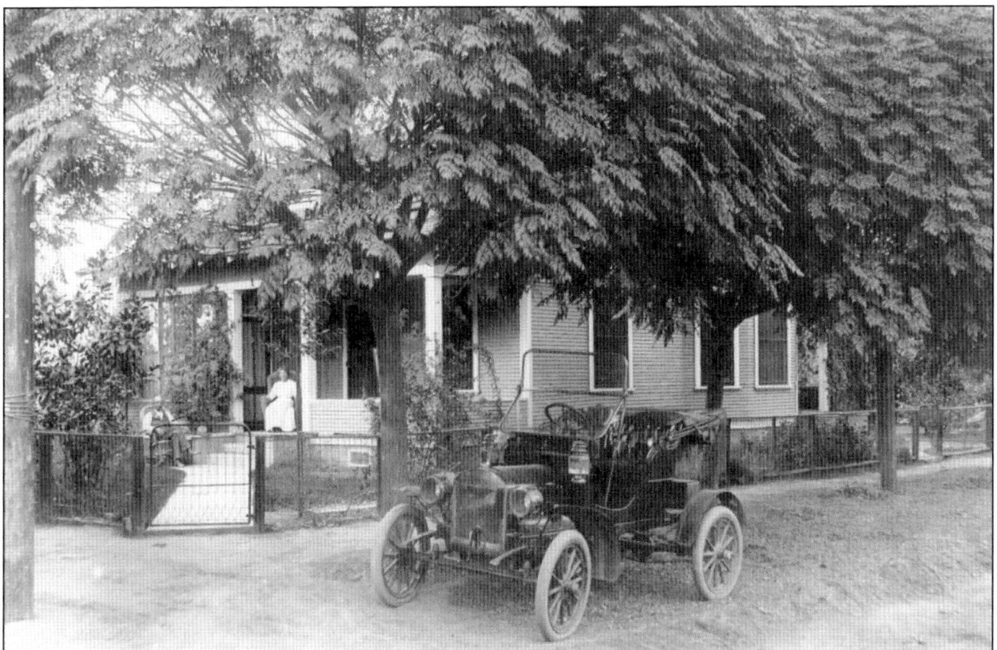

Reedley jeweler Joseph B. Moomaw sits in the front yard while Mrs. Moomaw sits on the front porch of their home at 756 G Street. Their Maxwell automobile is ready and waiting, but Joseph's commute was only two and a half blocks up G Street. A medical office now occupies the corner of G and Eighth Streets, where the Moomaws' home once stood. (Photograph by Drath Studio.)

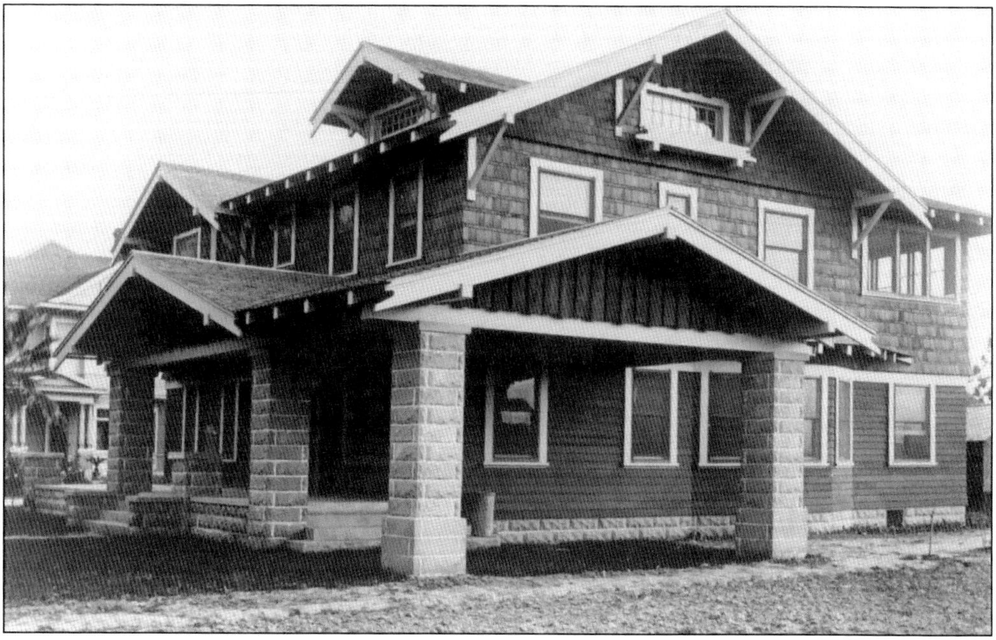

The A.P. Wedel house is an example of the large homes that were built on West (now Reed) Avenue during the early part of the century. This 1915 residence has had the benefit of caring owners through the years. Today, the home is still admired by all who have occasion to drive by its location at 259 South Reed Avenue.

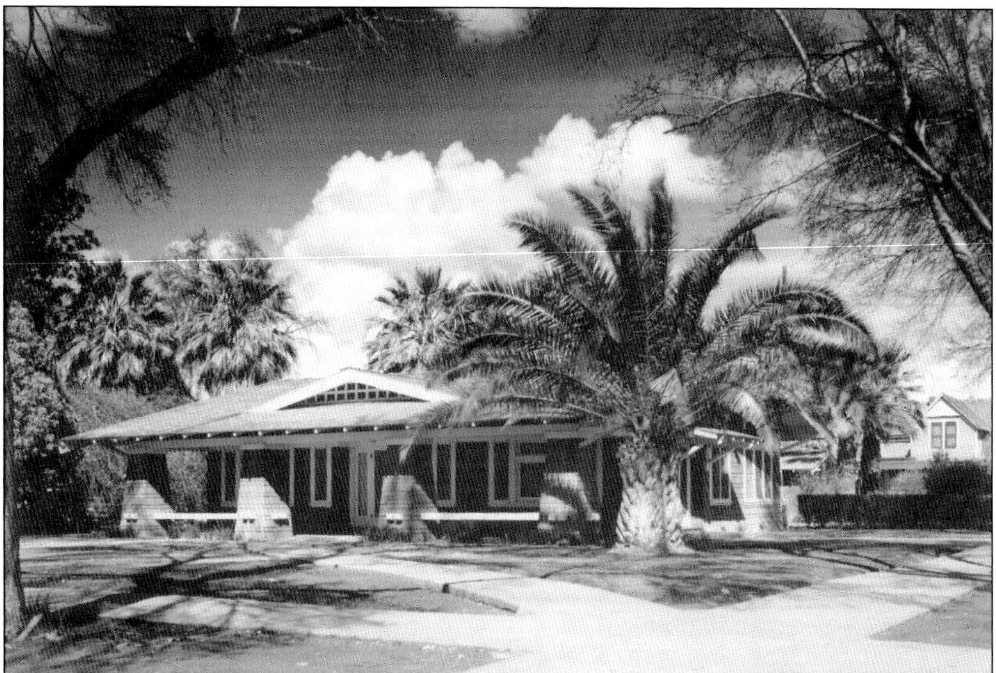

Chester W. and Elizabeth Tackaberry built their home, designed by Ernest J. Kump Sr., at 856 F Street in 1925. Tackaberry was an attorney and, for a time, served as city attorney for Reedley. Kump was also the architect of Reedley's St. Anthony's Church rectory.

The Baptist church was Reedley's second house of worship. The church was built at the corner of Eleventh and E Streets in 1891 and was enlarged in 1927. In 1951, the old section was moved to the rear of the property to make room for a new sanctuary. The congregation traces its roots to a group that first met at Wahtoke School in 1888. This photograph was taken around 1908. (Photograph by George Besaw.)

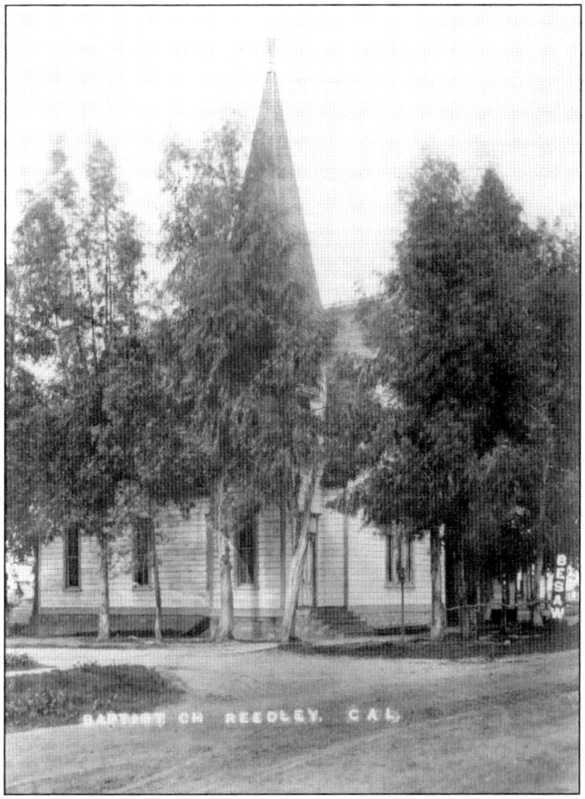

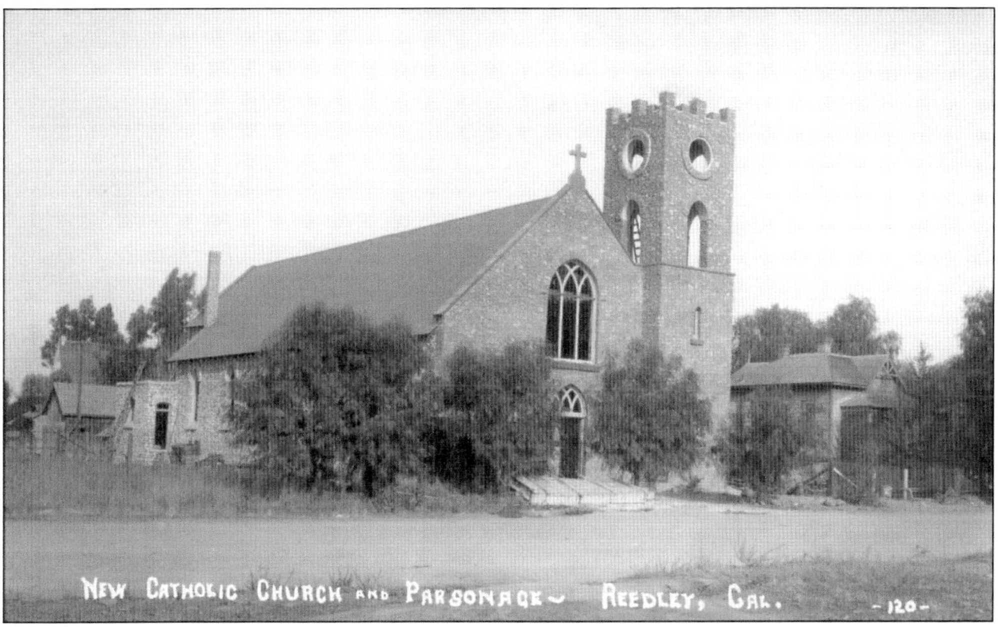

St. Anthony's Catholic Church was under construction at the corner of F and Eleventh Streets when this photograph was taken about 1909. Built with stone hauled in by parish families from nearby Smith Mountain, the church was finished and consecrated in 1911. (Photograph by George Besaw.)

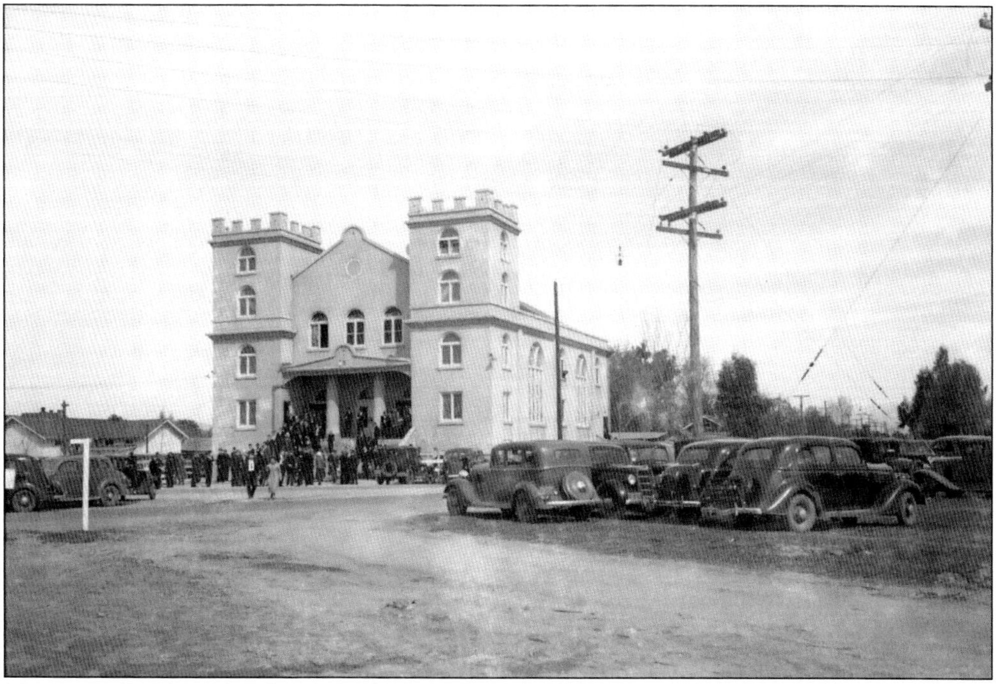

Mennonite Brethren families started meeting in Reedley in 1904. They built their first church in the 1300 block of L Street in 1909. Their second church (pictured) was built on adjacent property in 1919 to accommodate the fast-growing congregation. This photograph was taken on February 26, 1938. (Photograph by Nelson Studio.)

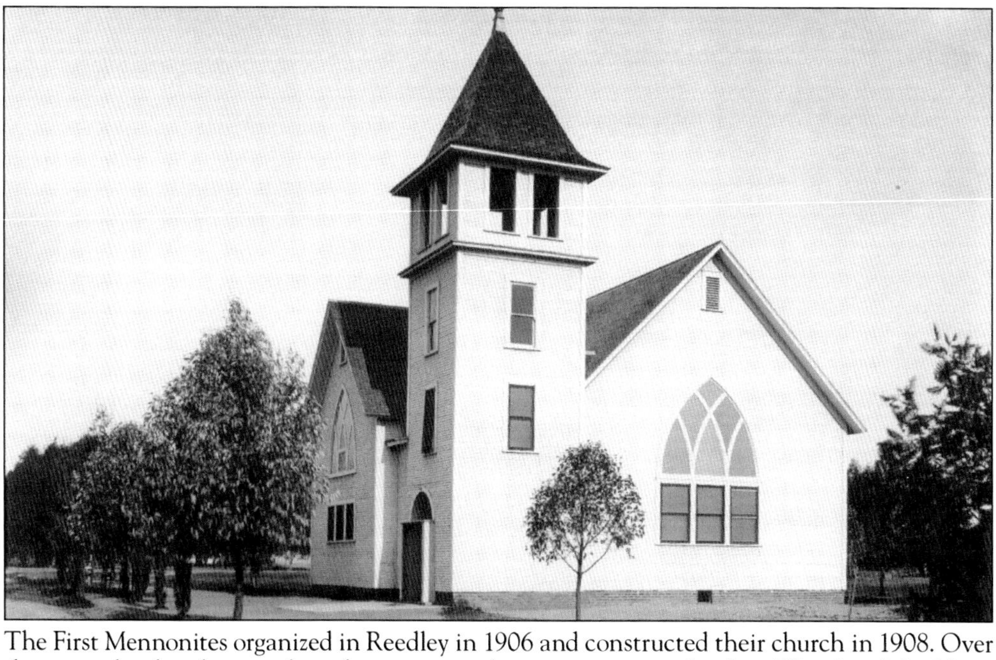

The First Mennonites organized in Reedley in 1906 and constructed their church in 1908. Over the years, the church was enlarged to accommodate a growing membership. The church building, at the corner of L and Twelfth Streets, still serves the First Mennonite congregation. (Photograph by George Besaw.)

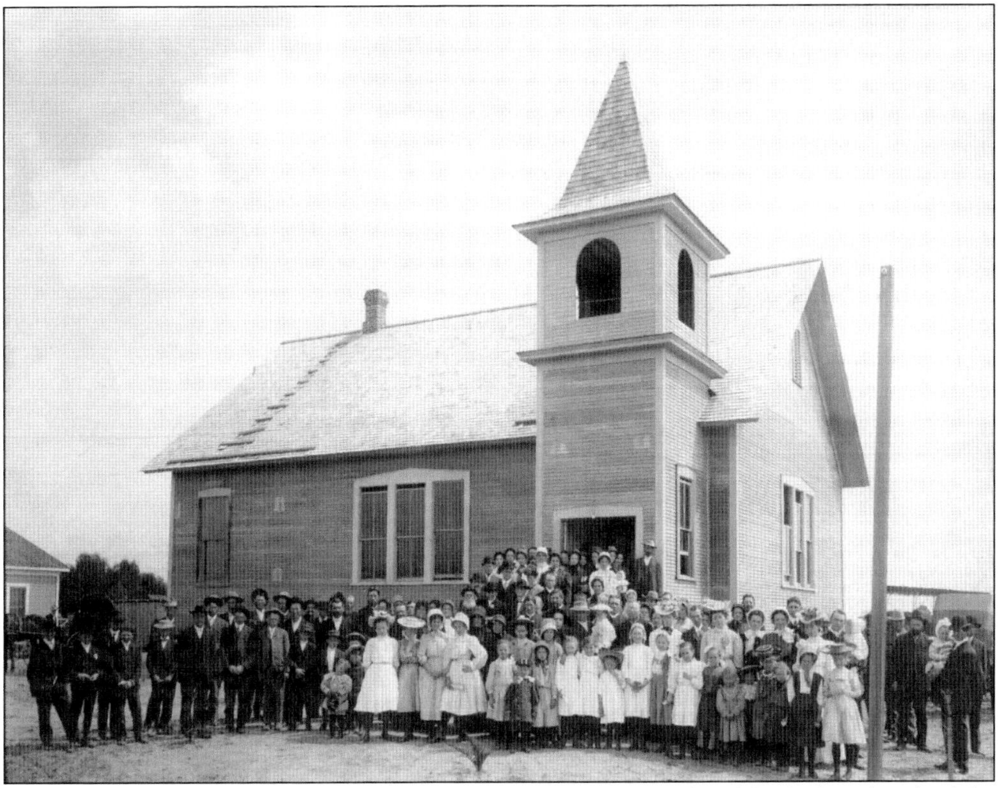

A group of German Baptist Brethren (also known as Dunker Brethren) built the Church of the Brethren at Eleventh and L Streets in 1906–1907. The congregation began meeting in the Reedley area in 1905. More recently, the congregation took the name Cornerstone Community Church. The congregation gathers for what is thought to be the church's dedication on March 31, 1907.

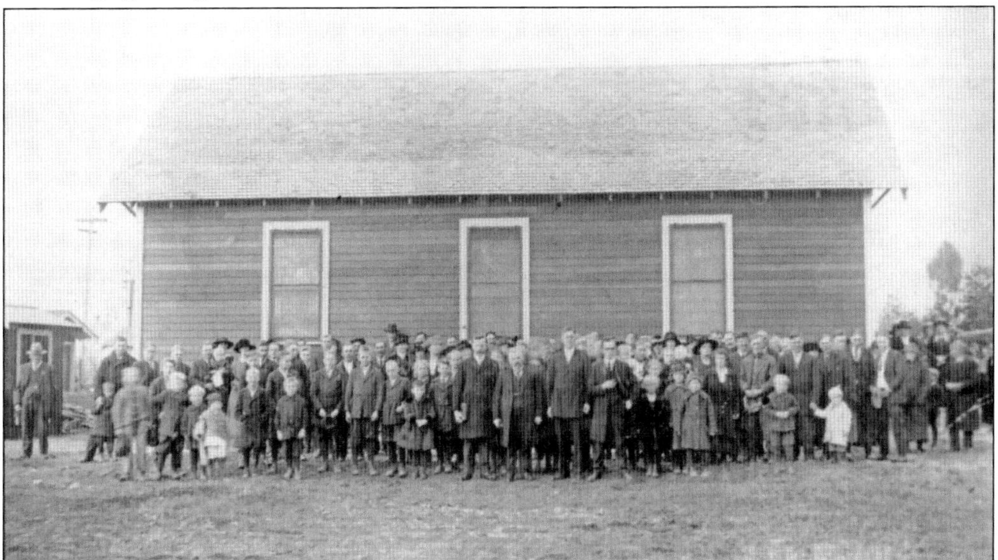

The Finnish Congregationalists organized in 1921. In that same year, they built this church at Acacia and Myrtle Avenues. The church was dismantled in 1971 after the congregation disbanded.

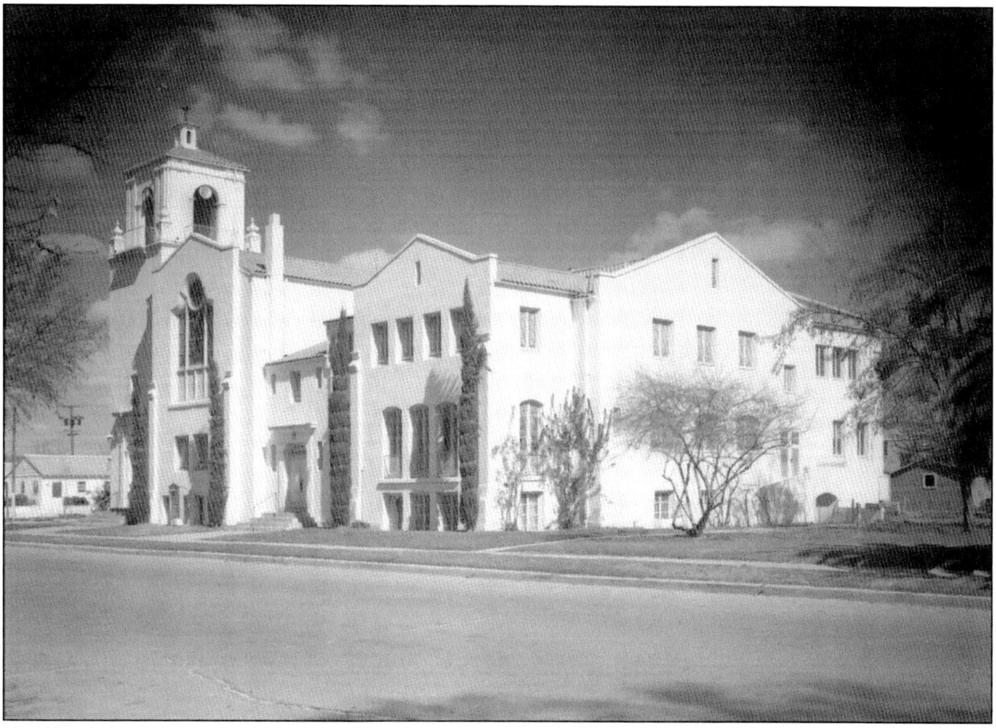

The beautiful First United Methodist Church was built at the corner of F and Twelfth Streets in 1921. Unfortunately, structural problems necessitated the demolition of the church in 1971. The congregation's original home, when it was known as Methodist Episcopal, had been just down the block, at F and Thirteenth Streets. (Photograph by Nelson Studio.)

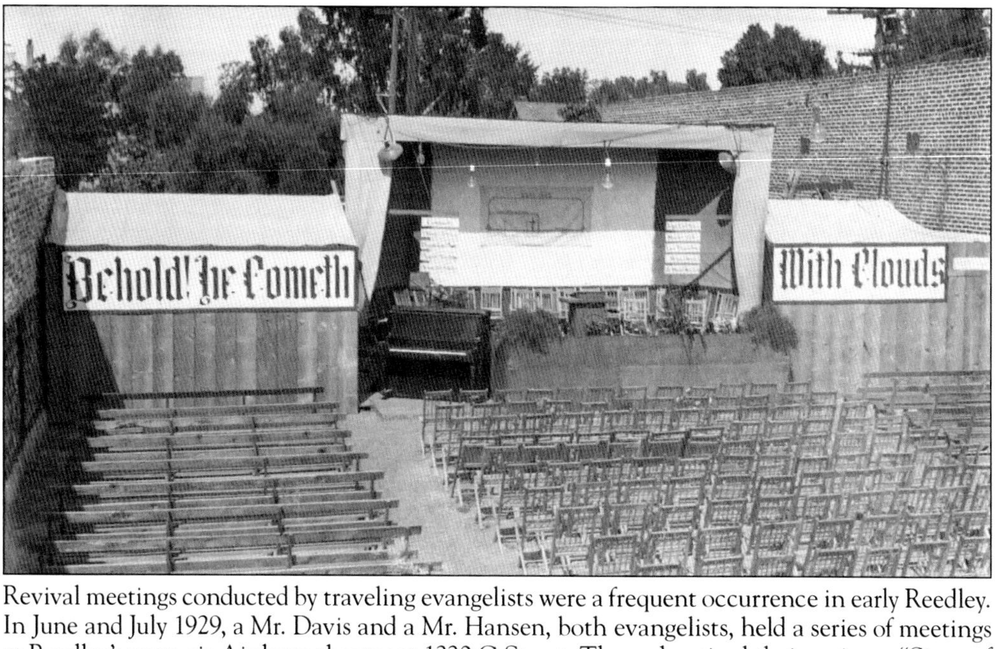

Revival meetings conducted by traveling evangelists were a frequent occurrence in early Reedley. In June and July 1929, a Mr. Davis and a Mr. Hansen, both evangelists, held a series of meetings at Reedley's open-air Airdome theater at 1220 G Street. They advertised their series as "Signs of the Times—Prophetic Lectures." (Photograph by Nelson Studio.)

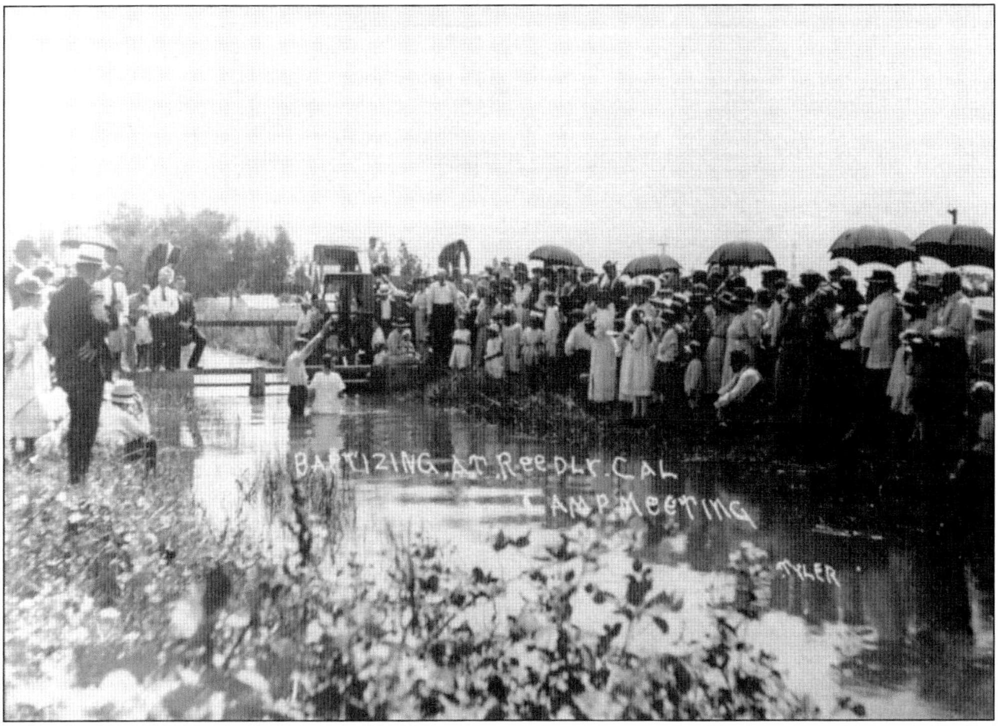

Camp meetings were another feature of Reedley's religious life in the 1920s. On this occasion, a nearby irrigation ditch was used to conduct baptisms.

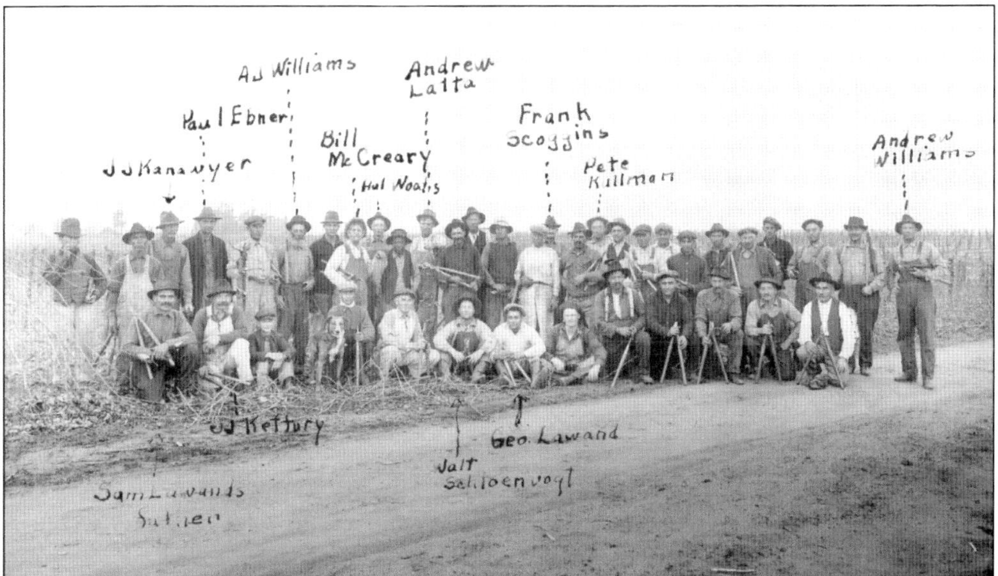

Mr. Saling had died, and his widow needed help pruning the vines. So neighbors and friends showed up to lend a hand, as seen here in 1934. These were Reedley people doing what Reedley people do. The Saling farm was just east of town.

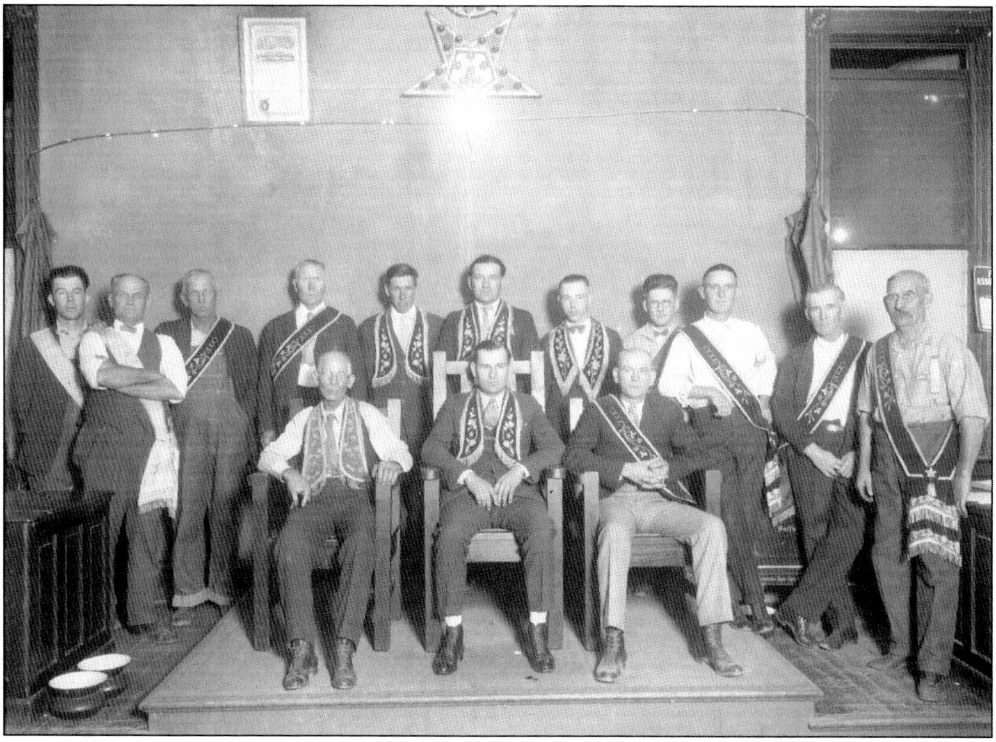

Numerous fraternal groups were organized in early Reedley, one of which was the Independent Order of Odd Fellows. Members of the Reedley lodge are seen here in 1927. (Photograph by Nelson Studio.)

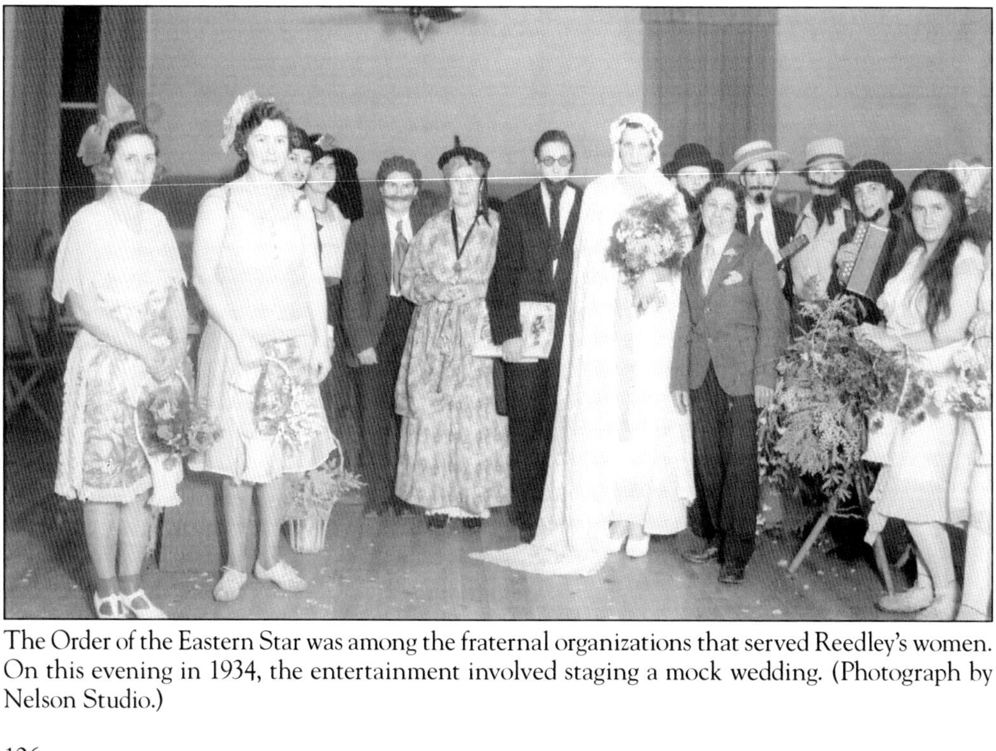

The Order of the Eastern Star was among the fraternal organizations that served Reedley's women. On this evening in 1934, the entertainment involved staging a mock wedding. (Photograph by Nelson Studio.)

The tradition of placing a Christmas tree at the intersection of G and Eleventh Streets goes back many years. This 1919 photograph shows local citizens gathering to decorate the tree. It is not known how they were able to decorate the top of the tree. (Photograph by Nelson Studio.)

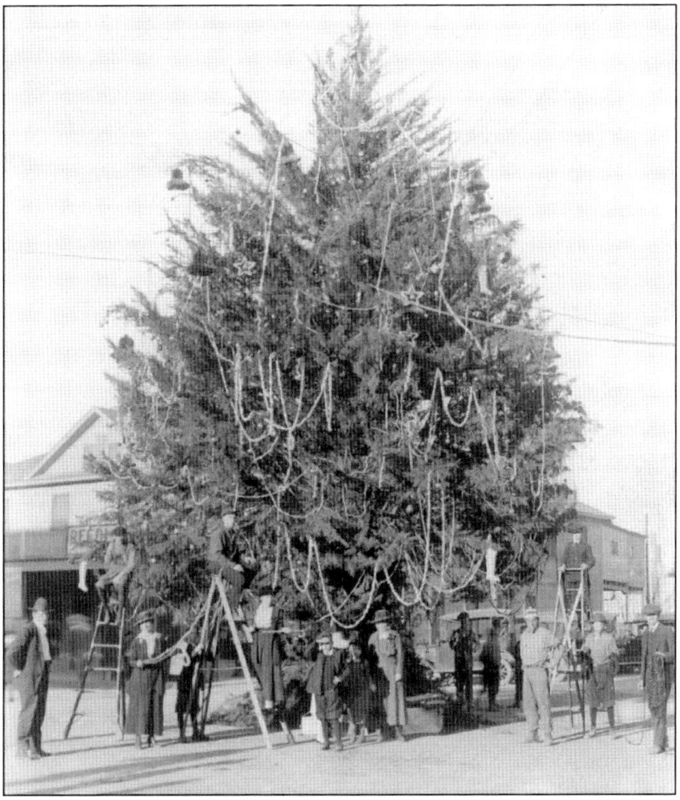

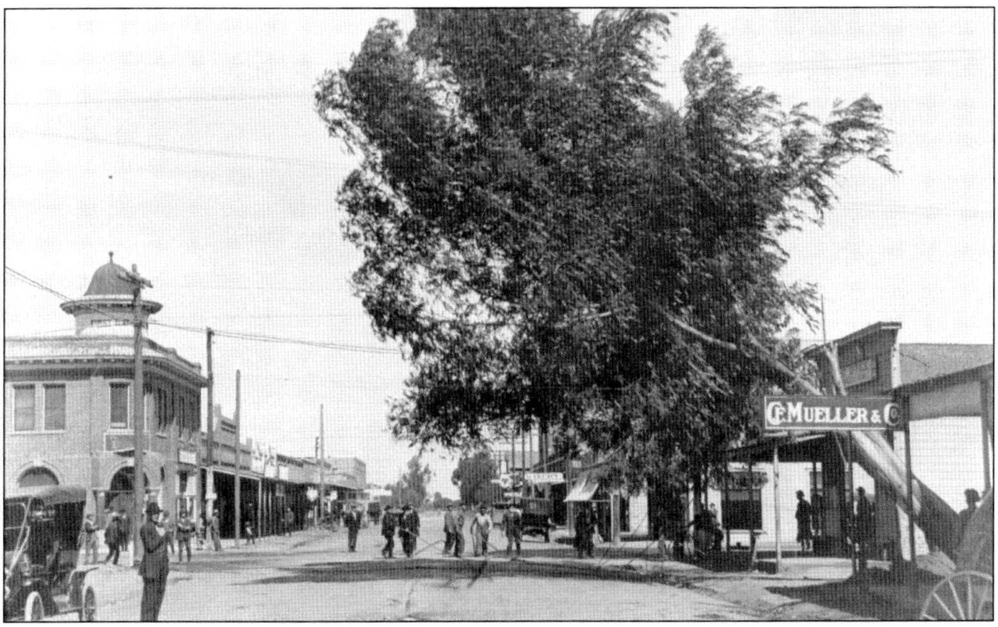

Men work to fell a large eucalyptus tree near the intersection of G and Eleventh Streets about 1909. There is no record as to whether the numerous overhead electrical wires survived the day's events. On the far right, behind the tree, is Reedley's post office. This was the second of five locations the post office occupied before moving to its current building. (Photograph by George Besaw.)

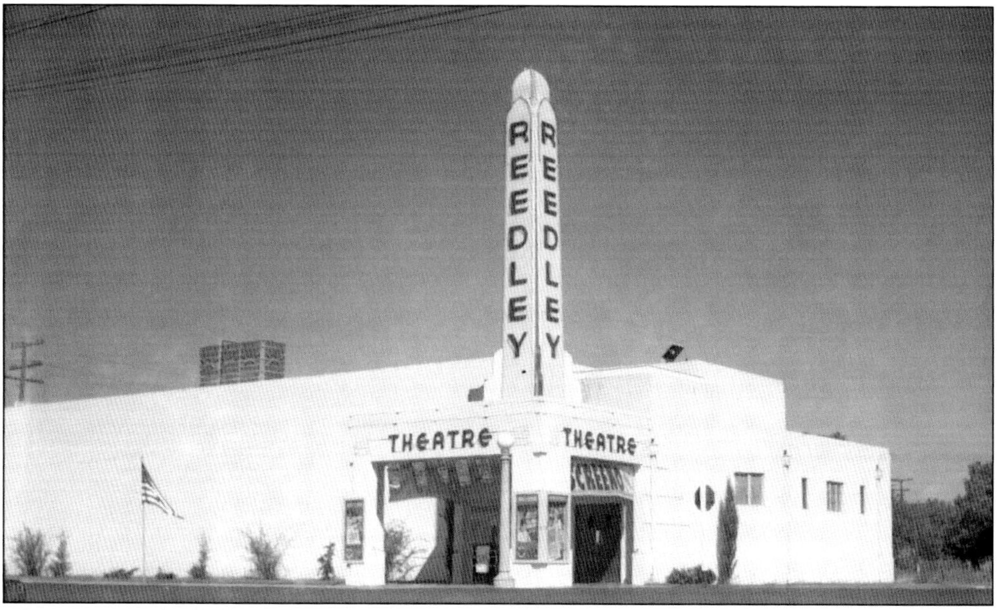

The town was thrilled when the modern Reedley Theatre opened its doors in May 1937. Its spire made this venue difficult to miss, but that big, boxy thing on the roof made it a particularly attractive destination. The theater was air-conditioned! The building, at the corner of Tenth and F Streets, was later converted to a bowling alley and now is a gym. (Photograph by Nelson Studio.)

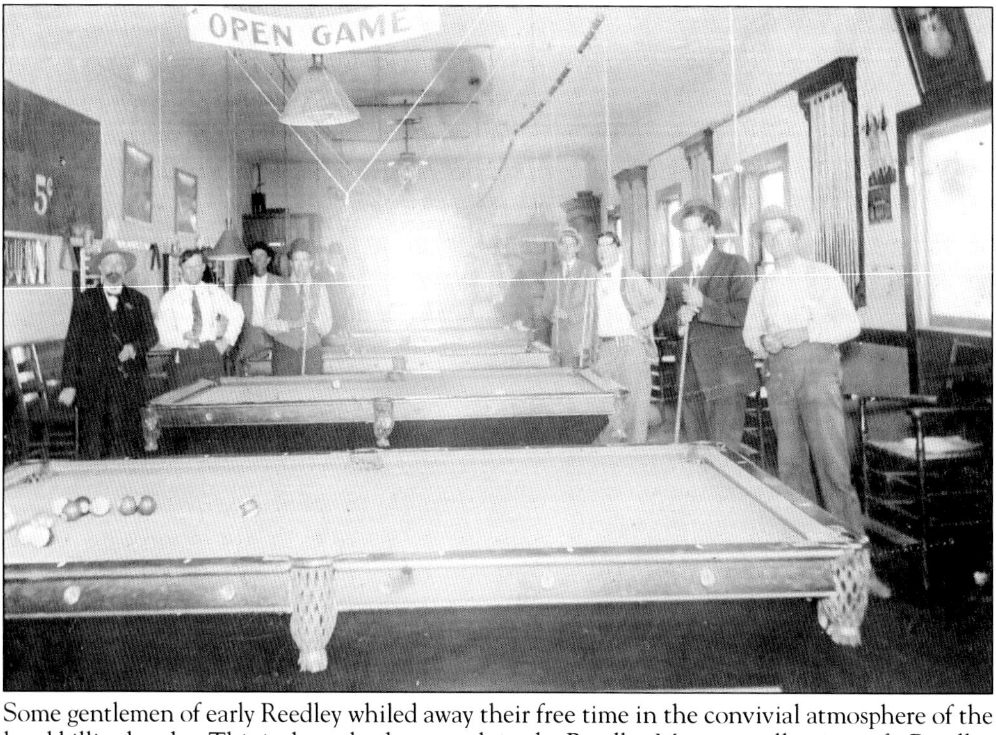

Some gentlemen of early Reedley whiled away their free time in the convivial atmosphere of the local billiard parlor. This is the only photograph in the Reedley Museum collections of a Reedley pool hall from the 1910s, even though the town supported at least two of these establishments during this period.

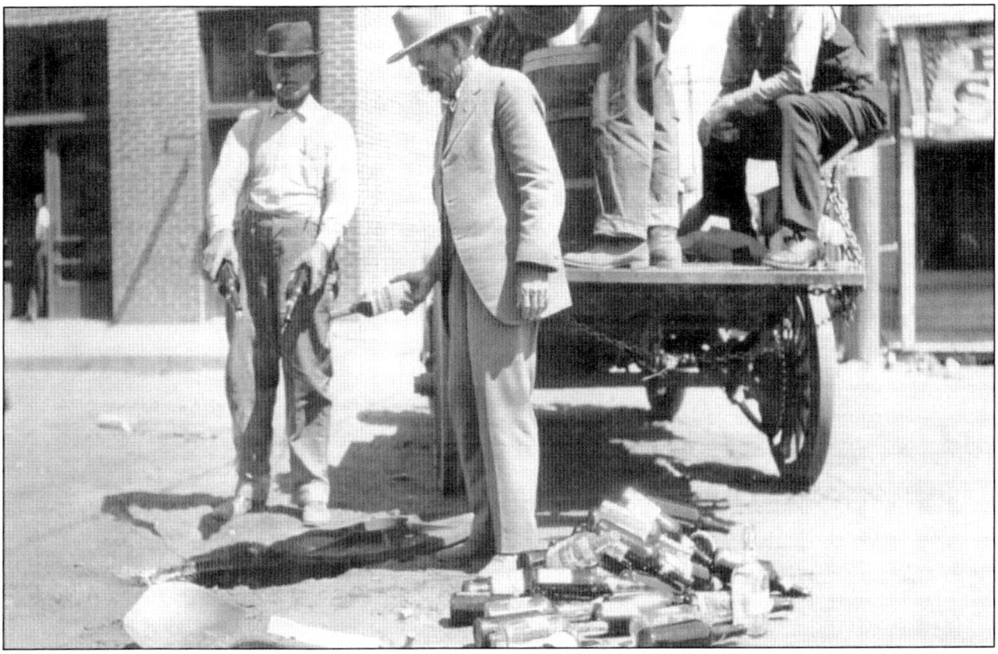

Marshal James Shipe makes a very public display of disposing of illegal liquor confiscated during a raid sometime in the 1910s. The booze was sent down the drain on Eleventh Street, across from the entrance to the Winnes Hotel.

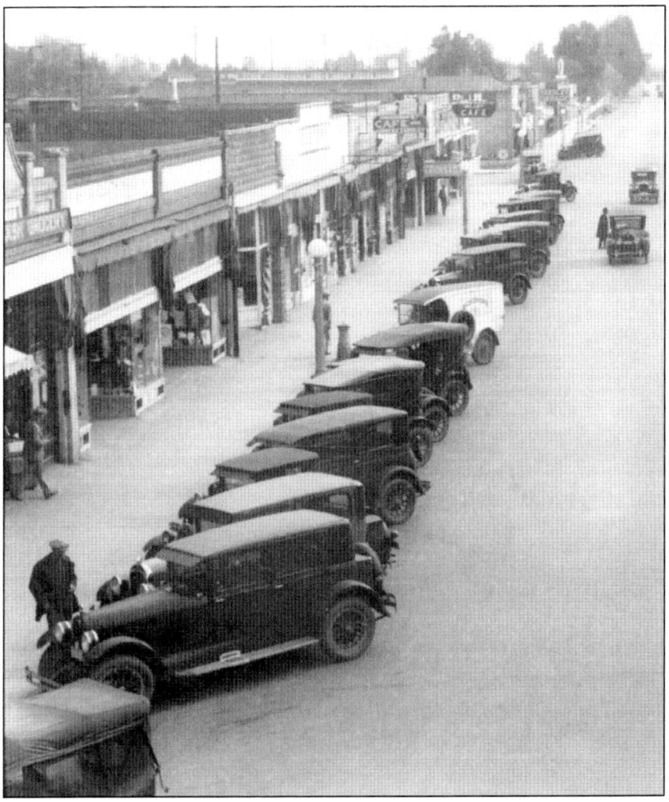

The local chapter of the Woman's Christian Temperance Union (WCTU) installed a water fountain in downtown Reedley in July 1909. (The stone fountain is at the curb in the center of the photograph.) This project was part of a national WCTU movement intended to keep women and children from having to go into a saloon to get a drink of water. The fountain was restored and can now be found in Pioneer Park. (Photograph by Nelson Studio.)

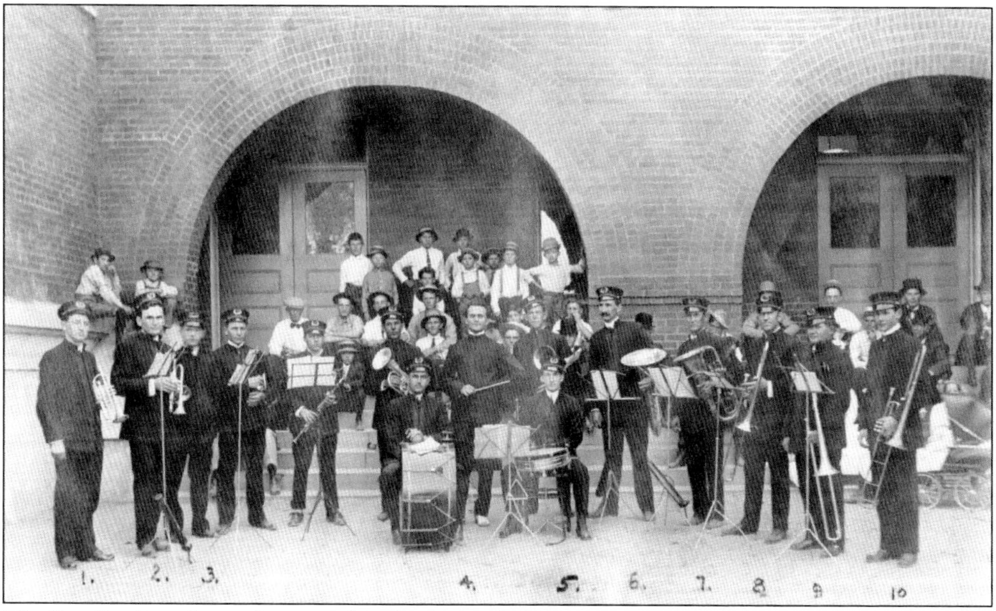

The Reedley Band was always on hand to provide music for community events and to entertain at summer concerts. Those identified here by number are the following: (1) Oliver Deffebach; (2) Jack Friesen, cleaner; (3) John Pugh, optometrist; (4) Pasquale Santa Emma, director; (5) Wendell Saile, standing; (6) Dr. George Wing, dentist; (7) Everett Crosby Sr., Santa Fe Railway agent; (8) Dr. Willard J. Ross, veterinarian; (9) Herman Dalke; and (10) Blaine Lyon. This c. 1913 photograph was taken in front of the grammar school.

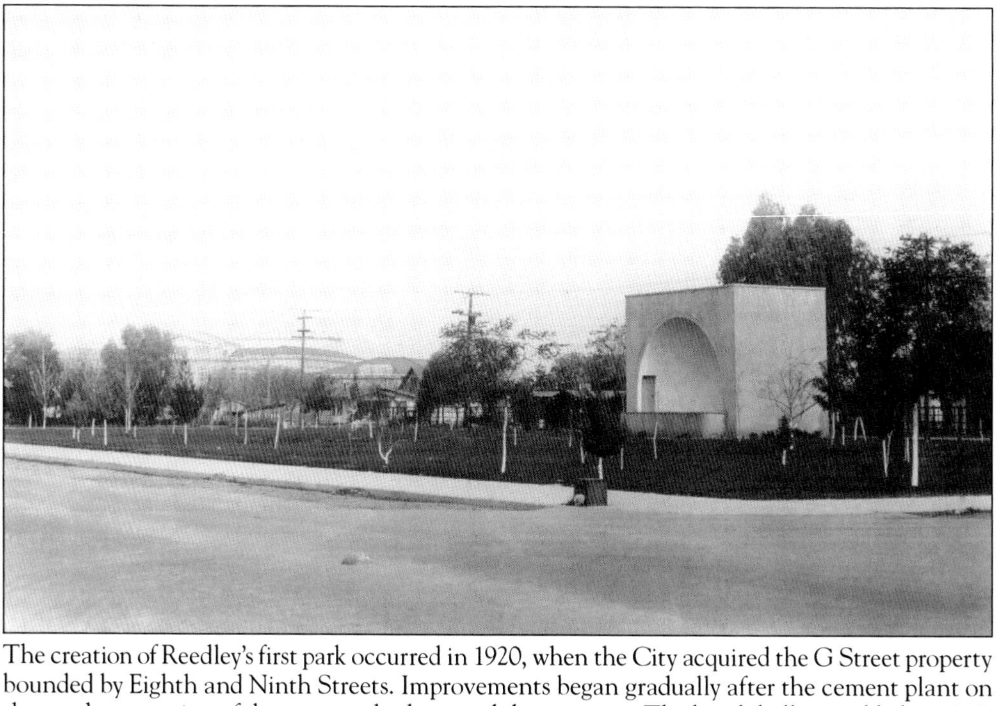

The creation of Reedley's first park occurred in 1920, when the City acquired the G Street property bounded by Eighth and Ninth Streets. Improvements began gradually after the cement plant on the southern portion of the property had vacated the premises. The band shell was added in 1923. What is now known as Pioneer Park continues to serve as a center for community celebrations.

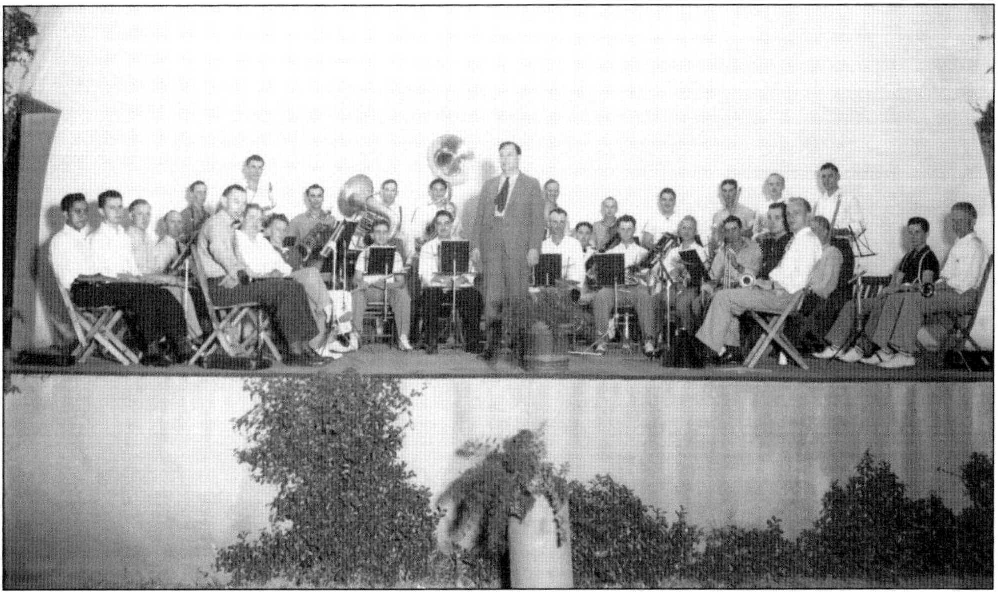

Summer band concerts in the city park were a tradition for many years. This photograph shows the city band ready to perform on the evening of July 22, 1937, under the baton of longtime director M.T. Garland. (Photograph by Nelson Studio.)

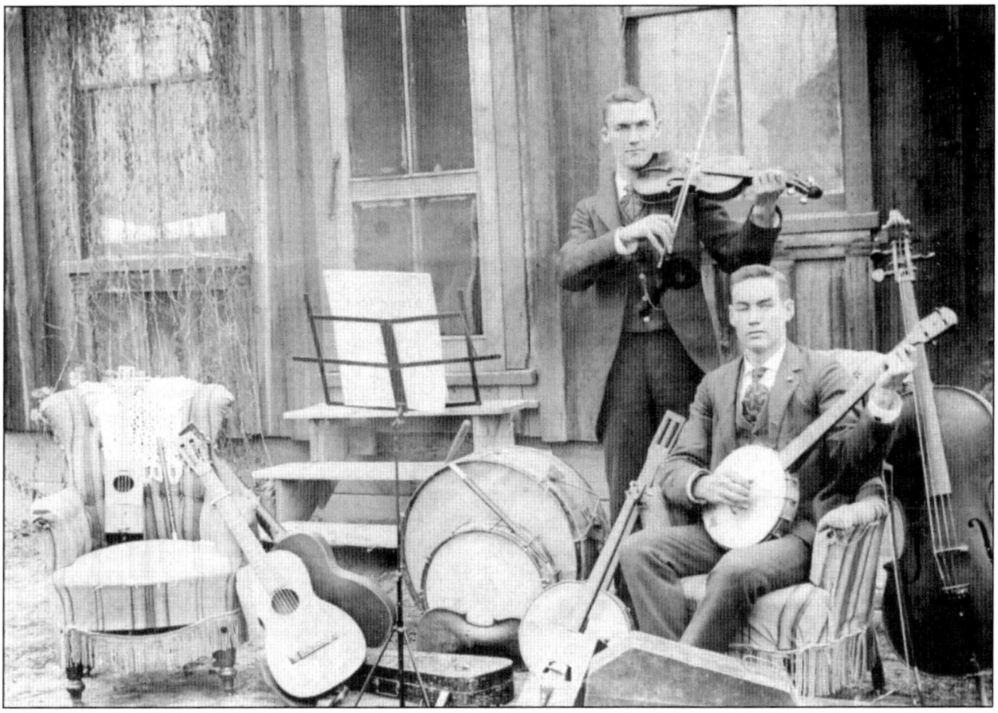

If people wanted music in the home in the 1910s, they could get a phonograph or, even better, make their own music. Singing and playing musical instruments like the piano were popular pastimes. Among Reedley's accomplished musicians were brothers Everett (left) and Albert Crosby. They are seen here at home with some of the instruments they played. One imagines the Crosby home always being filled with music.

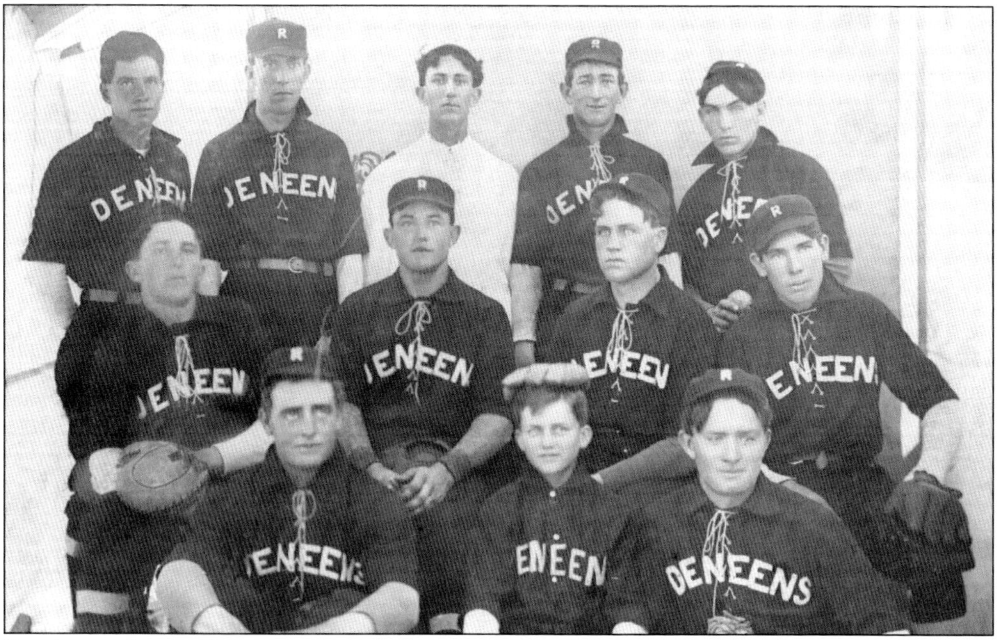

Residents of turn-of-the-century Reedley enjoyed competitive sports, and no sport was more popular than America's pastime, baseball. In the earliest years, local businesses would sponsor teams. Marion Deneen's butcher shop sponsored this 1904 team. A note on the back of the photograph states that two of the Segrue boys were on the team.

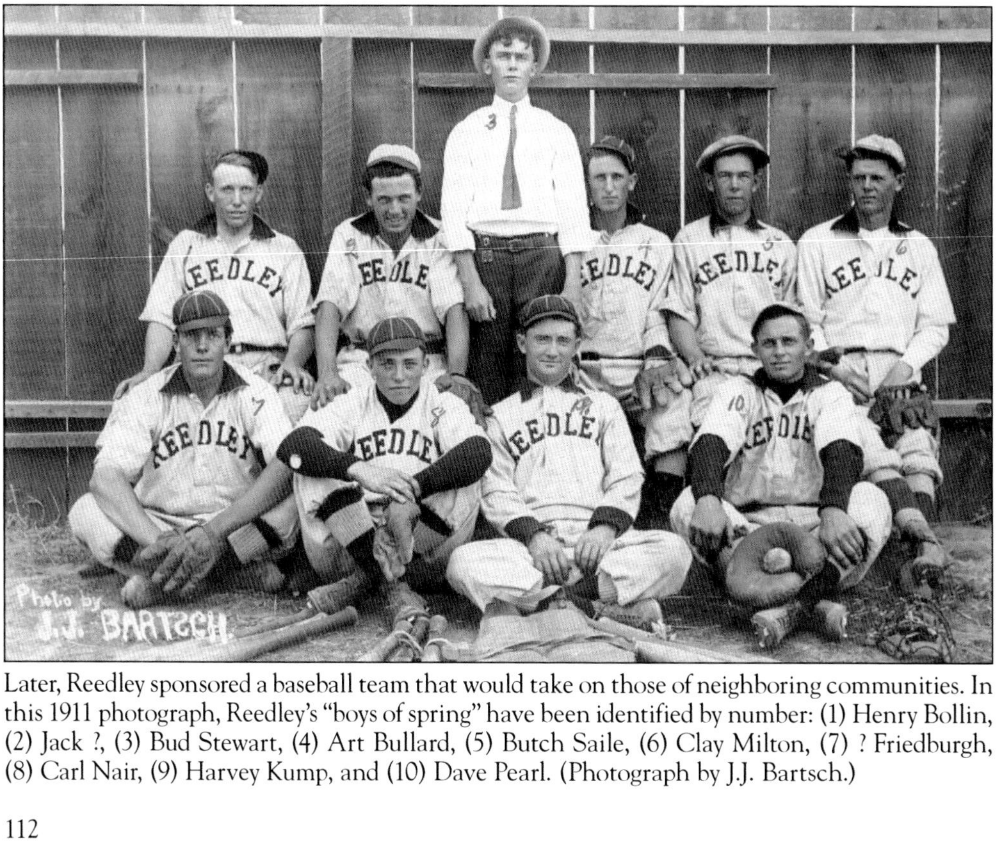

Later, Reedley sponsored a baseball team that would take on those of neighboring communities. In this 1911 photograph, Reedley's "boys of spring" have been identified by number: (1) Henry Bollin, (2) Jack ?, (3) Bud Stewart, (4) Art Bullard, (5) Butch Saile, (6) Clay Milton, (7) ? Friedburgh, (8) Carl Nair, (9) Harvey Kump, and (10) Dave Pearl. (Photograph by J.J. Bartsch.)

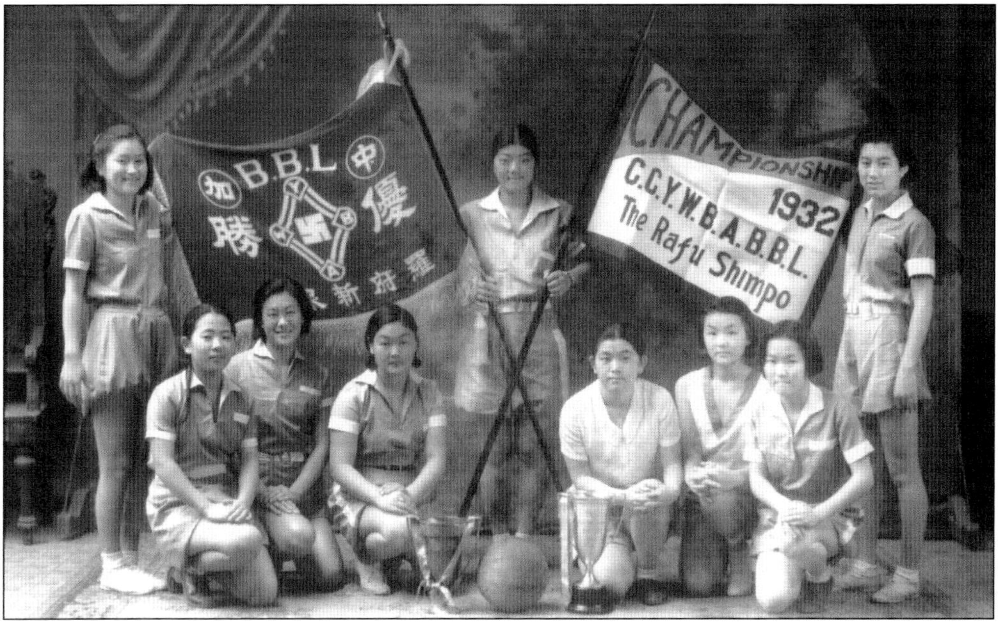

The Manjiettes, Reedley's Young Women's Buddhist Association basketball team, commemorated their 1932 victory with a visit to the photographer. The Manjiettes, founded in 1931, won the Central California championship 10 times in their first 11 years. From left to right are (first row) Kathleen Mitsuoka, Miyeko Kawamoto, Ethel Sasaki, Mae Yokota, Akiko Kodama, and Misao Oda; (second row) Patsy Kodama, Toshi Nishinaka, and Mitzi Hirashima. (Photograph by Nelson Studio.)

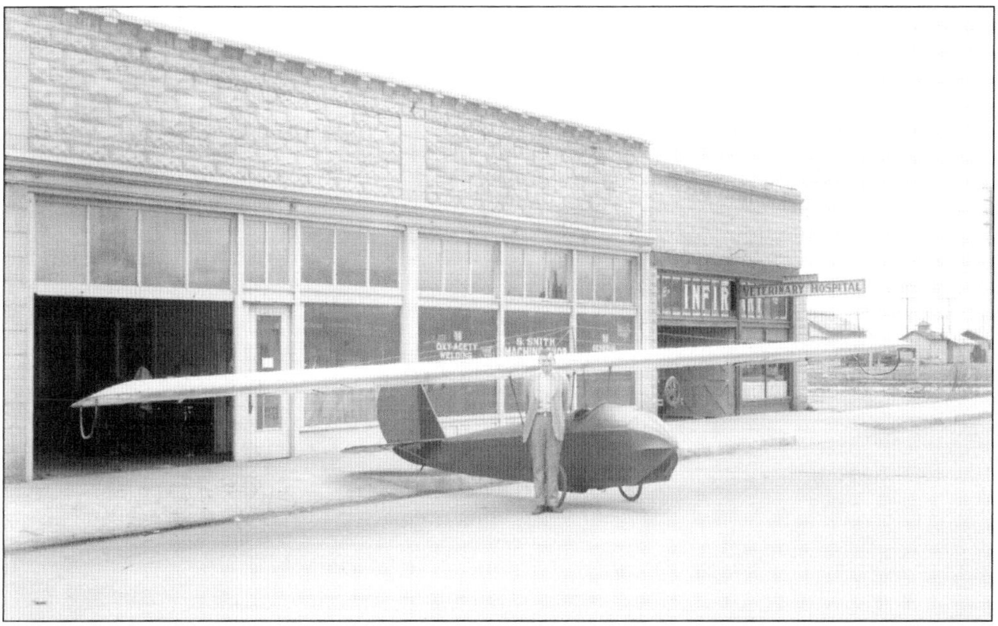

Dale Drake poses with his glider in front of Smith's machine shop at 917 G Street. Drake received national attention in 1929 when he set a world record for distance in a piloted, towed glider. It is said that 6,000 people witnessed his takeoff north of Reedley. The intended destination was Long Beach, but the towrope failed near Van Nuys. *Time* magazine reported, "Undaunted, he coasted ten miles and landed safely in a barley field." (Photograph by Nelson Studio.)

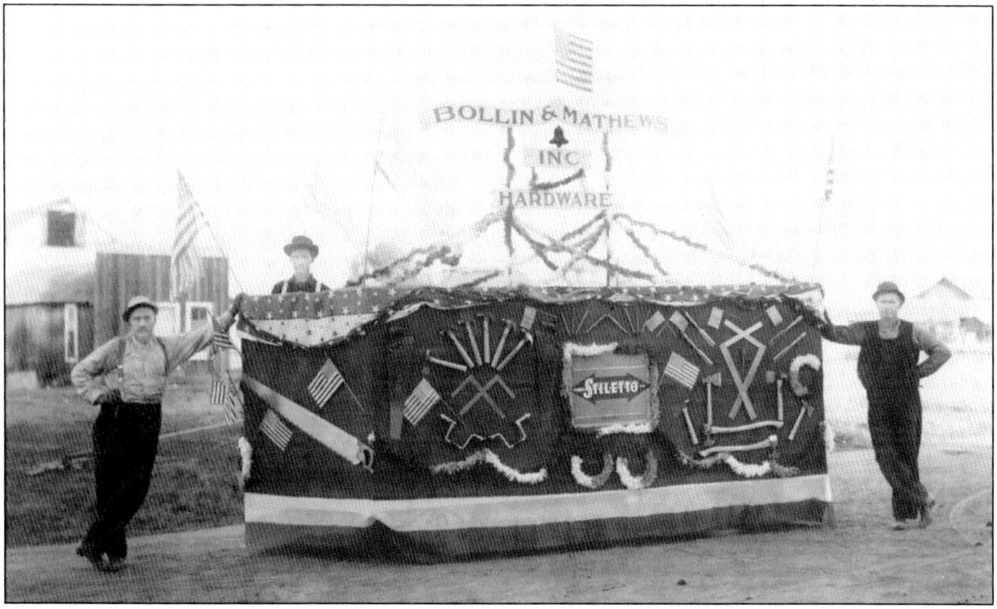

The Fourth of July parade in 1911 was the occasion of a spectacular celebration in the young community of Reedley. It was also the opportunity to tout one's business. The Bollin & Matthews Hardware float was an imaginative display of the various tools available at the establishment. H.D. Bollin is on the left, and James Besaw is next to him. The man at right is unidentified.

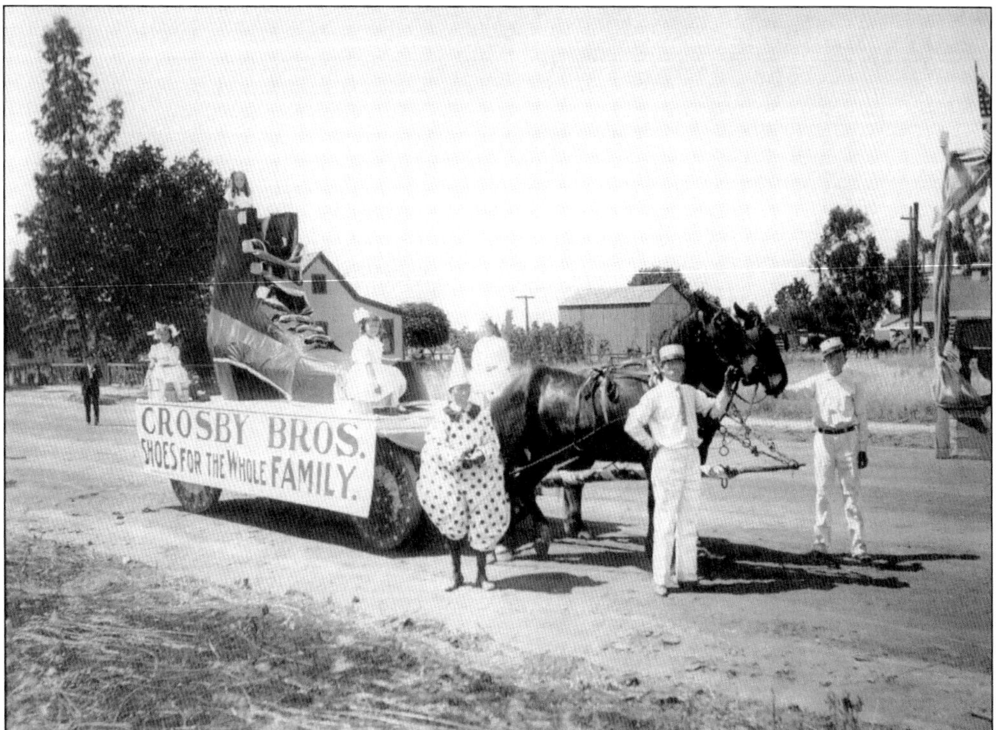

Crosby Brothers general merchandise store fashioned an extraordinarily large shoe for its horse-drawn float in the parade on July 4, 1911. Little Lucille Crosby is perched at the top of the shoe.

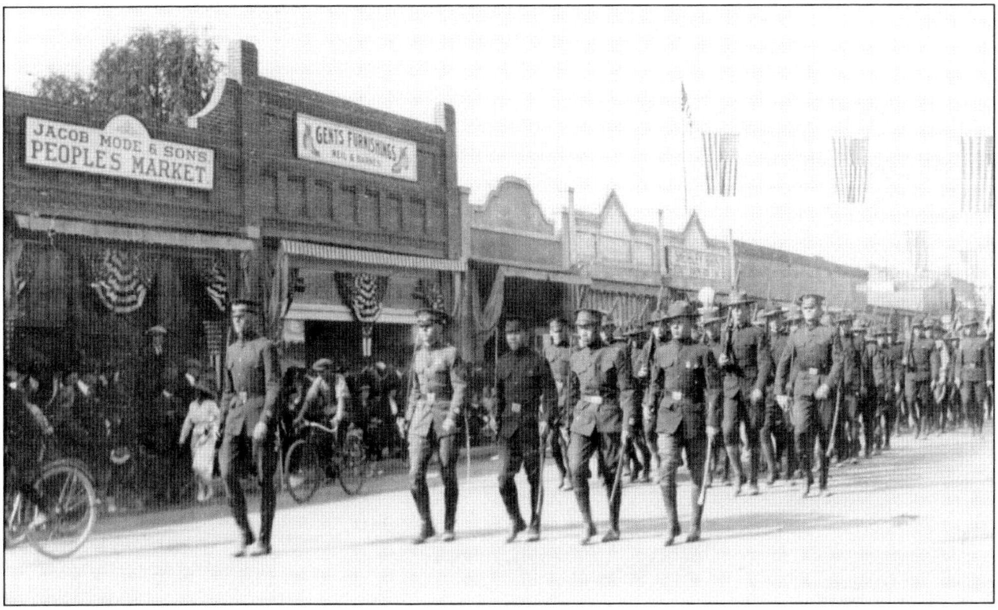

When Reedley hosted the official Fresno County Armistice Day celebration in 1921, memories of the World War (not yet known as World War I) were still fresh. The elation of the war's end and the recognition of the sacrifices made by those who had served made this an important day on the community's calendar. High school cadets from Fresno march up G Street in this photograph.

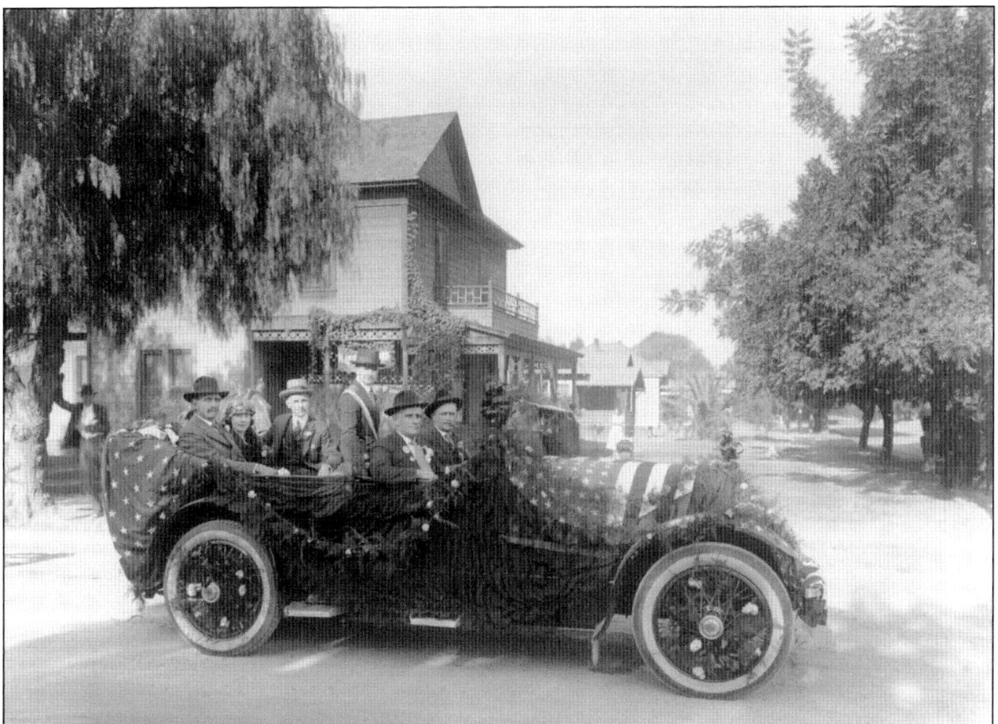

The *Exponent* reported that "fully fifteen thousand people witnessed the parade" on that special Armistice Day of 1921. Here, the Reedley city trustees prepare to motor down the parade route.

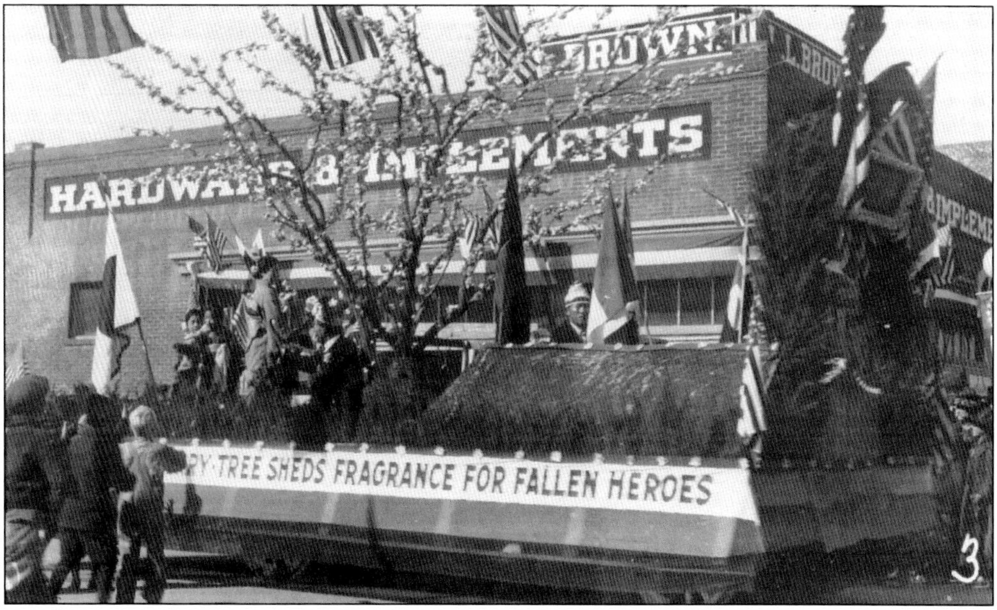

Reedley's Japanese community created a beautifully decorated float featuring a cherry tree for the 1921 Armistice Day Parade. The side of the float expressed the sentiment "A Cherry Tree Sheds Fragrance for Fallen Heroes." This photograph was taken on Tenth Street, near G Street.

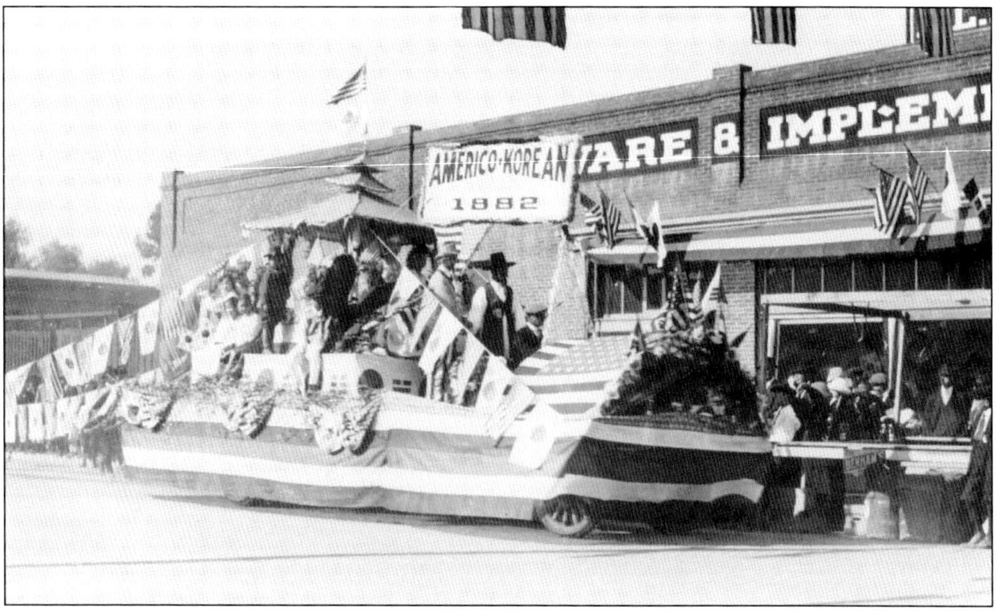

The Korean community's entry in the 1921 Armistice Day Parade celebrated the signing of the 1882 treaty between the United States and Korea. This was the first treaty Korea had ever negotiated with a Western nation.

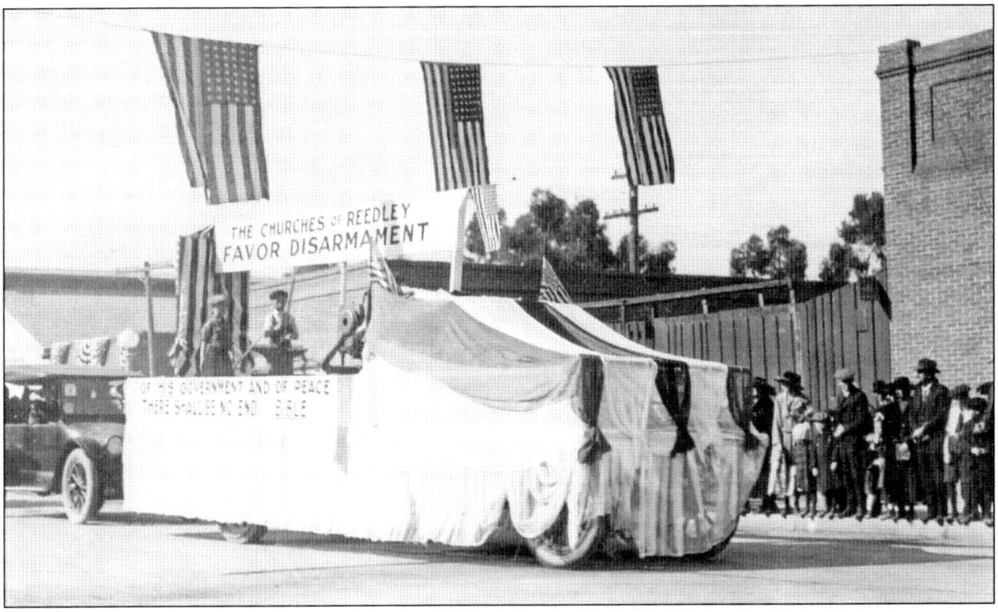

The message "The Churches of Reedley Favor Disarmament" adorns this float of the 1921 Armistice Day Parade. An explicit goal of the League of Nations, founded in the aftermath of World War I, was gradual disarmament. The convictions of many Reedley residents found expression with this float, sponsored by the local ministerial association.

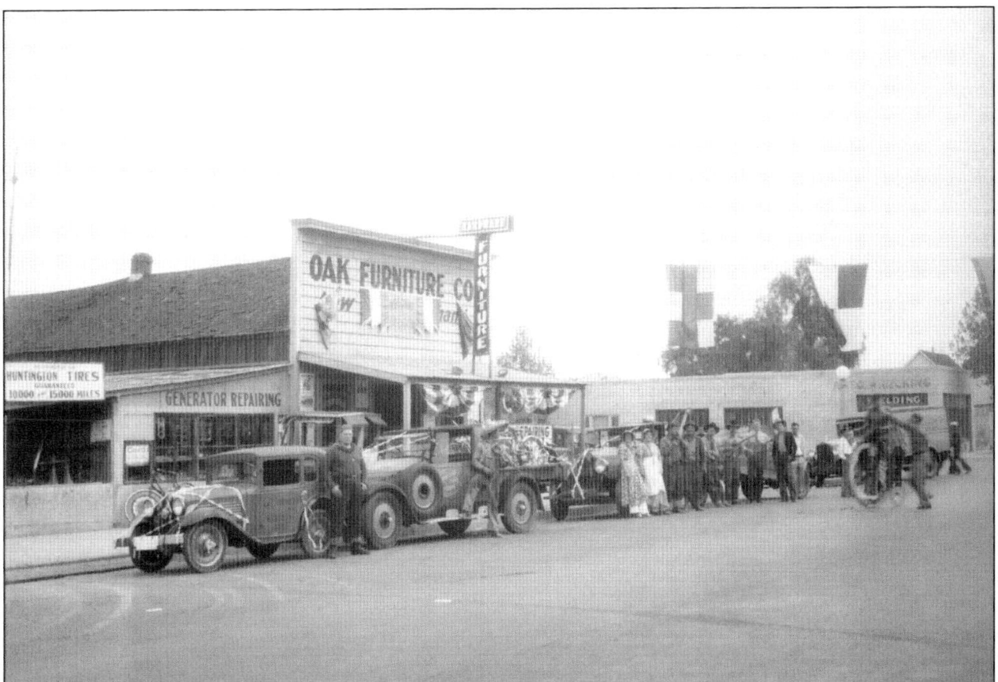

Unfortunately, no details are available about this 1936 parade or what occasion prompted the folks at Oak Furniture and Auto Wrecking Company to get all dressed up, recruit musicians, and ride the penny-farthing. The business was located at 1252 G Street. (Photograph by Nelson Studio.)

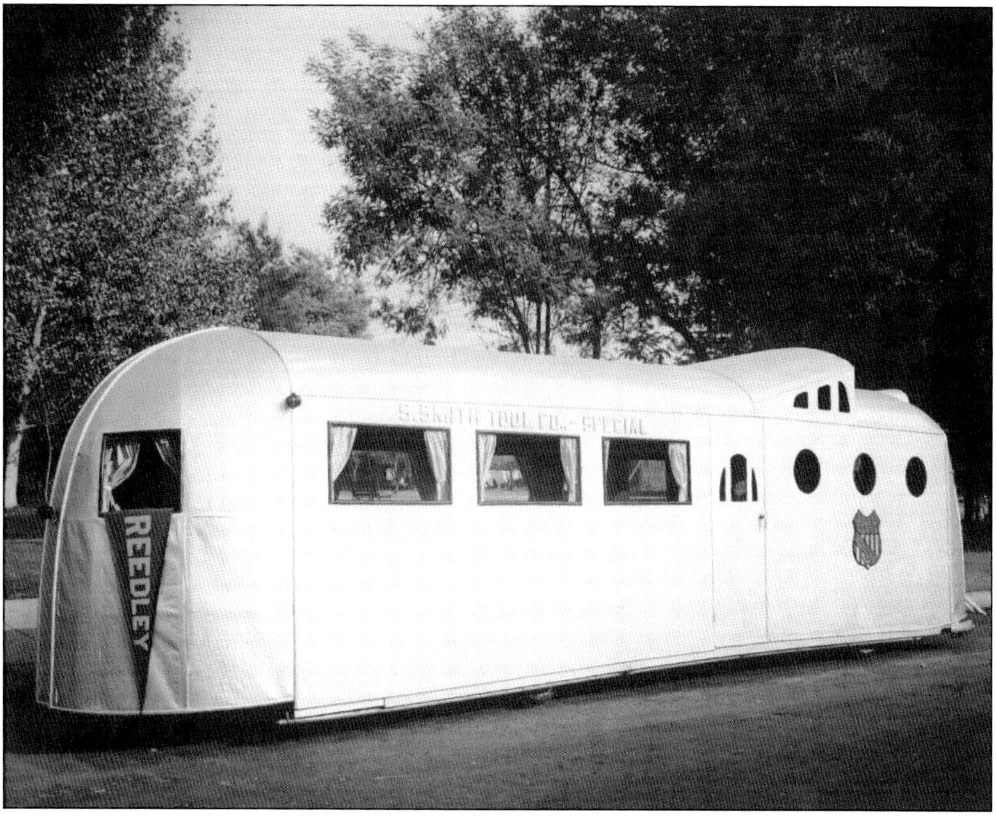

Sylvester "Tib" Smith, owner of a machine shop and tool company, constructed this elaborate float to resemble a modern, streamlined railcar for a Reedley parade. (Photograph by Nelson Studio.)

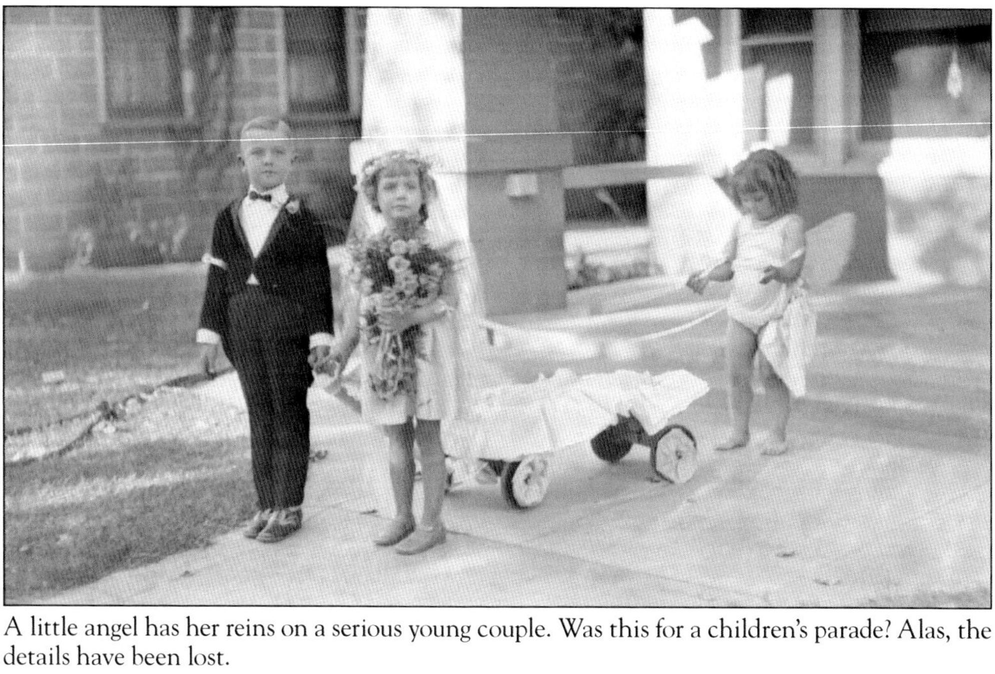

A little angel has her reins on a serious young couple. Was this for a children's parade? Alas, the details have been lost.

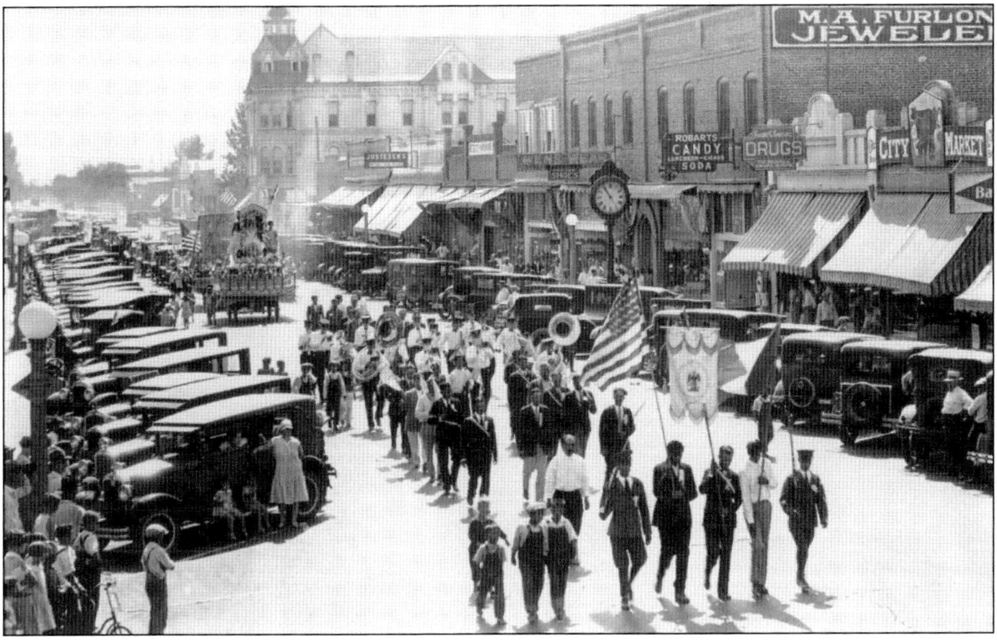

Reedley's Mexican American community held its first official celebration of Mexican Independence Day during a two-day event on September 14–15, 1928. The *Exponent* reported that the parade was several blocks long and featured decorated floats and automobiles. Falkenstein's band of Fresno marched at the front, followed by a float carrying Angelina Valdivia, queen of the celebration.

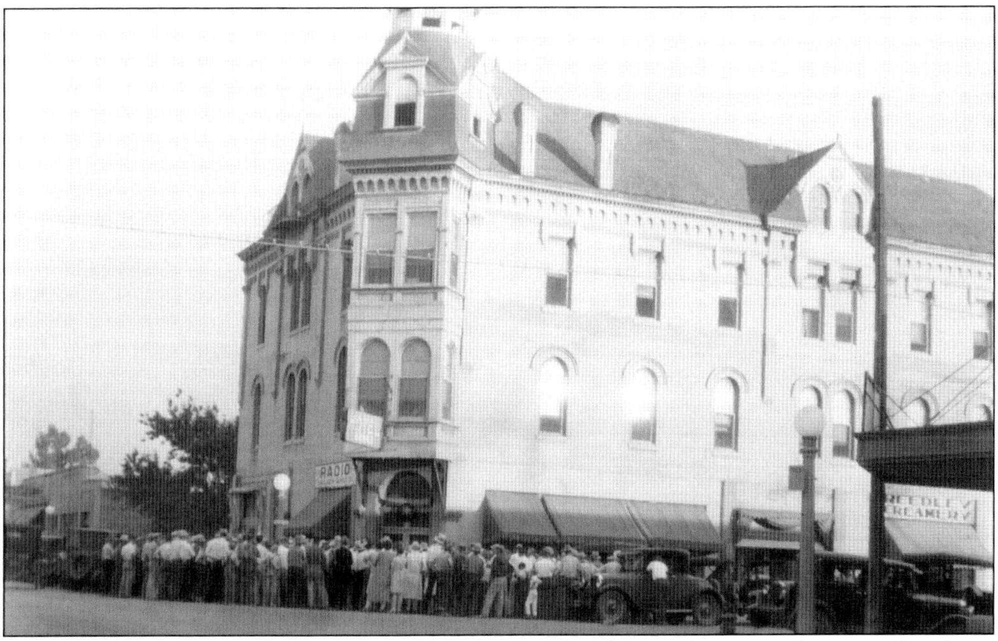

A crowd has gathered in the street in front of the David Radio Supply store to listen to a broadcast from an Atwater Kent radio that has been set up on the corner. Having a radio at home was still a rarity. What were they listening to? It might have been a World Series game, or perhaps an important political speech. This photograph was taken between 1922 and 1929. (Photograph by Nelson Studio.)

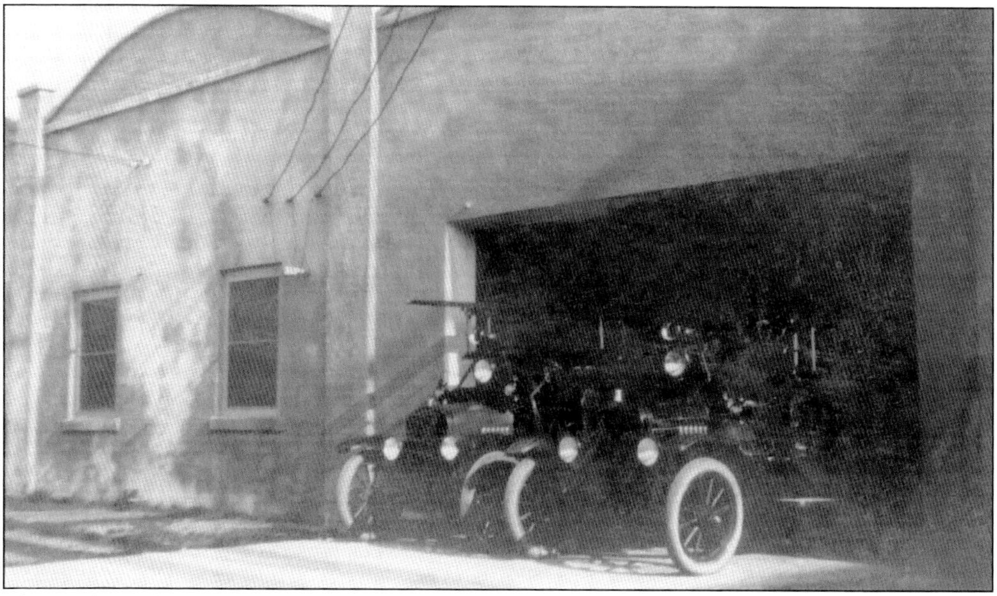

This is the earliest-known photograph of Reedley's first city hall and the fire department's first two motorized fire trucks. City hall was built in 1917, and these trucks were acquired in 1919. The old city hall building at 1752 Tenth Street is now home to the Reedley Museum.

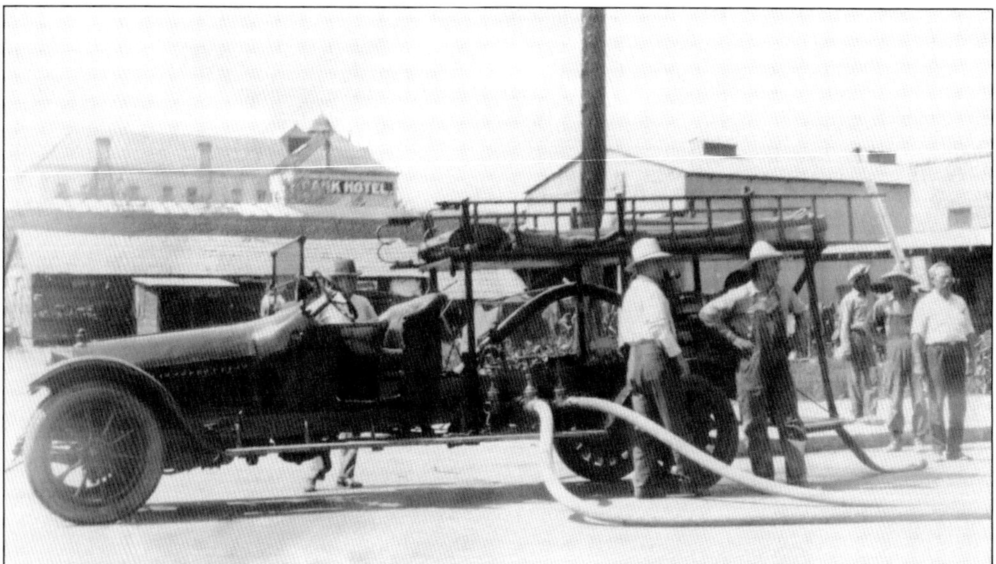

One of Reedley's first motorized fire trucks is seen at work on Thirteenth Street, between G and H Streets. This photograph dates from the early 1920s, when the Hotel Grand (in the background) was known as the Park Hotel. This photograph was found in an early fire department record book that is in the archives of the Reedley Historical Society.

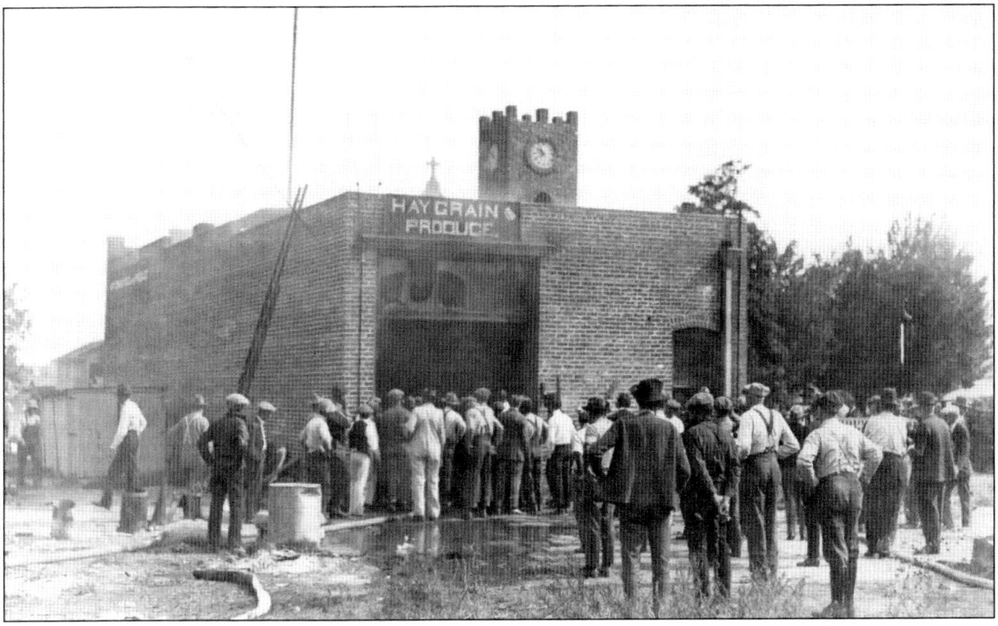

A fire always seems certain to generate a crowd of onlookers. Residents of Reedley in 1924 were no exception to this tendency. As soon as the flames were doused, spectators crowded the rear of the Reedley Feed and Produce store to view the damage. The store was located on F Street, across from the Catholic church.

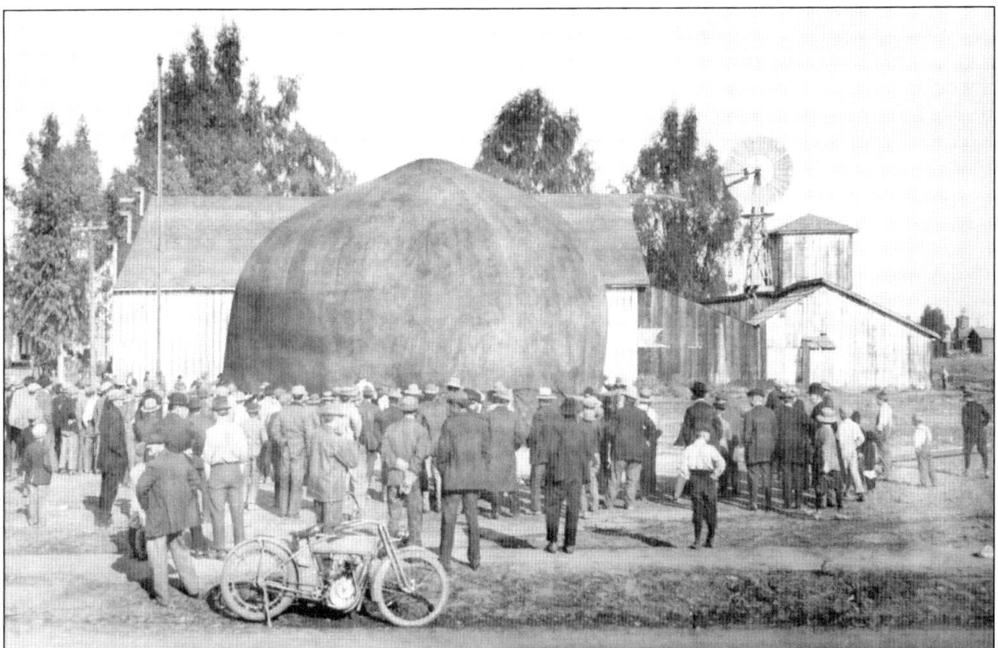

The novelty of a hot-air balloon in the early 1910s was another sure way to produce a crowd of the curious. It appears that those congregated are men and boys. Where were the women? Yes, that is a Harley Davidson motorcycle parked in the foreground. (Photograph by George Besaw.)

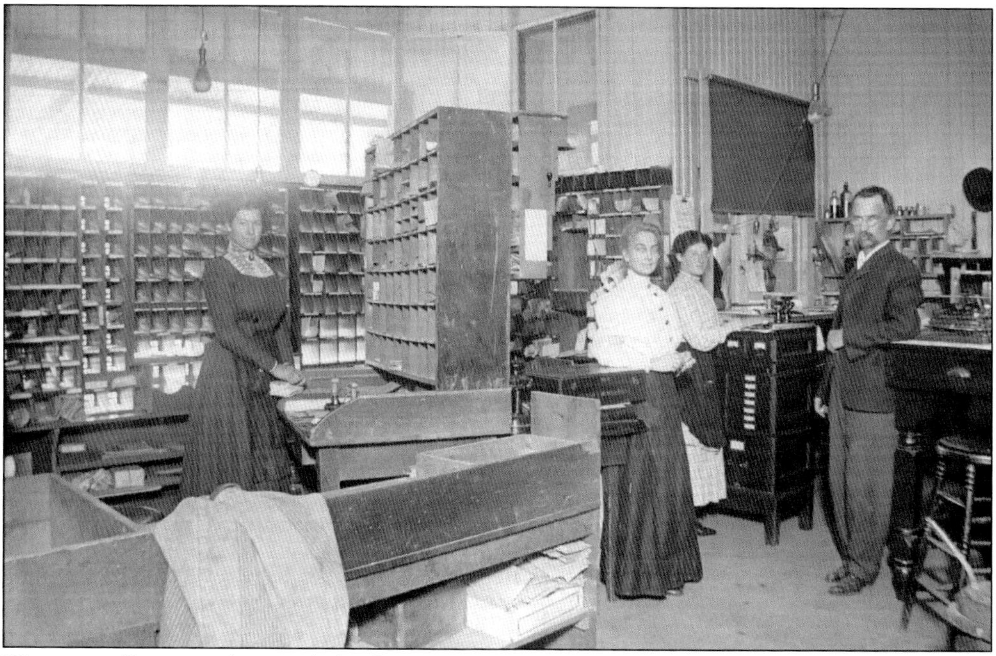

The post office was always a hub of activity in a small community. The lobby was a place for friends to catch up on the latest news. Behind the counter, the business of moving the mail took precedence. Postmaster Flora Knauer is second from left, and her husband, Frank Knauer, stands at right. This photograph dates from 1917–1923, when the post office was located in the Winnes Hotel building.

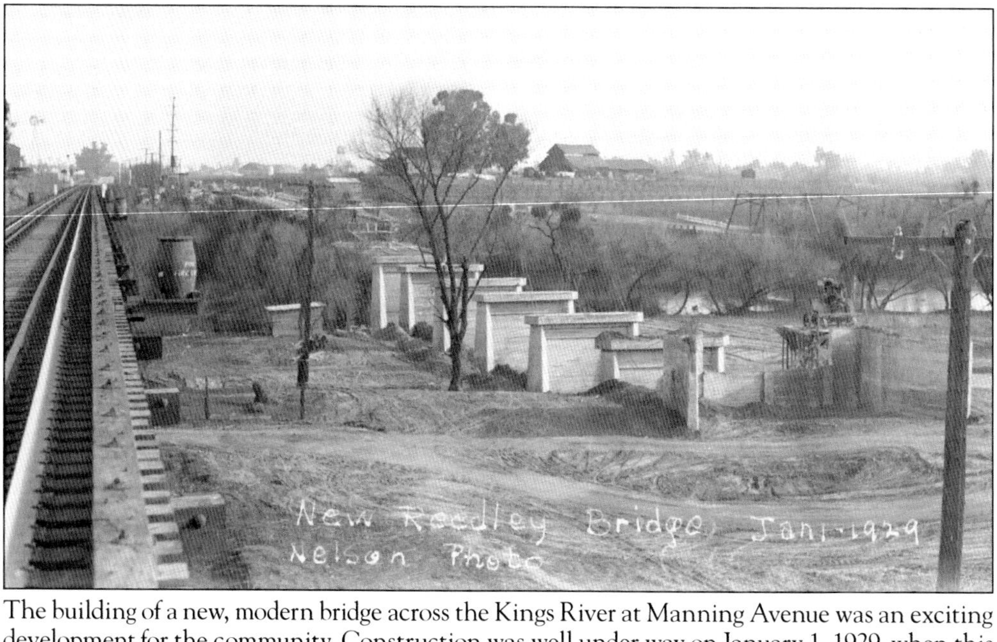

The building of a new, modern bridge across the Kings River at Manning Avenue was an exciting development for the community. Construction was well under way on January 1, 1929, when this photograph was taken from the west side of the river. The bridge that it would replace is seen on the far right. In the distance, just left of center, are Reedley's twin water towers. (Photograph by Nelson Studio.)

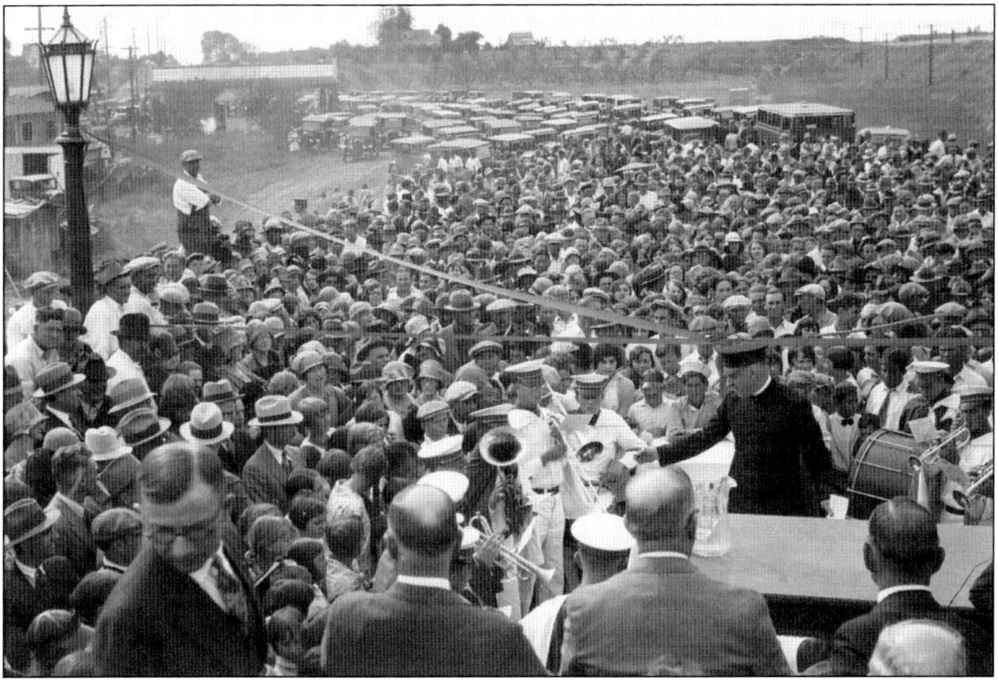

Politicians and various other dignitaries, along with hundreds of citizens, made the trek to the west side of the new Manning Avenue bridge for its dedication on April 15, 1929. The Reedley High School band provided music for the occasion. (Photograph by Nelson Studio.)

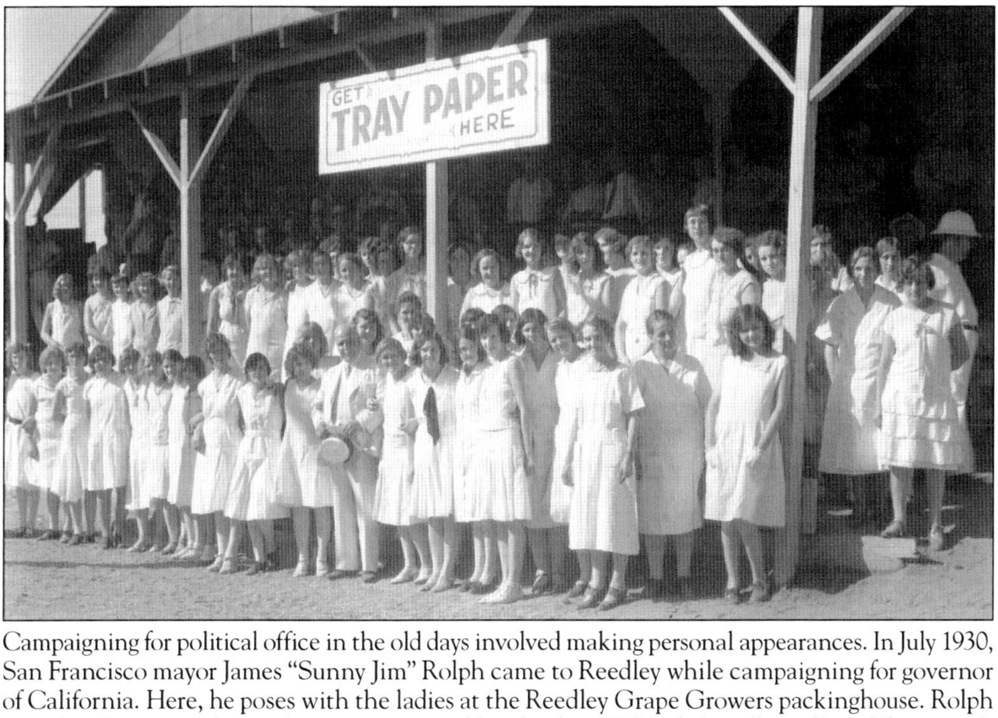

Campaigning for political office in the old days involved making personal appearances. In July 1930, San Francisco mayor James "Sunny Jim" Rolph came to Reedley while campaigning for governor of California. Here, he poses with the ladies at the Reedley Grape Growers packinghouse. Rolph won the election and served as governor until his death in 1934 while still in office. (Photograph by Nelson Studio.)

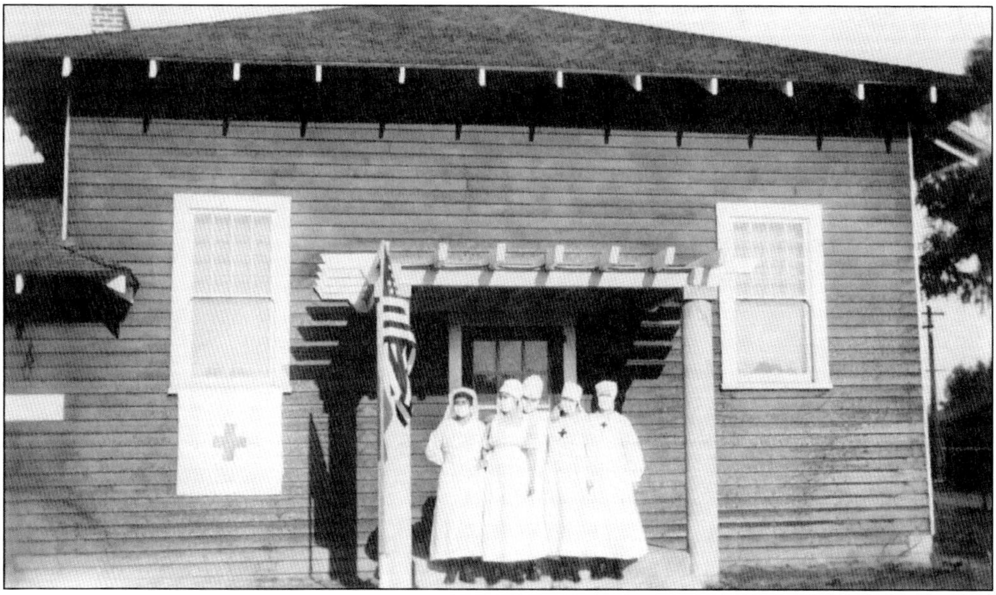

The Spanish influenza epidemic of 1918 struck Reedley with particular severity in November of that year. A central location was needed where doctors and nurses, weary of rushing from one house to another, could attend to their ill patients. The Study and Civic Club House, located at F and Eighth Streets, was pressed into service as a makeshift hospital.

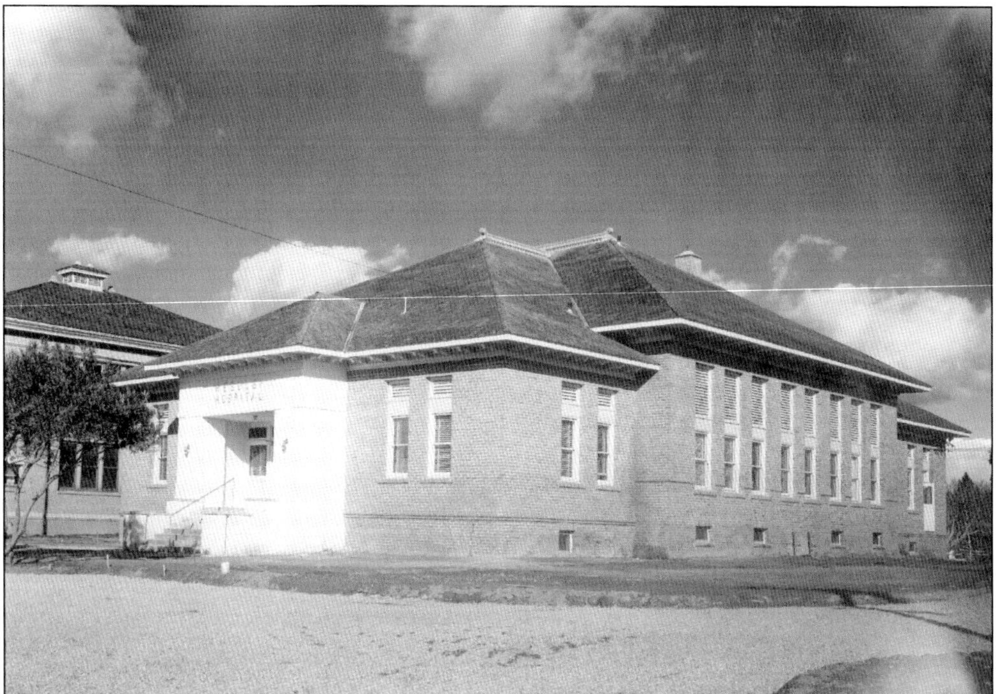

A group of concerned citizens first organized in 1937 with the intention of establishing a hospital in Reedley. They formed a nonprofit corporation that acquired the old high school building at West (now Reed) and Dinuba Avenues. The doors to the 17-bed facility opened in March 1939. The old science building to the north was used for medical offices.

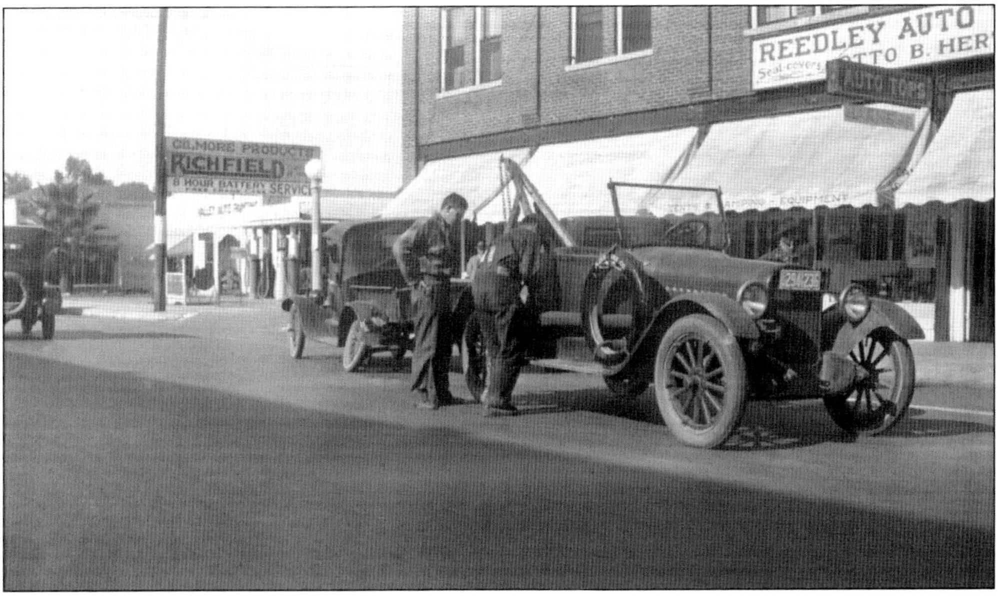

The emergence of the automobile age gave people a new set of aggravations. The example here is that of a disabled automobile. In 1916, a Tennessee entrepreneur recognized a viable business opportunity: he invented the tow truck. This photograph, taken 10 years after that invention, shows an unfortunate Reedley motorist in need of such a truck to attend to his vehicle, which has gone "lame" on Eleventh Street. (Photograph by Nelson Studio.)

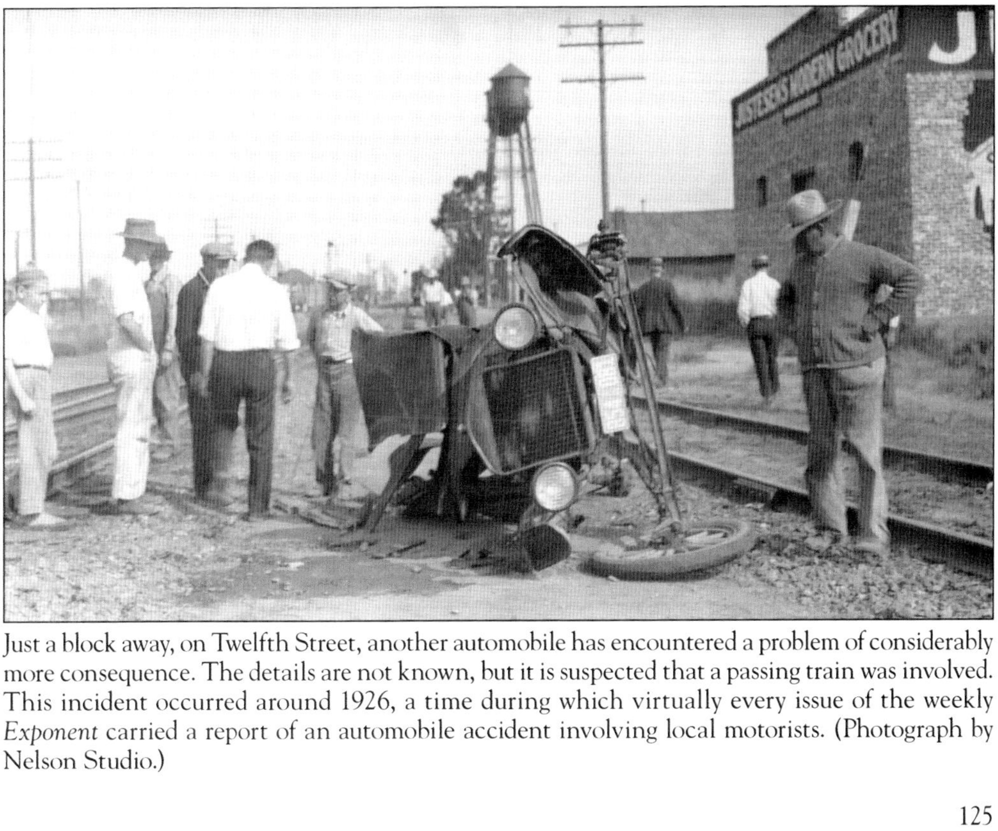

Just a block away, on Twelfth Street, another automobile has encountered a problem of considerably more consequence. The details are not known, but it is suspected that a passing train was involved. This incident occurred around 1926, a time during which virtually every issue of the weekly *Exponent* carried a report of an automobile accident involving local motorists. (Photograph by Nelson Studio.)

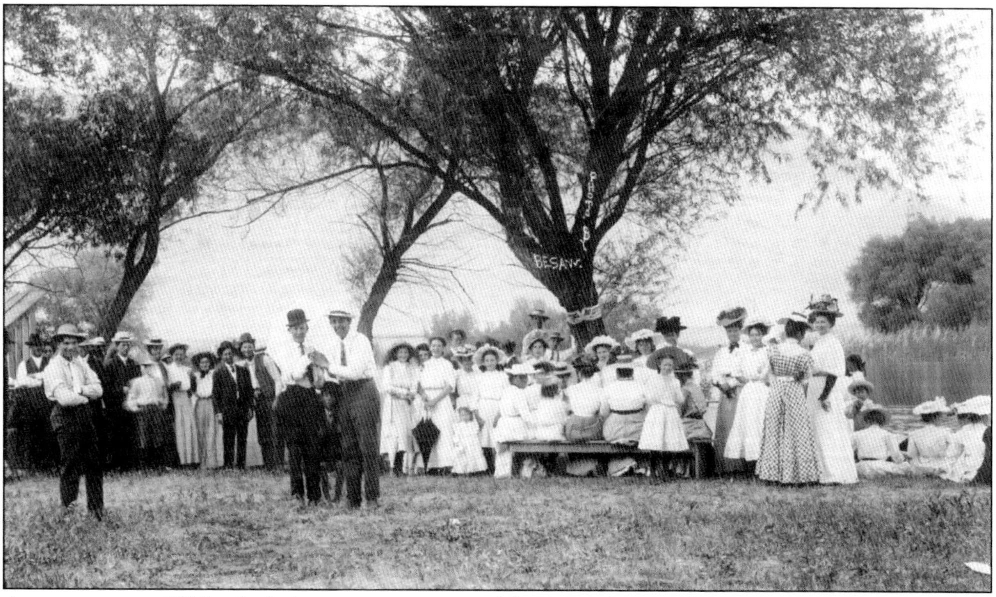

An excursion to Wahtoke Lake was an occasional diversion for Reedley citizens. One could picnic, swim, boat, or fish. At one time, there was a dance hall and concessions at the site. Located just a few miles north of town, the lake was formed when the 76 Land and Water Company built a restraining dam on Wahtoke Creek to allow the main Alta Canal to cross over the creek. (Photograph by George Besaw.)

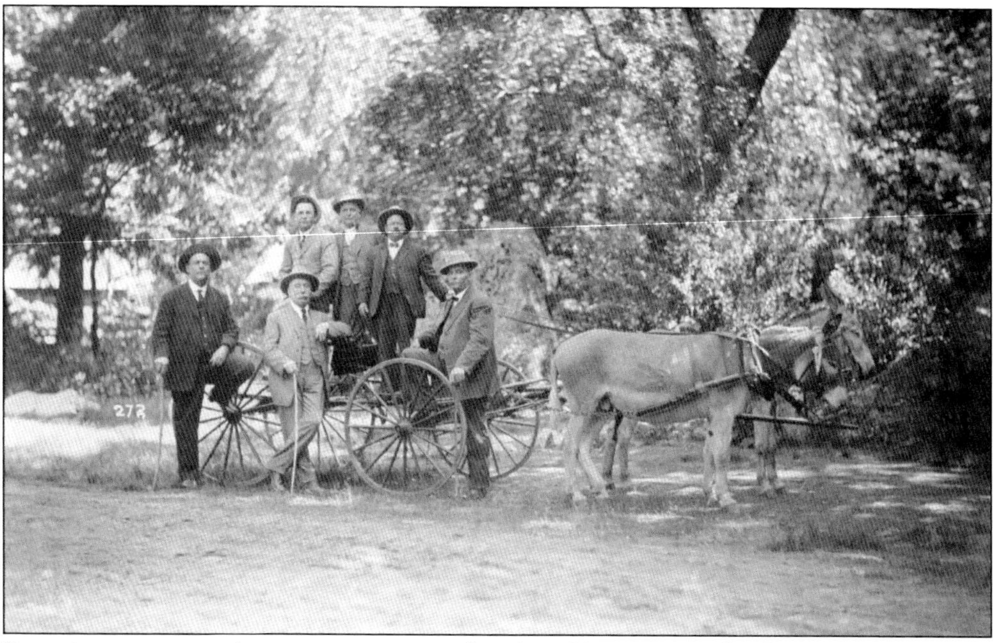

Sometimes a more ambitious outing was undertaken. Here, six Reedley businessmen visit the spectacular sites of Yosemite in 1912. They are, from left to right, (first row) E. Saile, Pat McDonald, and Frank Thomas; (second row) Bill Parlier, H.G. Williams, and O.D. Lyon. (Photograph by Pillsbury Photo Co.)

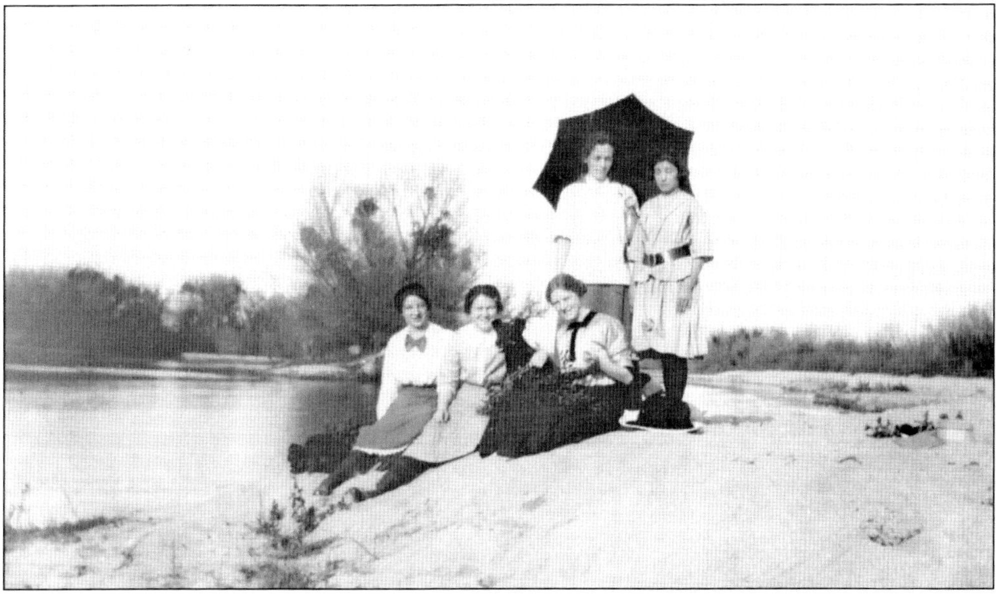

Even if one did not swim, a visit to Kings River beach on a warm summer day was bound to refresh the mind. On this particular day, a very happy pooch got to accompany these young ladies on their outing.

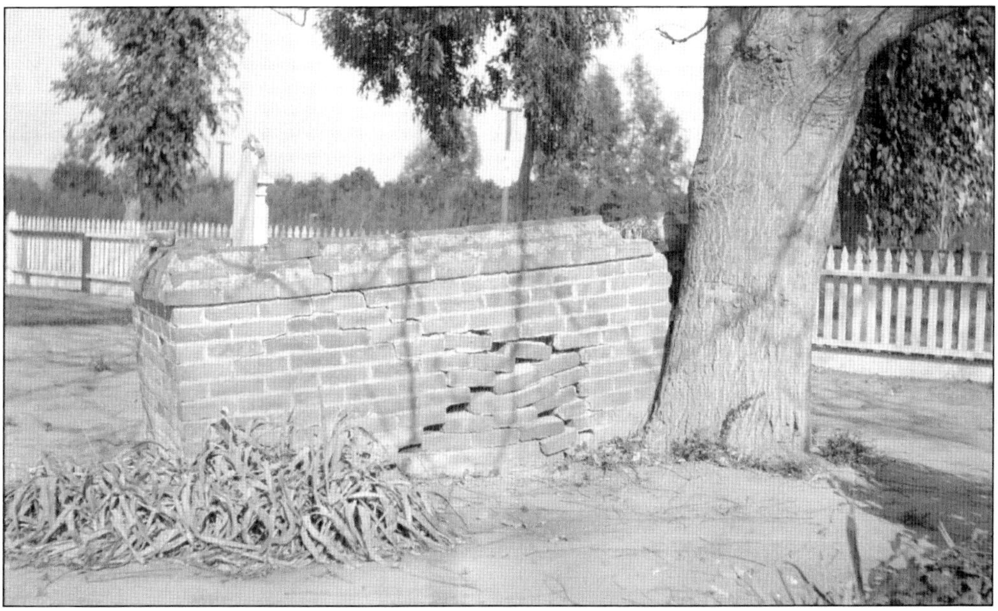

The mortal remains of many pioneers reside in Reedley Cemetery. The first burial, in what would officially become Reedley Cemetery 27 years later, was that of ferryman James Smith in 1862. He died of pneumonia at age 41. The second was that of Smith's two-year-old son, who died a month later. A brick wall once surrounded the gravesites of this father and son. The wall fell into disrepair and was removed in the 1920s.

Consistent with our mission to preserve history on a local level, this book was printed in South Carolina on American-made paper and manufactured entirely in the United States. Products carrying the accredited Forest Stewardship Council (FSC) label are printed on 100 percent FSC-certified paper.